The
ESSAYIST
AT WORK

D1015918

The
ESSAYIST
AT WORK

Profiles of
Creative Nonfiction
Writers

edited by Lee Gutkind

HEINEMANN
PORTSMOUTH, NH

Heinemann
A division of Reed Elsevier Inc.
361 Hanover Street
Portsmouth, NH 03801-3912
Offices and agents throughout the world.

Library of Congress Cataloging-in-Publication Data
The essayist at work : profiles of creative nonfiction writers / edited by Lee Gutkind.
p.   cm.
ISBN 0-435-07037-1 (acid-free paper)
1. American essays—20th century—History and criticism—Theory, etc.   2. Essay—Authorship.   I. Gutkind, Lee.
PS428.E86   1998
814'.5409—dc21
97-34958
CIP

Editor: Lisa A. Barnett
Cover design: Jenny Jensen Greenleaf
Manufacturing: Louise Richardson

Printed in the United States of America on acid-free paper.

00 99 98 97   DA   1 2 3 4 5 6

We would like to thank those who have given their permission to include material in this book.

"The Five Rs" from "The Immersion Journalism/Creative Nonfiction Interplay: Living and Writing the Literature of Reality," by Lee Gutkind reprinted by permission of Heinemann. In *More Than the Truth: Teaching Nonfiction Writing Through Journalism*, edited by Dennie Palmer Wolf and Julie Craven (Heinemann, A division of Reed Elsevier Inc., Portsmouth, NH, 1996).

"Schedules," by Annie Dillard. © copyright by Annie Dillard. Reprinted by permission of the author.

"Twenty Questions: A Conversation with John McPhee," by Michael Pearson was originally published in *Creative Nonfiction* (issue 1). © copyright 1996. Reprinted by permission of *Creative Nonfiction*.

"Son of Spoon River," by Hilary Masters was originally published in *Creative Nonfiction* (issue 5). © copyright 1996. Reprinted by permission of *Creative Nonfiction*.

Credits continued on page 232

CONTENTS

The
ESSAYIST
AT WORK

Introduction
The Five Rs of Creative Nonfiction

LEE GUTKIND

IT IS THREE A.M. AND I AM STANDING ON A STOOL IN THE operating room at the University of Pittsburgh Medical Center in scrubs, mask, cap, and paper booties, peering over the hunched shoulders of four surgeons and a scrub nurse as a dying woman's heart and lungs are being removed from her chest. This is a scene I have observed frequently since starting my work on a book about the world of organ transplantation, but it never fails to amaze and startle me: to look down into a gaping hole in a human being's chest, which has been cracked open and emptied of all of its contents, watch the monitor and listen to the rhythmic sighing sounds of the ventilator, and know that this woman is on the fragile cusp of life and death and that I am observing what might well be the final moments of her life.

Now the telephone rings; a nurse answers, listens for a moment and then hangs up. "On the roof," she announces, meaning that the helicopter has set down on the hospital helipad and that a healthy set of organs, a heart, and two lungs, en bloc, will soon be available to implant into this woman, whose immediate fate will be decided within the next few hours.

With a brisk nod, the lead surgeon, Bartley Griffith, a young man who pioneered heart-lung transplantation and who at this point has lost more patients with the procedure than he has saved, looks up, glances around and finally rests his eyes on me: "Lee," he says, "would you do me a great favor?"

I was surprised. Over the past three years I had observed Bart Griffith in the operating room a number of times, and although a great deal of conversation takes place between doctors and nurses during the long and intense surgical ordeal, he had only infrequently addressed me in such a direct and spontaneous manner.

Our personal distance is a by-product of my own technique as an immersion journalist—my fly-on-the-wall or living-room-sofa concept of immersion: Writers should be regular and silent observers, so much so that they are virtually unnoticed. Like walking through your living room dozens of times, but paying attention to the sofa only when suddenly you realize that it is missing. Researching a book about transplantation, *Many Sleepless Nights* (W.W. Norton), I had been accorded great access to the OR, the transplant wards, ethics debates, and the most intimate conversations between patients, family members, and medical staff. I had jetted through the night on organ donor runs. I had witnessed great drama—at a personal distance.

But on that important early morning, Bartley Griffith took note of my presence and requested that I perform a service for him. He explained that this was going to be a crucial time in the heart-lung procedure, which had been going on for about five hours, but that he felt obligated to make contact with this woman's husband who had traveled here from Kansas City, Missouri. "I can't take the time to talk to the man myself, but I am wondering if you would brief him as to what has happened so far. Tell him that the organs have arrived, but that even if all goes well, the procedure will take at least another five hours and maybe longer." Griffith didn't need to mention that the most challenging aspect of the surgery—the implantation—was upcoming; the danger to the woman was at a heightened state.

A few minutes later, on my way to the ICU waiting area where I would find Dave Fulk, the woman's husband, I stopped in the surgeon's lounge for a quick cup of coffee and a moment to think about how I might approach this man, undoubtedly nervous—perhaps even hysterical—waiting for news of his wife. I also felt kind of relieved, truthfully, to be out of the OR, where the atmosphere was so intense.

Although I had been totally caught-up in the drama of organ transplantation during my research, I had recently been losing my passion and curiosity; I was slipping into a life-and-death overload in which all of the sad stories from people all across the world seemed to be congealing into the same muddled dream. I recognized this feeling from experience— a clear signal that it was time to abandon the research phase of this book and sit down and start to write. Yet, as a writer, I was confronting a serious and frightening problem: Overwhelmed with facts and statistics, tragic and triumphant stories, I felt confused. I knew, basically, what I wanted to say about what I learned, but I didn't know how to structure my message or where to begin.

And so, instead of walking away from this research experience and sitting down and starting to write my book, I continued to return to the scene of my transplant adventures waiting for lightning to strike . . . inspiration for when the very special way to start my book would make itself known. In retrospect, I believe that Bart Griffith's rare request triggered that magic moment of clarity I had long been awaiting.

DEFINING THE DISCUSSION

Before I tell you what happened, however, let me explain what kind of work I do as an immersion journalist/creative nonfiction writer and define what I am doing, from a writer's point of view, in this essay.

But first some definitions: Immersion journalists immerse or involve themselves in the lives of the people about whom they are writing in ways that will provide readers with a rare and special intimacy.

The other phrase to define, a much broader term, creative nonfiction is a concept that offers great flexibility and freedom, while adhering to the basic tenets of nonfiction writing and/or reporting. In creative nonfiction, writers can be poetic and journalistic simultaneously. Creative nonfiction writers are encouraged to utilize fictional (literary) techniques in their prose—from scene to dialogue to description to point of view—and be cinematic at the same time. Creative nonfiction writers write about themselves and/or capture real people and real life in ways that can and have changed the world. What is most important and enjoyable about creative nonfiction is that it not only allows but encourages the writer to become a part of the story or essay being written. The personal involvement creates a special magic that alleviates the suffering and anxiety of the writing experience; it provides many outlets for satisfaction and self-discovery, flexibility, and freedom.

When I refer to creative nonfiction, I include memoir (autobiography), and documentary drama, a term more often used in relation to film, as in *Hoop Dreams*, which captures the lives of two inner-city high school basketball players over a six-year period. Much of what is generically referred to as literary journalism or, in the past, "new journalism," can be classified as creative nonfiction. Although it is the current vogue in the world of writing today, the combination of creative nonfiction as a form of writing and immersion as a method of research has a long history. George Orwell's famous essay, "Shooting an Elephant" combines personal experience and high quality literary writing techniques. The Daniel DeFoe classic, *Robinson Crusoe*, is based upon a true story of a physician who was marooned on a desert island. Ernest Hemingway's paean to bullfighting, *Death in the Afternoon*, comes under the creative nonfiction umbrella, as does Tom Wolfe's, *The Right Stuff*, which was made into an award-winning film.

In fact, many of the current masters of the creative nonfiction genre are represented in this collection, where the essay form is discussed and profiles of the creative nonfiction essayist at work are presented: John McPhee; Tracy Kidder; Gay Talese; Diane Ackerman; William Least Heat-Moon; Phillip Lopate; Annie Dillard; and others. Currently, many of our best magazines—*The New Yorker*, *Harper's*, *Vanity Fair*, *Esquire*—publish more creative nonfiction than fiction and poetry combined. Universities offer Master of Fine Arts degrees in creative nonfiction. Newspapers are publishing an increasing amount of creative nonfiction, not only as features, but in the news and op-ed pages as well. Most important, from my personal point of view, a literary journal—the triquarterly I edit called (quite appropriately) *Creative Nonfiction*—is devoted entirely to original new work of dramatic nonfiction prose.

THE FIVE Rs

Reading, 'Riting, 'Rithmitic—the three Rs—was the way in which basic public school education was once described. The "five Rs" is an easy way to remember the basic tenets of creative nonfiction/immersion journalism.

The first "R" has already been explained and discussed: the immersion or *real life* aspect of the writing experience. As a writing teacher, I design assignments that force my students out into their communities for an hour, a day, or even a week so that they see and understand that the foundation of good writing emerges from personal experience. Some writers (and students) may utilize their own personal experience rather than immersing themselves in the experiences of others. In a recent introductory class I taught, one young man working his way through school as a sales person wrote about selling shoes, while another student, who served as a volunteer in a hospice, captured a dramatic moment of death, grief, and family relief. I've sent my students to police stations, bagel shops, golf courses; together, my classes have gone on excursions and participated in public service projects—all in an attempt to re-create from personal experience real life.

In contrast to the term *reportage*, the word *essay* usually connotes a more personal message from writer to reader. "An essay is when I write what I think about something," students will often say to me. Which is true, to a certain extent—and also the source of the meaning of the second R for *reflection*. A writer's feelings and responses about a subject are permitted and encouraged, as long as what they think is written to embrace the reader in a variety of ways.

As editor of *Creative Nonfiction*, I receive approximately one hundred fifty unsolicited essays, book excerpts and profiles a month for possible publication. Of the many reasons the vast majority of these submissions are rejected, two are most prevalent, the first being an overwhelming egocentrism; in other words, writers write too much about themselves without seeking a universal focus or umbrella so that readers are properly and firmly engaged. Essays that are so personal that they omit the reader are essays that will never see the light of print. The overall objective of the personal essayist is to make the reader tune in—not out.

The second reason *Creative Nonfiction* and most other journals and magazines reject essays is a lack of attention to the mission of the genre, which is to gather and present information, to teach readers about a person, place, idea, or situation combining the creativity of the artistic experience with the essential third R in the formula: *Research*.

Even the most personal essay is usually full of substantive detail about a subject that affects or concerns a writer and the people about whom he or she is writing. Read the books and essays of the most renowned nonfiction writers in this century and you will read about a writer engaged in a quest for information and discovery. From George Orwell to Ernest Hemingway to John McPhee, books and essays written by these writers are invariably about a subject other than themselves, although the narrator will be intimately included in the story. Personal experience and spontaneous intellectual discourse—an airing and exploration of ideas—are equally vital. In her first book, *Pilgrim at Tinker Creek*, which won the Pulitzer Prize, and in her other books and essays, Annie Dillard repeatedly overwhelms her readers with factual information, minutely detailed descriptions of insects, botany and biology, history, anthropology, blended with her own feelings about life.

One of my favorite Dillard essays, "Schedules," which appears in this collection, focuses on the importance of writers working on a regular schedule rather than writing only intermittently. In "Schedules," she discusses, among many other subjects, Hasidism, chess, baseball, warblers, pine trees, june bugs, writers' studios, and potted plants—not to mention her own schedule and writing habits and that of Wallace Stevens and Jack London.

What I am saying is that the genre of creative nonfiction, although anchored in factual information, is open to anyone with a curious mind and a sense of self. The research phase actually launches and anchors the creative effort. Whether it is a book or essay I am planning, I always begin my quest in the library—for three reasons. First, I need to familiarize myself with the subject. If it is something about which I do not know, I want to make myself knowledgeable enough to ask intelligent questions. If I can't display at least a minimal understanding of the subject about which I am writing, I will lose the confidence and the support of the people who must provide access to the experience.

Secondly, I will want to assess my competition. What other essays, books, and articles have been written about this subject? Who are the experts, the pioneers, the most controversial figures? I want to find a new angle, not write a story similar to one that has already been written. And finally, how can I reflect and evaluate a person, subject, or place unless I know all of the contrasting points of view? Reflection may permit a certain amount of speculation, but only when based upon a solid foundation of knowledge.

So far in this essay I have named a number of well-respected creative nonfiction writers and discussed their work, which means I have satisfied the fourth R in our *five-R* formula: *Reading*. Not only must writers read the research material unearthed in the library, but they also must read the work of the masters of their profession. I have heard some very fine writers claim that they don't read too much anymore—or that they don't read for long periods, especially during the time they are laboring on a lengthy writing project. But almost all writers have read the best writers in their field and are able to converse in great detail about their stylistic approach and intellectual content. An artist who has never studied Picasso, Van Gogh, Michelangelo, even Warhol, is an artist who will quite possibly never succeed.

To this point, we have mostly discussed the nonfiction or journalistic aspects of the immersion journalism/creative nonfiction genre. The fifth R the *riting* part is the most artistic and romantic aspect of the total experience. After all of the preparatory (nonfiction) work is complete, writers will often create in two phases. Usually, there is an inspirational explosion, a time when writers allow instinct and feeling to guide their fingers as they create paragraphs, pages, and even entire chapters of books or complete essays. This is what art of any form is all about—the passion of the moment and the magic of the muse. I am not saying that this always happens; it doesn't. Writing is a difficult labor, in which a regular schedule, a daily grind of struggle, is inevitable. But this first part of the experience for most writers is rather loose and spontaneous and therefore more creative and fun. The second part of the writing experience—the craft part, which comes into play after a basic essay is written—is equally important—and a hundred times more difficult.

WRITING IN SCENES

Vignettes, episodes, slices of reality are the building blocks of creative nonfiction—the primary distinguishing factor between traditional reportage/journalism and literary and/or creative nonfiction and between good, evocative writing and ordinary prose. The uninspired writer will tell the reader about a subject, place, or personality, but the creative nonfiction writer will show that subject, place, or personality in action. Before we discuss the actual content or construction of a scene, let me suggest that you perform what I like to call the "yellow test."

Take a yellow Hi-Liter or Magic Marker and leaf through a favorite magazine—*Vanity Fair, Esquire, The New Yorker*, or *Creative Nonfiction*. Or return to favorite chapters in books by Dillard, Ackerman, etc. Yellow-in the scenes, just the scenes, large and small. Then return to the beginning and review your handiwork. Chances are, anywhere from 50 to 80 percent of each essay, short story, novel selected will be yellow. Plays are obviously constructed with scenes, as are films. Most poems are very scenic.

Jeanne Marie Laskas, the talented columnist for the *Washington Post Magazine*, once told me: "I only have one rule from start to finish. I write in scenes. It doesn't matter to me in which order the scenes are written; I write whichever scene inspires me at any given time, and I worry about the plot or frame or narrative later. The scene—a scene—any scene—is always first."

THE ELEMENTS OF A SCENE

First and foremost, a scene contains action. Something happens. I jump on my motorcycle and go helter-skelter around the country; suddenly, in the middle of July in Yellowstone National Park I am confronted with twenty inches of snow. Action needn't be wild, sexy, and death-defying, however. There's also action in the classroom. A student asks a question, that requires an answer, that necessitates a dialogue, that is a marvelously effective tool to trigger or record action. Dialogue represents people saying things to one another, expressing themselves. It is a valuable scenic building block. Discovering dialogue is one of the reasons to immerse ourselves at a police station, bagel shop, or at a zoo. To discover what people have to say spontaneously—and not in response to a reporter's prepared questions.

Another vehicle or technique of the creative nonfiction experience may be described as intimate and specific detail. Through use of intimate detail, we can hear and see how the people about whom we are writing say what is on their minds; we may note the inflections in their voices, their elaborate hand movements and any other eccentricities. "Intimate" is a key distinction in the use of detail when crafting good scenes. Intimate means recording and noting detail that the reader might not know or even imagine without your particular inside insight. Sometimes intimate detail can be so specific and special that it becomes unforgettable in the reader's mind. A very famous intimate detail appears in a classic creative nonfiction profile, "Frank Sinatra Has a Cold," written by Gay Talese in 1962 and published in *Esquire Magazine*.

In this profile, Talese leads readers on a whirlwind cross-country tour, revealing Sinatra and his entourage interacting with one another and with the rest of the world and demonstrating how the Sinatra world and the world inhabited by everyone else will often collide. These scenes are action-oriented; they contain dialogue and evocative description with great specificity and intimacy such as the gray-haired lady spotted in the shadows of the Sinatra entourage—the guardian of Sinatra's collection of toupées. This tiny detail—Sinatra's wig lady—loomed so large in my mind when I first read the essay that even now, thirty-five years later, anytime I see Sinatra on TV or spot his photo in a magazine, I find myself unconsciously searching the background for the gray-haired lady with the hatbox. Gay Talese's contribution to this collection provides essential background behind the researching and writing of this classic essay.

THE NARRATIVE OR FRAME

The frame represents a way of ordering or controlling a writer's narrative so that the elements of his book, article, or essay are presented in an interesting and orderly fashion with an interlaced integrity from beginning to end.

Some frames are very complicated, as in the movie, Pulp Fiction; Quentin Tarantino skillfully tangles and manipulates time. But the most basic frame is a simple beginning-to-end chronology. The dramatic documentary (which is also classic creative nonfiction) Hoop Dreams, for example, begins with two African-American teenage basketball stars living in a ghetto and sharing a dream of stardom in the NBA and dramatically tracks both of their careers over the next six years.

As demonstrated in Pulp Fiction, writers don't always frame in a strictly chronological sequence. My book, One Children's Place, begins in the operating room at a children's hospital. It introduces a surgeon, whose name is Marc Rowe, his severely handicapped patient, Danielle, and her mother, Debbie, who has dedicated her every waking moment to Danielle. Two years of her life have been spent inside the walls of this building with parents and children from all across the world whose lives are too endangered to leave the confines of the hospital. As Danielle's surgery goes forward, the reader tours the hospital in a very intimate way, observing in the emergency room; participating in helicopter rescue missions as part of the emergency trauma team; attending ethics meetings, well-baby clinics, child abuse examinations—every conceivable activity at a typical high-acuity children's hospital so that readers will learn from the inside out how such an institution and the people it services and supports function on an hour-by-hour basis. We even learn about Marc Rowe's guilty conscience about how he has slighted his own wife and children over the years so that he can care for other families.

The book ends when Danielle is released from the hospital. It took two years to research and write this book, returning day and night to the hospital in order to understand the hospital and the people who made it special, but the story in which it is framed begins and ends in a few months.

BACK TO THE BEGINNING—THAT RARE AND WONDERFUL MOMENT OF CLARITY

Now let's think about this essay as a piece of creative nonfiction writing, especially in relation to the concept of framing. It begins with a scene. We are in an operating room at the University of Pittsburgh, the world's largest organ transplant center, in the middle of a rare and delicate surgery that will decide a dying woman's fate. Her heart and both lungs have been emptied out of her chest and she is maintained on a heart-bypass system. The telephone alerts the surgical team that a fresh and potentially lifesaving set of organs has arrived at the hospital via helicopter. Suddenly the lead surgeon looks up and asks an observer (me) to make contact with the woman's husband. I agree, leave the operating room and then stop for a coffee in the surgeon's lounge.

Then, instead of moving the story forward, fulfilling my promise to Dr. Griffith and resolving my own writing dilemma, I change directions, move backwards (flashback) in time and sequence and begin to discuss this genre: immersion journalism/creative nonfiction. I provide a mountain of information—definitions, descriptions, examples, explanations. Basically, I am attempting to satisfy the nonfiction part of my responsibility to my readers and my editors while hoping that the suspense created in the first few pages will provide an added inducement for readers to remain focused and interested in this Introduction from the beginning to the end where, (the reader assumes) the two stories introduced in the first few pages will be completed.

In fact, my meeting with Dave Fulk in the ICU waiting room that dark morning was exactly the experience I had been waiting for, leading to that precious and magic moment of clarity for which I was searching and hoping. When I arrived, Mr. Fulk was talking with an elderly man and woman from Sacramento, California, who happened to be the parents of a twenty-one-year-old US Army private named Rebecca Treat who, I soon discovered, was the recipient of the liver from the same donor who gave Dave's wife (Winkle Fulk) a heart and lungs. Rebecca

Treat, life-flighted to Pittsburgh from California, had been in a coma for ten days by the time she arrived in Pittsburgh; the transplanted liver was her only hope of ever emerging from that coma and seeing the light of day.

Over the next half hour of conversation, I learned that Winkle Fulk had been slowly dying for four years, had been bedridden for three of those years, as Dave and their children watched her life dwindle away, as fluid filled her lungs and began to destroy her heart. Rebecca's fate had been much more sudden; having contracted hepatitis in the army, she crashed almost immediately. To make matters worse, Rebecca and her new husband had separated. As I sat in the darkened waiting area with Dave Fulk and Rebecca's parents, I suddenly realized what it was I was looking for, what my frame or narrative element could be. I wanted to tell about the organ transplant experience—and what organ transplantation can mean from a universal perspective—medically, scientifically, personally for patients, families, and surgeons. Rebecca's parents and the Fulk family, once strangers, would now be permanently and intimately connected by still another stranger—the donor—the person whose tragic death provided hope and perhaps salvation to two dying people. In fact, my last quest in the research phase of the transplant book experience was to discover the identity of this mysterious donor and literally connect the principal characters. In so doing, the frame or narrative drive of the story emerged.

Many Sleepless Nights begins when fifteen-year-old Richie Becker, a healthy and handsome teenager from Charlotte, North Carolina, discovers that his father is going to sell the sports car that he had hoped would one day be his. In a spontaneous and thoughtless gesture of defiance, Richie, who had never been behind the wheel, secretly takes his father's sports car on a joy ride. Three blocks from his home, he wraps the car around a tree and is subsequently declared brain dead at the local hospital. Devastated by the experience, but hoping for some positive outcome to such a senseless tragedy, Richie's father, Dick, donates his son's organs for transplantation.

Then the story flashes back a half century, detailing surgeons' first attempts at transplantation and all of the experimentation and controversy leading up to the development and acceptance of transplant techniques. I introduce Winkle Fulk and Private Rebecca Treat. Richie Becker's liver is transplanted into Rebecca, while his heart and lungs are sewn into Mrs. Fulk by Dr. Bartley Griffith. The last scene of the book three hundred seventy pages later is dramatic and telling and finishes the frame three years later when Winkle Fulk travels to Charlotte, North Carolina, a reunion I arranged to allow the folks to personally thank Richie's father for his son's gift of life.

> At the end of the evening, just as we were about to say goodbye and return to the motel, Dick Becker stood up in the center of the living room of his house, paused, and then walked slowly and hesitantly over toward Winkle Fulk, who had once stood alone at the precipice of death. He eased himself down on his knees, took Winkle Fulk by the shoulder and simultaneously drew her closer, as he leaned forward and placed his ear gently but firmly between her breasts and then at her back.
>
> Everyone in that room was suddenly and silently breathless, watching as Dick Becker listened for the last time to the absolutely astounding miracle of organ transplantation: the heart and the lungs of his dead son Richie, beating faithfully and unceasingly inside this stranger's warm and loving chest.

Lee Gutkind's award-winning Many Sleepless Nights, *an inside chronicle of the world of organ transplantation, has been reprinted in Italian, Korean, and Japanese editions, while his most recent nonfiction book, a Book-of-the-Month Club selection,* An Unspoken Art, *was published by Henry Holt in 1997. He is a professor of English at the University of Pittsburgh.*

Schedules

ANNIE DILLARD

What if man could see Beauty Itself, pure, unalloyed, stripped of mortality and all its pollution, stains, and vanities, unchanging, divine, . . . the man becoming, in that communion, the friend of God, himself immortal; . . . would that be a life to disregard? —Plato

I HAVE BEEN LOOKING INTO SCHEDULES. EVEN WHEN we read physics, we inquire of each least particle, "What then shall I do this morning?" How we spend our days is, of course, how we spend our lives. What we do with this hour, and that one, is what we are doing. A schedule defends from chaos and whim. It is a net for catching days. It is a scaffolding on which a worker can stand and labor with both hands at sections of time. A schedule is a mock-up of reason and order—willed, faked, and so brought into being; it is a peace and a haven set into the wreck of time; it is a lifeboat on which you find yourself, decades later, still living. Each day is the same, so you remember the series afterward as a blurred idyll.

The most appealing daily schedule I know is that of a certain turn-of-the-century Swedish aristocrat. He got up at four and set out on foot to hunt black grouse, wood grouse, woodcock, and snipe. At eleven he met his friends who had also been out hunting alone all morning. They converged "at one of these babbling brooks," he wrote. He outlined the rest of his schedule.

Take a quick dip, relax with a schnapps and a sandwich, stretch out, have a smoke, take a nap or just rest, and then sit around and chat until three. Then I hunt some more until sundown, bathe again, put on white tie and tails to keep up appearances, eat a huge dinner, smoke a cigar and sleep like a log until the sun comes up again to redden the eastern sky. This is living. . . Could it be more perfect?

There is no shortage of good days. It is good lives that are hard to come by. A life of good days living in the senses is not enough. The life of sensation is the life of greed; it requires more and more. The life of the spirit requires less and less; time is ample and its passage sweet. Who would call a day spent reading a good day? But a life spent reading—that is a good life. A day that closely resembles every other day for the past ten or twenty years does not suggest itself as a good one. But who would not call Pasteur's life a good one, or Thomas Mann's?

Wallace Stevens in his forties, living in Hartford, Connecticut, hewed to a productive routine. He rose at six, read for two hours, and walked another hour—three miles— to work. He dictated poems to his secretary. He ate not lunch; at noon he walked for another hour, often to an art gallery. He walked home from work—another hour. After dinner he returned to his study; he went to bed at nine. On Sundays, he walked in the park. I don't know what he did on Saturdays. Perhaps he exchanged a few words with his wife, who posed for the Liberty dime. (One would rather read these people, or lead their lives, than be their wives. When Swedish aristocrat Wilhelm Dinesen shot birds all day, drank schnapps, napped, and dressed for dinner, he and his wife had three children under three. The middle one was Karen, later known as Isak Dinesen.)

Like Stevens, Osip Mandelstam composed poetry on the hoof. So did Dante. Nietzsche, like Emerson, took two long walks a day. "When my creative energy flowed most freely, my muscular activity was always greatest . . . I might often have been seen dancing; I used to walk through the hills for seven or eight hours on end—I was perfectly vigorous and patient" (Nietzsche). On the other hand, A. E. Housman, almost predictably, maintained, "I have seldom written poetry unless I was rather out of health." This makes sense, too, because in writing a book you can be too well for your own good.

Jack London claimed to write twenty hours a day. Before he undertook to write, he obtained the University of California course list and all the syllabi; he spent a year reading the textbooks in philosophy and literature. In subsequent years, once he had a book of his own under way, he set his alarm to wake him after four hours sleep. Often he slept through the alarm, so, by his own account, he rigged it to drop a weight on his head. I cannot say I believe this, though a novel like *The Sea Wolf* is strong evidence that some sort of wright fell on his head with some sort of frequency—though you wouldn't think a man would claim credit for it. London maintained that every writer needed experience, a technique, and a philosophical position. Perhaps the position need not be an airtight one; London himself felt comfortable with a weird amalgam of Karl Marx and Herbert Spencer (Marks & Sparks).

I write these words in my most recent of many studies—a pine shed on Cape Cod. The pine lumber is unfinished inside the study; the pines outside are finished trees. I see the pines from my two windows. Nuthatches spiral around their long, coarse trunks. Sometimes in June a feeding colony of mixed warblers flies through the pines; the warblers make a racket that draws me out the door. The warblers drift loosely through the stiff pine branches, and I follow through the thin long grass between the trunks.

The study—sold as a prefabricated toolshed—is eight feet by ten feet. Like a plane's cockpit, it is crammed with high-tech equipment. There is no quill pen in sight. There is a computer, a printer, and a photocopying machine. My backless chair, *aprie-dieu* on which I kneel, slides under the desk; I give it a little kick when I leave. There is an air conditioner, a heater, and an electric kettle. There is a low-tech bookshelf, a shelf of gull and whale bones, and a bed. Under the bed I stow paints—a one-pint can of yellow to touch up the window's trim, and five or six tubes of artists' oils. The study affords ample room for one. One who is supposed to be writing books. You can read in the space of a coffin, and you can write in a space of a toolshed meant for mowers and spades.

I walk up here from the house every morning. The study and its pines, and the old summer cottages nearby, and the new farm just north of me, rise from an old sand dune high over a creeky salt marsh. From the bright lip of the dune I can see oyster farmers working their beds on the tidal flats and sailboats under way in the saltwater bay. After I have warmed myself standing at the crest of the dune, I return under the pines, enter the study, slam the door so the latch catches— and then I cannot see. The green spot in front of my eyes outshines everything in the shade. I lie on the bed and play with a bird bone until I can see it.

Appealing workplaces are to be avoided. One wants a room with no view, so imagination can dance with memory in the dark. When I furnished this study seven years ago, I pushed the long desk against a blank wall, so I could not see from either window. Once, fifteen years ago, I wrote in a cinder-block cell over a parking lot. It overlooked a tar-and-gravel roof. This pine shed under trees is not quite so good as the cinder-block study was, but it will do.

"The beginning of wisdom," according to a West African proverb, "is to get you a roof."

It was on summer nights in Roanoke, Virginia, that I wrote the second half of a book, *Pilgrim at Tinker Creek*. (I wrote the first half in the spring, at home.) Ruefully I noted then that I would possibly look back on those times as an idyll.

I slept until noon, as did my husband, who was also writing. I wrote once in the afternoon, and once again after our early dinner and a walk. During those months, I subsisted on that dinner, coffee, Coke, chocolate milk, and Vantage cigarettes. I worked till midnight, one, or two. When I came home in the middle of the night I was tired; I longed for a tolerant giant, a person as big as a house, to hold me and rock me. In fact, an exhausted daydream—almost a hallucination—of being rocked and soothed sometimes forced itself upon me, and interrupted me even when I was talking or reading.

I had a room—a study carrel—in the Hollins College library, on the second floor. It was this room that overlooked a tar-and-gravel roof. A plate-glass window, beside me on the left, gave out a number of objects: the roof, a parking lot, a distant portion of Carvin's Creek, some complicated Virginia sky, and a far hilltop where six cows grazed around a ruined foundation under red cedars.

From my desk I kept an eye out. Intriguing people, people I knew, pulled into the parking lot and climbed from their cars. The cows moved on the hilltop. (I drew the cows, for they were made interestingly; they hung in catenary curves from their skeletons, like two-man tents.) On the flat roof just outside the window, sparrows pecked gravel. One of the sparrows lacked a leg; one was missing a foot. If I stood and peered around I could see a feeder creek running at the edge of a field. In the creek, even from that great distance, I could see muskrats and snapping turtles. If I saw a snapping turtle, I ran downstairs and out of the library to watch it or poke it.

One afternoon I made a pen drawing of the window and the landscape it framed. I drew the window's aluminum frame and steel hardware; I sketched in the clouds and the far hilltop with its ruined foundation and wandering cows. I outlined the parking lot and its tall row of mercury-vapor lights; I drew the cars, and the graveled rooftop foreground.

If I craned my head, I could see a grassy playing field below. One afternoon I peered around at that field and saw a softball game. Since I happened to have my fielder's glove with me in my study, I thought it would be a generous thing to join the game. On the field, I learned there was a music camp on campus for two weeks. The little boys playing softball were musical whizzes. They could not all play ball, but their patter was a treat. "All right, MacDonald," they jeered when one kid came to bat, "that pizzicato won't help you now." It was slightly better than no softball, so I played with them every day, second base, terrified that I would bust a prodigy's fingers on a throw to first or the plate.

I shut the blinds one day for good. I lowered the venitian blinds and flattened the slats. Then, by lamplight, I taped my drawing to the closed blind. There, on the drawing, was the window's view: cows, parking lot, hilltop, and sky. If I wanted a sense of the world, I could look at the stylized outline drawing. If I had possessed the skill, I would have painted, directly on the slats of the lower blind, in meticulous colors, a *trompe l'oeil* mural view of all that the blinds hid. Instead, I wrote it.

On the Fourth of July, my husband and our friends drove into the city, Roanoke, to see the fireworks. I begged off; I wanted to keep working. I was working hard, although of course it did not seem hard enough at the time—a finished chapter every few weeks. I castigated myself daily for writing too slowly. Even when passages seemed to come easily, as though I were copying from a folio held open by smiling angels, the manuscript revealed the usual signs of struggle—blood stains, teeth marks, gashes, and burns.

This night, as on most nights, I entered the library at dusk. The building was locked and dark. I had a key. Every night I let myself in, climbed the stairs, found my way between the tall stacks in the dark, located and unlocked my study's door, and turned on the light. I remember how many stacks I had to hit with my hand in the dark before I turned down the row to my study. Even if I left only to get a drink of water, I felt and counted the stacks with my hand again to find my room. Once in daylight I glanced at a book on a stack's corner, a book I presumably touched every night with my hand. The book was *The World I Live In*, by Helen Keller. I read it at once; it surprised me by its strong and original prose.

When I flicked on my carrel light, there it all was: the bare room with yellow cinder-block walls; the big, flattened venitian blind and my drawing taped to it; two or three quotations taped up on index cards; and on a far table some books, the fielder's mitt, and a yellow bag of chocolate-covered peanuts. There was the long, blonde desk and its chair, and on the desk a dozen different-colored pens, some big index cards in careful, splayed piles, and my messy yellow legal pads. As soon as I saw that desktop, I remembered the task: the chapter, its problems, its phrases, its points.

This night I was concentrating on the chapter. The horizon of my consciousness was the contracted circle of yellow light inside my study—the lone lamp in the enormous, dark library. I leaned over the desk. I worked by hand. I doodled deliriously in the legal-pad margins. I fiddled with the index cards. I reread a sentence maybe a hundred times, and if I kept it I changed it seven or eight times, often substantially.

Now a June bug was knocking at my window. I was wrestling inside a sentence. I must have heard it a dozen times before it registered, before I noticed that I had been hearing a bug knock for half an hour. It made a hollow, bunking sound. Some people call the same fumbling, heavy insects May beetles. It must have been attracted to my light, what little came between the slats of the blind. I dislike June bugs. Back to work. Knock again, knock again, and finally, to learn what monster of a fat, brown June bug could fly up to a second story and thump so insistently at my window as though it wanted admittance, at last, unthinkingly, I parted the venitian blind slats with my fingers, to look out.

And there were the fireworks, far away. It was the Fourth of July. I had forgotten. They were red and yellow, blue and green and white; they blossomed bright in the black sky many miles away. The fireworks seemed as distant as the stars, but I could hear the late banging their bursting made. The sound, those bangs so muffled and out of synch, accompanied at random the silent, far sprays of color widening and raining down. It was the Fourth of July, and I had forgotten all of wide space and all of historical time. I opened the blinds a crack like eyelids, and it all came exploding in on me at once—oh yes, the world.

My working the graveyard shift in Virginia affected the book. It was a nature book full of sunsets; it wholly lacked dawns, and even mornings.

I was reading about Hasidism, among other things. If you stay awake one hundred nights, you get the vision of Elijah. I was not eager for it, although it seemed to be just around the corner. I preferred this: "Rebbe Shmelke of Nickolsburg, it was told, never really heard his teacher, the Maggid of Mezritch, finish a thought because as soon as the latter would say 'and the Lord spoke,' Shmelke would begin shouting in wonderment, 'The Lord spoke, the Lord spoke,' and continue shouting until he had to be carried from the room."

The second floor of the library, where I worked every night, housed the rare book room. It was a wide, carpeted, well-furnished room. On an end table, as if for decoration, stood a wooden chess set.

One night, stuck on an intractable problem in the writing,

I wandered the dark library looking for distraction. I flicked on the lights in the rare book room and looked at some of the books. I saw the chess set and moved white's king's pawn. I turned off the light and wandered back to my carrel.

A few nights later, I glanced into the rare book room and walked in, for black's queen's pawn had moved. I moved out my knight.

We were off and running. Every day, my unseen opponent moved. I moved. I never saw anyone anywhere near the rare book room. The college was not in session; almost no one was around. Late at night I heard the night watchmen clank around downstairs in the dark. The watchmen never came upstairs. There was no one upstairs but me.

When the chess game was ten days old, I entered the rare book room to find black's pieces coming toward me on the carpet. They seemed to be marching, in rows of two. I put them back as they had been and made my move. The next day, the pieces were all piled on the board. I put them back as they had been. The next day, black had moved, rather brilliantly.

Late one night, while all this had been going on, and while the library was dark and locked as it had been all summer and I had accustomed myself to the eeriness of it, I left my carrel to cross the darkness and get a drink of water. I saw a strange chunk of light on the floor between stacks. Passing the stacks, I saw the light spread across the hall. I held my breath. The light was coming from the rare book room; the door was open.

I approached quietly and looked in the room from an angle. There, at the chess table, stood a baby. The baby had blond curls and was wearing only a diaper.

I paused, considering that I had been playing a reasonable game of chess for two weeks with a naked baby. After a while I could make out the sound of voices; I moved closer to the doorway and peered in. There was the young head librarian and his wife, sitting on chairs. I pieced together the rest of it. The librarian stopped by to pick something up. Naturally, he had a key. The couple happened to have the baby along. The baby, just learning to walk, had cruised from the chairs to the table. The baby was holding on to the table, not studying the chess pieces' positions. I greeted the family and played with the baby until they left.

I never did learn who or what was playing chess with me. The game went on until my lunatic opponent scrambled the board so violently the game was over.

During that time, I let all the houseplants die. After the book was finished I noticed them; the plants hung completely black, dead in their pots in the bay window. For I had not only let them die, I had not moved them. During that time, I told all my out-of-town friends they could not visit for a while.

"I understand you're married," a man said to me at a formal lunch in New York that my publisher had arranged. "How do you have time to write a book?"

"Sir?"

"Well," he said, "you have to have a garden, for instance. You have to entertain." And I thought he was foolish, this man in his seventies, who had no idea what you must do. But the fanaticism of my twenties shocks me now. As I feared it would.

Annie Dillard is the author of The Writing Life, American Childhood, Teaching a Stone to Talk, *and other books.* Pilgrim at Tinker Creek *won the Pulitzer prize in general nonfiction for 1975.*

Twenty Questions
A Conversation with
John McPhee

MICHAEL PEARSON

During his four collegiate years he appeared on "Twenty Questions," a weekly television and radio program originating from New York. The producers wanted one young person on the show's panel. Fond of games, he rapidly mastered the art of identifying mystery items—animal, vegetable, or mineral—with questions that could only be answered Yes or No. The training was probably useful for a future journalist; it taught him how to assemble facts and infer their hidden meanings.

—William Howarth, *The John McPhee Reader*

THE ROOM IS LONGER THAN A MONK'S CELL BUT NOT MUCH wider. It even has the requisite ascetic's cot, narrow and uncomfortable looking. The corridor outside is bland and featureless, and the doors are made of the sort of pressboard that would probably splinter under a loud "Amen." But even though the East Pyne Building has the stony elegance of a medieval monastery, it's actually the Center for Humanities on the Princeton University campus, where on most days for twelve hours or so John McPhee uses that cot in Room 311 to "work horizontally," writing on a clipboard until "everything tumbles into the right slot."

Perhaps more consistently and dramatically than any other nonfiction writer today, McPhee has been able to find the right slot, producing over twenty books in little more than a quarter of a century. At sixty-one years old, he is still slim and athletic, and although after an Achilles tendon injury a few years ago he no longer plays basketball or tennis, he still rides his bicycle when he's not off marching with the Swiss army, standing aboard a Merchant Marine vessel or roaming the geological backroads of America. The final book in his quartet on geology, *Assembling California*, has recently been published. He is already involved in another project about the cattle business in Utah.

A handwritten sign over the inside of his office door reads, "My patience is not inexhaustible," but my suspicion is that patience may be a big part of his genius. In conversation, as in his books, McPhee is a lover of small details. He is the kind of man who draws intricate directions on the backs of cocktail napkins. He is a connoisseur of topographic maps, a passionate list maker, a reverent collector of facts. He seems to have as much patience with people as he does with the materials he shapes into his stories. This is my second talk with him. A few months ago he met with me to discuss my project on the New Jersey Pine Barrens, a return to the place twenty-five years after his account, using his book as an imaginative guide. Of course, he's not an easy man to get in touch with— no one who has written a book virtually every year since his mid-thirties can have much time for anything but writing or family (four daughters by his first marriage and four step-children). This time we meet to discuss the writing process in general. I have in mind a *Paris Review* style of interview, a question-and-answer format, and I have specific things to ask him. Because I feel lucky to have the chance to speak with him, to catch him for the second time between travel and writing, I don't even murmur dissent when he says he doesn't want me to use a tape recorder. "This is strictly a professional decision," he says. "You'll get a better story without a tape recorder. Besides, the question-and-answer format is the most primitive form of writing, you realize. Writing is selection. It's better to start choosing right here and right now."

However, he tells me that, despite the myth that he never uses such machines, he uses tape recorders "with some frequency." He uses them when a person speaks so rapidly or technically that it is difficult to get the words otherwise. He used a tape recorder, and made that fact clear in "Looking for a Ship," a book about the United States Merchant Marine, in his conversations with Captain Washburn, for instance. Finally, though, he feels that such machines have a tendency to "slavishly reproduce Bushisms," and he seems happy to tell me about the reporter who interviewed him some years back—with a tape recorder. The reporter didn't bother to take notes, and McPhee got a call that night: "The man was in a deep gloom. The machine hadn't recorded anything."

Therefore, as I hesitate for a moment in front of East Pyne, the stone archways looking like the entranceway to a forbidding castle, I can't stop myself from having some serious doubts about interviewing a writer who has been described by one reviewer as a man with "total recall." I check my bag—three pens, two notebooks, questions, extra batteries for the tape recorder left behind—and bound down the hall, past television newscaster Roger Mudd, who is having a conference with a student, and knock on 311. The man who answers the door is slight, but there is nothing fragile about him. He looks like a man who might have recently explored Alaska, traveled through the orange groves in Florida, or canoed the rivers of northern Maine. He has dark gray hair, a slightly grayer beard, and a healthy, weathered face. Canted ever so slightly to the right, his glasses sit a bit crookedly on his nose. His eyes are clear, and although they are laced underneath with lines, they have a smile that seems to dismiss the possibility of weariness. He is dressed casually, in an orderly disarray—corduroy pants, a faded green shirt, black socks, and brown walking shoes. It's hard to imagine him in a white suit, à la Tom Wolfe, or on the talk show circuit, like Truman Capote, or loudly proclaiming his character, in the blaring tones of Norman Mailer. He seems more like Joan Didion, inconspicuous. It's possible to see how his description of Frank L. Boyden in *The Headmaster* might fit him as well: "People walk right by him sometimes without seeing him."

His office seems to fit him, too. It is casual and unpretentious but neat and organized even in its motley look. On one wall is a physical map of the world, on another a tectonic map of North America, and on another a series of geological maps with a sign "Public toilet 440 yards" thumbtacked over it. The far end of the room looks like a version of Fred Brown's yard in *The Pine Barrens*—a small refrigerator, an ancient typewriter, a coffee maker—but unlike Brown's collection, everything here seems in good working order. "At one time," McPhee says, "I had the idea that the room where you worked on a piece of writing would be filled exclusively with stuff related to what you were working on, covering the walls."

"But," he says, looking at the pictures of his family and the memorabilia from friends and various assignments, "that's been violated more than once, as you can see." However, the room seems less a violation than a representation of the man. There are a number of desks and bookcases bridging one end of the room and the other, and a cot with papers placed in carefully separated piles—letters from his publisher, a note pad from *The New Yorker*, even a paperback copy of *The Pine Barrens* lying there as if it's waiting for me to pick it up. The dictionary on the desk near the door just happens to be open to the phrase *legal cap*, and a sign near the ceiling warns:

Danger
Bear Trap
Do Not Approach

Clearly the private and public man are entwined in all this, in the photographs of Captain Washburn standing alone or Bill Bradley towering over McPhee, in the canvas bags—saying Princeton English Department or Department of Geology/Princeton University—in the picture of his daughter, Laura, with the inscription "Portrait of the Artist as a Young(ish) Teacher." A metal statue of a basketball player and a plastic cube with photographs of his daughters serve as bookends for a shelf of books by former students. McPhee graduated from Princeton University and spent a year abroad studying literature and playing basketball at Cambridge University, but his dream was to write for *The New Yorker*. When he was eighteen he decided that he would one day write a long fact piece for the magazine. For the next fourteen years he collected rejection slips from *The New Yorker*, wrote television scripts, and became a staff reporter for *Time* magazine. In 1963, at the age of thirty-two, he received his first acceptance from *The New Yorker* for "Basketball and Beefeaters," a story about his adventures playing basketball in Great Britain. His first book, *A Sense of Where You Are*, a profile of Bill Bradley, was published two years later. It was not long before William Shawn, then editor of *The New Yorker*, offered McPhee a position as a staff writer.

There is a separate bookcase for works of nonfiction that he uses in the course he teaches at Princeton titled "The Literature of Fact"—*In Cold Blood, Joe Gould's Secret, Blue Highways, Let Us Now Praise Famous Men, Armies of the Night, Hiroshima, The Right Stuff, In Patagonia, Five Seasons, The Sea Around Us, The Soul of a New Machine*, and others. The first book on the shelf, *Alive*, and the last, *The Journalist and the Murderer*, are both, ironically, it seems, about forms of cannibalism and perhaps the pitfalls of writing nonfiction.

But, as McPhee sits back in his chair, hands behind his head and feet propped up on his desk, his voice is calm and self-assured. He gives his beard a meditative scratch and takes his time, mulling things over, structuring his ideas like the pieces of one of his stories, and answers in a voice that is rasping and slightly nasal but pleasant, with just a whisper of his New Jersey upbringing. It's a voice that has a rough lyrical clarity which seems perfectly tuned for communicating long passages of information. And behind every sentence, pushing each vowel and consonant out a fraction faster than you would expect, is the source of McPhee's writing: a curiosity about the world and a boyish exuberance about what he has learned out there.

I wish I hadn't asked my first question as soon as it leaves my mouth: Many critics see *Coming into the Country* as your best work. What do you see as the best things you've done? His warm eyes grow a little cool, and he appears to glance at the "Bear Trap" sign. "I find this sort of question mildly irritating," he says. "There seems to be a need in people to use words like *best*." He looks out the window as if he's trying to locate the individuals who do this kind of thing. I'm glad he doesn't direct his gaze at me. "I'm pleased with *Coming into the Country*, but it's not my best work. I've received letters from readers about each of my books saying *Oranges* or *Giving Good Weight* or whatever was their favorite. Each one is unique, itself. You do your best with the materials that you have to work with in each piece or you don't turn it in. You can't compare *The Deltoid Pumpkin Seed* and *Looking for a Ship*. I wouldn't differentiate between them any more than I would compare my daughters." He pauses over this thought and cocks his head to the right as if he's looking for another angle. "Nonfiction writers go out not knowing what to expect. In a way you're like a cook foraging for materials, and in many ways, like a cook, you're only as good as your materials. You go out looking for characters to sketch, arresting places to describe, dialogue to capture—the way you would gather berries. You hope for the greatest variety. Perhaps the work that best exemplifies what I'm talking about, this sort of variety, is *The Deltoid Pumpkin Seed*. I'm not saying it's the best, but it is a good example of what I reach for in my writing."

I glance down at those lonely batteries in my bag, lying like two displaced persons, and ask him about the critic who suggested he had total recall. "I don't have it," he says simply. "Truman Capote said that when he was working on *In Cold Blood* he trained himself to listen in the day and remember that night exactly what people said." Once again he pauses, and the lines around his eyes thread together as he smiles. "Good for him! That's a dazzling skill. It's no skill, though, that I'd associate with a normal human being." He reaches into the shadows of the bookcase next to him and takes out three small note pads and fans them in the air. "I write in notebooks like these. If I interview you, you know what I'm doing. I make it clear to you, what I'm working on, where it's going to be published. My notebook is always visible, a factor between us. It's like a film crew, only less obtrusive." I wonder aloud about a particular passage from *Coming into the Country*, asking how he recorded a long conversation with John Kauffmann as they paddled along an Alaskan river. "That's easy," he tells me. "He paddled. I wrote . . . fast."

I decided to push a bit further in the same direction and mention William Howarth's idea from *The John McPhee Reader* that creating a true replica of an informant's conversation demanded a ventriloquist's skill. Then I quoted Kathy Smith's interpretation of his work in *Literary Journalism in the Twentieth Century*: "McPhee's fictionalizing act, whether he acknowledges it or not, is grounded in the same logic as all narrative, one that seeks, through illusion, a perfect apprehension of the world." I can tell he doesn't like this question any more than he did my first one, but this time we both glance out the window, as if we might catch a glimpse of this nefarious Kathy Smith. When he looks at me, he says, "That's just academic air. Of course, there's definite truth in it, the idea that all writing is fiction. I agree with the idea if you express it in a certain way. You can't exactly reproduce human life; everything is a little bit of illusion. So what? Ho, hum. Basically, the whole thing is academic air. Everyone knows that at the start. The important gradation in the whole thing is that you get as close as you can to what you saw and heard."

What about works like *In Cold Blood* or *The Electric Kool-Aid Acid Test*? In your discussion with Norman Sims in *The Literary Journalists* you say, "You don't make up dialogue. . . . And you don't get inside their heads and think for them." Have Capote, Wolfe, and others gone too far?

"I greatly admire *In Cold Blood*, especially in terms of structure, particularly the first three quarters. But it falls apart, for me, at the conclusion, kind of like a burlap bag spilling grain at the end. But on the matter of the dialogue, clearly I have my doubts that you can train yourself to remember verbatim hours later." About Tom Wolfe, all he will say is that he is a stylistic marvel, "interesting, funny." But about creating characters in nonfiction, he is direct: "Nonfiction writers have a real debt to one another and to their readers. When that *Washington Post* reporter won the Pulitzer Prize a few years back for a story that turned out to be a complete fiction, she did the whole business a serious disservice. The debt we owe to one another in this form of writing has to do with credibility. Nonfiction writing is like an aquifer: One pollutant can spread through it and taint it all."

One of the four calls he receives during our conversation interrupts our talk now. Each call, some of them from other writers, he handles with tact and care, but each time he explains that he is busy speaking with me right now. I've been doing what any book lover does sitting in a person's office waiting for him to get off the phone: I eye the titles in the bookcase. When he hangs up the receiver, I ask him if he has read William Least Heat-Moon's book *PrairyErth*. He tells me that he admires it a great deal, that "it was a good choice to go deep this time." He says, "Bill is a friend of mine, and I feel guilty that I haven't written him yet to tell him how much I like the book, the stories of the people he found."

It seems natural to ask him about the people he writes about in his books, those individuals the critics call the "McPhee hero," people like Fred Brown in *The Pine Barrens* or the Gelvins in *Coming into the Country*, a sort of endangered species. "I write about real people in real places," he says. "All of my work is about that. It's not the unusual person that is most interesting—the eccentric. I don't have any predilection about that. In Alaska there are lots of unusual people. But within the context of Alaska the Gelvins are not unusual or eccentric or odd. I remember saying to myself as I worked on *Coming into the Country* that if I don't succeed in describing them, in capturing their character, then the whole thing will fall apart. They were the real McCoy; they were so uneccentric. Fred Brown, too, was the solid stuff of the place where he lived."

McPhee's skill over the years has been in taking that solid stuff of the world and reshaping it into narratives, and I ask him about William Howarth's description of his method of composition that appears in the introduction to *The John McPhee Reader*. Is structure, as Howarth suggests, the main ingredient in your work? Have advances in computer technology changed your methods?

"The reader is not necessarily conscious of structure," he says. "Readers are not supposed to be aware of structure. But the logic may bring them in. My computer has been adapted to what I did before. There is a computer genius at Princeton—Howard Strauss—who has written programs to do the same thing I did in the tenth century, when I started writing. One of his programs implodes information, the other explodes it. I've told him: If he leaves Princeton, I leave, too. . . . I still do note cards, though. I move them around until I get them in the right order. I write the lead first, then work on the rest. And I always know what the ending is going to be. This may sound mechanistic, but it liberates you to write."

As if the word *liberate* has triggered his memory, he stands up and suggests we go to the Annex to have lunch. We walk past Roger Mudd and make a five-minute walk across campus through a sea of dappled leaves and past strolling students. The restaurant is an unpretentious place in the basement of a building which stands near the intersection of Nassau and Tulane streets. Across the street is the Midlantic Bank, in the brick building where McPhee once had his office over a hardware store. In that rented office he wrote *Coming into the Country* and a number of other books. Next door to the Annex is the Rialto Barber Shop, where McPhee gets his hair cut and his beard trimmed. On the wall near the front door is a faded 1975 newspaper photograph of a beardless McPhee, a handsome, square face. When Ed Cifelli, one of the owners of the barber shop, sees me looking at it, he says, "He won't shave off his beard. His wife likes it. He's afraid if he shaves it off she's gonna leave him." The other barber, Rich Pinelli, tells me to look at the drawing of the Midlantic Bank Building that is hanging on the far wall. "That's where he had his office, you know. He wrote about everything up there—oranges, canoes—but never about barbers. We're too boring." I have to say the drawing is interesting, well, not so much the drawing as the postcards that almost completely cover it—naked women from Aruba, Florida, Hawaii, and other tropical paradises. It seems that these barbers, like McPhee, have a diverse sense of adventure.

In the Annex we find a quiet spot, a few tables away from a group of cartoonists, one of whom—Henry Martin—regularly contributes to *The New Yorker*. The restaurant reminds me of Walker Percy's description of Princeton in *The Last Gentleman*: Everyone seemed to have "a certain Princeton way of talking . . . and a certain way of sticking their hands in their pockets and setting their chins in their throats." There is a club atmosphere but, as Percy says, a "muted Yankee friendliness" too, so I follow McPhee's lead and order a turkey club sandwich, but not even my admiration for his writing skill or his gentle humanity can induce me to order, as he does, the lima bean soup.

I ask him about the writing course he teaches at Princeton, the "Literature of Fact." It is a course that he has taught once every year or so since 1975 as the Ferris Professor of Journalism. I wonder how he gets his students to view things differently, to enhance their powers of seeing. "Nothing that I know of directly," he says, looking into the swampy-green bowl in front of him, "I tell them that I'm not a real professor. I'm a writer, brought here by the university to look at the writing that they do. I look over their shoulders at what they do and they can look over mine at what I do. As far as being observant is concerned, I am observant when I have a notebook in my hand. But when I'm not working, that part of me shuts off. As a matter of fact, my family teases me about my not noticing things. Six elephants could walk through the kitchen, they say, and I'd never notice."

A bit later he says, "Writing teaches writing. Writing begets writing. It doesn't make any difference what the form is as long as the person who talks to the students about it is interested in their writing and knows something about the genre."

Do you read the reviews of your work? I'm thinking in particular of Edward Hoagland's 1975 *New York Times Book Review* criticism of McPhee that he didn't take enough risks. "I read them. Usually I ask Farrar to collect them and send me a batch. That way I place them in a larger context. But I can't say that I've read anything in a review that caused a great swerve in my writing. I've seen everything from soup to nuts, from highly intelligent comments to truly dumb remarks. If you are a writer and you are reading reviews of your work, you have a unique view of the process—reviewers, you see, are doing a sketch of themselves. Therefore, it's not a good idea, generally speaking, to let any of them be a pilot fish for your work."

Who, then, is your ideal reader? I remind him of John Cheever's teasing response to the same question in which he offered height, weight, and other specifics. "Cheever's was a creative and humorous response to a pretty amorphous question," he says and pauses to choose his words. "Obviously, many of the people who will be reading what I write will be smarter, more sensitive, more subtle than I am. I know that when I'm writing. I write with them in mind. You often have a problem when you are trying to describe something and you know some readers will know all about it in advance while others will not. You have to find a way to negotiate this road—especially when you're writing about science. One way to do it is to get at the information through children. For instance, to write something like—'When Ted was sixteen he learned about particles in physics.' Bring it in through characters, through what interested or inspired them."

For his own inspiration, McPhee draws on the things that interested him before he was twenty. "Much of it came from Camp Keewaydin in Vermont, eight miles south of Middlebury," he tells me. "A few years back I was giving a talk at Vassar and a young man raised his hand and asked me what academic institution had influenced me the most. Well, I had gone to Princeton High School and Princeton University and Cambridge, but I didn't hesitate for a second. I said Keewaydin; it was a real educational institution. I started going there in the summers when I was six and I was working as a camp counselor when I was in college. There are lots of good ideas for pieces of writing, but you still have to sell them. Someone has to want them, and it's far more likely that something you have an emotional commitment to will work out than some Hessian piece of writing."

The Keewaydin Camp director, Alfred Hare, Jr., still remembers Johnny McPhee quite well and confirms the writer's sense that the camp was an important influence on his life. Recently, Hare said to me, "He [McPhee] was an outstanding camper and a superior staff person. He was the best writer we ever had for the camp newspaper, The Kicker. He had a wonderful sense of humor. He dressed those stories up in his special style and read them with great dramatic flair. Right here may have been where he got his start in the sort of literary journalism that he does so well now."

But writing is hard work for McPhee, and like most writers he invents ways to avoid writing, until the pressure builds up and some words leak out. I wonder if he's ever thought of shedding the "lonely, nerve-wracking" writing activity to do something else. I'm thinking particularly of the conclusion of the essay he wrote about the ranger in Maine named John McPhee whom he met a few years ago. The writer ends up "wishing he were John McPhee."

Once again he confirms that there is no other profession that he is genuinely drawn toward and says that his daughter

Jenny tells him that he overemphasizes the negative aspects of the daily life of a writer. "There are many rewards," he says. "Making something that you have a compulsion to make and being glad when it's done. At least a few months later you're glad. The biggest reward for me is that those books of mine exist. I'm still a little bit surprised and awfully pleased that people seem to like them."

And, of course, many people do, among them some of the most gifted younger practitioners of literary journalism. I bring up Tracy Kidder's and Mark Kramer's citing his influence on their work and ask about influences on his. But he won't name individual books or writers. He received a B.A. in English from Princeton and read English literature at Cambridge, but as a teenager it was the long fact pieces that drew him to *The New Yorker*. "But I didn't rule out anything as a younger writer," he explains. "I tried everything, sometimes with hilarious results. I think that young writers have to roll around like oranges on a conveyor belt. They have to try it all. If they are lucky, they'll fall into the right hole. There are plenty of writers in the wrong holes, that's for sure. Even with my reading, I take whatever the hell comes along. I read haphazardly and usually in the dead of night. I've taken in the last few years to listening to books on tape as I drive in my car. Now, my ignition comes on, a voice comes on with it."

Just as he finishes his sentence, a tweedy-looking, gray-haired gentleman comes up to our table, says "Hi, John," and relates a story about an aunt with Alzheimer's. "That's a story you should write about," he says as he waves goodbye.

"Do you get that suggestion often?" I ask him.

"Sure," he replies, then shrugs, "but he's just an English professor."

As we walk up the stairs toward a sunny, brisk afternoon, I ask him about a profile written a few years ago that described him as a "slightly eccentric recluse with a beard."

"Does that sound right?" I ask.

"It's perfect," he says and smiles.

"So, is it some eccentricity that keeps your photograph off your book jackets?"

"Actually, that's a complicated thing," he says. "I think authors can get between the reader and the work. A piece of writing is something in which the figure of the author is just one component. When I see this figure of an author on television, for instance, coming between the reader and the work, I think the reader loses something. The reader is the most creative thing in a piece of work. The writer puts down the words and the reader creates a scene. Writing is literally in the eye of the beholder. Therefore, the writer who is embedded in the text can distract the reader by coming forward."

"Do you feel any kinship with the new journalists or the practitioners of creative nonfiction?"

"I'm not one of the new journalists. I'm an old journalist. I have some sympathy for the term *creative nonfiction*, however. It's an attempt to sort out the too numerous things that will be placed under the same category—everything from the telephone book and an instructional manual to the work of Joseph Mitchell. It's an attempt to recognize something, that a piece of writing can be creative while using factual materials, that creative work can respect fact."

We stand for a few more minutes on the corner of Tulane and Nassau, discussing the new *New Yorker*, the possible effects of Tina Brown's editorship, but he is reserving judgment, hoping that the magazine will nurture new writers the way it nurtured him.

"Things have always been allowed to grow there and not grow to fit the circumstances," he says. "A piece of writing is a piece of writing, whether it's a haiku or the Anglo-Saxon Chronicle, but when I started at the magazine I never had the onerous sense that my stories had to fit a mold. They had to be as long as they had to be and not a smidgen more. If that changes, *The New Yorker* will not be the same kind of seedbed. If that's the case, I feel sorry for younger writers."

Just one final question before the light turns green and he heads back onto Princeton campus: "How does it feel to have the tables turned, to be interviewed rather than do the interviewing?"

"Well," he says as he begins to cross the street, heading back toward the monk's cell with the cot, "anything beats writing."

Michael Pearson's most recent book is a biographical-critical study titled John McPhee, published in 1997 by Twayne Publishers, an imprint of Simon & Schuster Macmillan. His first book, Imagined Places: Journeys into Literary America, published in 1991, was named a notable book by the New York Times Book Review. He is the head of the Creative Writing Program at Old Dominion University in Norfolk, Virginia.

The Power of Self-Revelation
A Conversation with
Mary Kay Blakely

CATHERINE WALD

"THE TRUTH WILL MAKE YOU FREE, BUT FIRST IT WILL MAKE you miserable."

It's one of Mary Kay Blakely's favorite sayings, and she ought to know. Telling truths, spilling secrets, breaking silences have become a profession and a way of life for the prolific essayist, author, feminist, teacher, and mother ever since she joined the fledgling women's movement in Indiana in the mid-1970s.

Blakely's first essay, "The Myths of Motherhood," and her first job as a columnist (for the Ft. Wayne Journal-Gazette), came out of a university lecture she gave in those days. After that first piece appeared, the letters to the editor flew fast and furious; and Blakely, who had never planned to become a writer, was hooked. "That connection with readers propelled me through the terrors of those first deadlines, when I really was feeling very unsteady in my skills as a writer." She also "discovered the pure pleasures of craft" and "how strongly I wanted not to be a bad writer."

Unsteady no longer, Mary Kay writes with "extraordinary compassion, intelligence, grace, and sensitivity," is how one editor, Amy Gross of Mirabella, described her. Blakely continues to forge strong emotional ties with readers of magazines ranging from Ms., Vogue, Reader's Digest, and the L.A. Times. She continues to bravely explore the nuances of the deeply personal, blowing the lids off as many myths and stereotypes as she can along the way.

On this windy November afternoon, the truth Blakely is preparing to tell (and she's on a deadline) has to do with authenticity as it plays out in the uniquely complicated life of an autistic woman named Donna Williams, the subject of several of Blakely's articles. Still, she doesn't seem the slightest bit miserable as she ushers me into her Upper West Side apartment with a warm, Midwestern smile that could melt the heart of even the most hard-boiled Manhattanite.

My thin, five foot six inch host is wearing a gray long-sleeved cotton T-shirt, black fleece pants, white running shoes, and, as usual, no makeup. In person, Blakely is much like her writing: She welcomes you in as if she's known you all her life, and her presentation is unencumbered by artifice, yet so natural that you suspect she must have taken some pains with it. With her sparkling blue eyes, clear pink complexion, and luminescent silver-white head of shoulder-length hair (it's a little bit shocking to see in a forty-eight-year-old, but it works), she almost fits a New Yorker's stereotype of a Midwestern farm girl, but not quite. You just know you're going to be interested in what she has to say.

I have a long list of questions, but first we stand in the long, narrow kitchen as Blakely fixes us tuna fish sandwiches for lunch, chopping pickles and spooning in mayonnaise with all the efficiency of a mother who has prepared, by her own estimate, two-and-a-half tons of that quintessential Midwestern comfort food, tuna noodle casserole, while raising two sons.

We chat about our kids, and I remember how I felt when I first read *American Mom*. (Working Publishing, 1994), a memoir in which Blakely took the musty, sacrosanct Victorian garment of motherhood and put it out for a good airing. I could practically hear women across the country breathing a collective sigh of relief. Blakely shared her worst mothering nightmares, as well as friends "bad mother stories" (the woman who left her kids at the grocery store, the one who fed her child Calamine lotion instead of Pepto Bismol). She affirmed what we all knew but never talked about: that motherhood is hard, that it doesn't come naturally to anyone, that you're bound to have "more bad days on the job than most other professionals, considering the hours: round-the-clock, seven days a week, fifty-two weeks a year."

After lunch, we arrange ourselves at either end of a huge couch in a living room/office that overlooks the Cathedral of St. John the Divine. Blakely tucks her legs under her and sips coffee as I admire the high-ceilinged apartment, which feels surprisingly quiet, despite the inevitable sirens, honks, and yells from the street. With its off-white walls and tastefully subdued floral wallpaper, this home could serve as a backdrop for a Ralph Lauren ad, if it weren't for the strange, quasi-religious mementos scattered throughout: a nun figurine sporting boxing gloves, a plastic Jesus from a local Botanic that lights up and moves its eye.

There are also several feminist posters, which point to Blakely's long-standing involvement in the women's movement. It was in the consciousness-raising group of the early '70s, that Blakely first learned about the value of revealing the hidden truths of everyday life. "The conventions of keeping secrets, of 'pretend you don't know what you know,' are so strong, that if you *do* say what you really think, it's really powerful," she says.

She also found out that "the act of keeping secrets takes a lot of energy. You always have to be careful, careful, careful. And I think a writer *can't* be careful, careful, careful. You have to avail yourself of all language, all passion. A writer has to entertain all possibilities and all ideas."

For a writer, even one secret can take a toll, she says. "If it starts to feel like a burden, if it's starting to make you have to cover up who you really are, then you're dampening a part of your voice and a part of your character that lends power to your writing.

"I talk a lot about that in my book (*Red, White and Oh, So Blue: A Memoir of a Political Depression*, Scribner, 1996): How the whole attitude of 'don't ask, don't tell,' doesn't just apply to gays in the military, it applies to the whole culture. Don't ask, don't tell, what your salary is, don't ask, don't tell the secret you can tell other women but not your husband. And of course, that's death for a writer: 'Don't ask, don't tell.'"

Some of Blakely's best articles have come from her ability

to both ask and tell. Even though she believes that "everybody on this planet has a story, a secret they feel burdened by and yearn to release," the questions can be difficult to ask. For example, she felt compelled to ask Donna Williams, who is averse to any kind of physical touch, about her sex life. "I had to be sure before I asked, that this vulnerable woman was not revealing more than she intended. So I told her what readers would be curious about, and asked how much she could tell us." Blakely adds that letters to the magazine later called that passage the most touching in the article.

But, I ask, what do you do when your secrets involve family members or close friends?

Blakely pauses to reflect. "When I first started writing about my brother's madness, that was hard," she says, referring to her brother, Frank, a manic depressive who committed suicide in 1981. "I really needed to write about what it was like growing up with a severely mentally ill brother, especially in the '50s, when no one was allowed to be mentally ill, and being mentally ill was the mother's fault, before we discovered that bipolar disorders were a result of biochemical conditions.

"There was no way to write this story without involving my mother and involving some of my family members through some of their most compromising and embarrassing scenes. But that's also how we learned. It was those embarrassing and compromising things that told us: Something's wrong here. And drove the will to discover what it was. And of course we *did* discover a lot. But I couldn't just make the revelation to readers without showing how it began, how this journey began and what were the terrible things that happened, things that were embarrassing to my family, terribly compromising to my brother.

The challenge in telling that story became "not to withhold the truth, but to tell it in a way that makes these stories accessible to readers without dehumanizing the very private people in them."

In the end, although she takes great pains to be considerate and fair, "mostly I feel a sense of doom about it. I have no choice but to call it as I see it in my writing. To be a writer is not to be liked, it's to tell what you have to tell."

Some of the courage to do that telling came after Blakely went into a coma for nine days in 1984 (described in the memoir, *Wake Me When It's Over*, Times Books, 1989). She later wrote:

> In those years after my close brush with death, I spent a lot of time thinking about, "What if this had been it?" . . . The sorriest parts of my life were not the things I had done badly or clumsily, sometimes hurting innocent bystanders. I most regretted the things I hadn't done because I lacked sufficient nerve to risk disapproval from people who were important to me.

Our conversation turns to craft. Blakely tells me that, after all these years, she still struggles with leads and the first drafts. "The first draft is hard because you're working not on language, but on logic. You have to be really hard on yourself the whole time. You have to tell yourself, 'This doesn't go here, this is not a developed thought, this is a really stupid joke.' You have to confront your own ineptitude over and over and over again. When people call me in that stage and I pick up the phone, it sounds like I'm swallowing dust balls under my desk."

Blakely affirms that there are no shortcuts to the writing process—it's slow and circuitous, no matter what. "I remember an editor once saying, 'It's too bad you have to spend so much time writing these beautiful tangents.' And I said, 'I know, but it's writing the tangents that actually puts you in touch with your own thinking. And some of the tangents become the body of the article.'"

When the going gets tough, "those really dismal days when you spend five hours in front of your computer and it still looks hopeless," Blakely admits to indulging in what she calls "writing avoidance activities." As an example, she points out two file cabinets which she once spent days painstakingly covering with red velvet upholstery and a matching braid trim. On other days, she'll play with e-mail or dash off to the movies.

"When writing is going badly, it's not just your work that's going badly, it's like your whole soul is on some kind of collision course with itself," Blakely says.

But in addition to the frustration and anxiety, writing does have its moments. "Sometimes, even when it's really hard, I do realize that I love it. That usually happens when I'm already into the middle of a piece and I know I'm going to finish it. On those days, I can go onto the computer and get lost for hours. Then I love my work, and I do feel lucky that my job is to think hard about things that matter to me."

What about her reading habits? Blakely takes me on a quick tour of her bookshelves, enthusiastically naming favorite writers Virginia Woolf, E.B. White, J.D. Salinger, and Kurt Vonnegut, Jr. 'This is the good sentence shelf, where I go whenever I need the taste of a good sentence in my mouth," she says pointing out Katha Pollitt, John Leonard, Barbara Kingsolver, Alix Kates Shulman, Harper Lee, Hunter Thompson. And Molly Ivins, she says, is there to remind her "not to be so formal that you forget to be outrageous."

I ask Blakely about writing for an audience: What is the relationship between writing your truths and seeing that they get published?

"I think it's terrifically important for writers to be published," she says, "because the act of publishing makes you say it harder, better, deeper, more than if you're just writing it for yourself." She adds: "I remember reading in Tillie Olsen's *Silences* the line that said, 'Not to have an audience for a writer is a kind of death.' I think that's really true, and I think, sadly, that women writers are far more deeply familiar with the death and the heartbreak of silence."

In closing, I remind Blakely about a story she once told: Years ago, in the process of writing an essay about eating ice cream with her husband, she suddenly realized that she couldn't stay married. Isn't it scary, I ask, that the simple act of writing has the potential to shake up your life like that?

"Very," she agrees. "Sometimes those sentences come into your head and your realize, 'Oh, this is really true!' That's what writing does. It makes your unconscious readable.

"I think sometimes that's what writer's block is all about. We don't want to know, because sometimes it's just plain too scary, or you're not ready to acknowledge that particular truth yet. Because I do think that once you know certain truths, they are so compelling that you've got to act on them."

Catherine Wald's articles and essays have appeared in The Baltimore Sun, Chicago Tribune, Newsday, Poets & Writers, Writer's Digest and Woman's Day, among other publications. Her translation from the French of Valery Larbaud's Childish Things was published by Sun & Moon Press in 1994. She has just completed her first novel, Woman in Flames.

Son of Spoon River

HILARY MASTERS

THE PHOTOGRAPHER FROM *NEWSWEEK* HAS WALKED ME around to the rear of St. Pat's and to a corner in the gothic masonry where the light is even. He has pulled a light meter out of his kit and holds it before my face.

"A Luna-Pro," I say. "I just got one myself."

"Oh, yeah? You a photographer, too?" He's begun shooting me with the heavy, black Nikon. The camera's film advance whirs disinterestedly, and I sense any subject, breathing or still, might excite its mechanism. Even the author of a newly published family biography.

"Yes, I do some," I answer. I was about to give him a short résumé: my time as a Naval Correspondent, using the old Kodak Medalist; the two or three shows I have mounted in pizza joints and basement galleries; the calendar shots I have sold to a stock agency. But his casual proficiency, his expertise with his equipment, makes me shy to suggest a collegiality.

Just last month, in an hubristic rush, I traded in my old Weston exposure meter, a reliable tool in my photo kit for many years, for one of these same nine-volt Gossens whose complex computations have made the mystery of illumination for me even darker. On the other hand, this new meter has revealed the deception the Weston has played upon me all the years I've held it up to subjects, allowing me to think its measurements of reflected light were simple factors rather than the complicated theories of phenomena which the Luna-Pro posits again and again. To be sure, the selenium photocell of the Weston had transposed available light into equations of shutter speeds and lens stops that had given me perfect exposures every time, but, clearly, the process has been too easy—incomprehensibly correct if not accidentally accurate. When I offered the Weston as part of a trade on the Luna-Pro, the owner of the photo shop was amused by its antique naiveté and finally, as a favor, took it off my hands.

This ambition to make better photographs can inspire a lust for more and more equipment, the most advanced gadgetry, because once the shutter is clicked, the image registered becomes permanent. In that instant, the subject has been taken for all time, so the picture should be *perfect*. This freeze of reality is perhaps a dubious achievement of photography and makes for a curious cannibalism of subject matter. For example, the monumental clay bulk of the St. Francis Church in Rachos de Taos, New Mexico, has been printed indelibly in our minds by Ansel Adams's photograph of its back wall, the eloquent play of shadow and light along the curve of its adobe buttress. No other photographer, professional or amateur, has been able to take that church from a different angle, though many have tried, and most end up with a photograph very similar to the one Adams made in 1929. He made the picture of it.

So, it comes down to who first holds the camera, puts the angle held on the object—the "third eye," as Cocteau observed about the relationship between camera and photographer. The ingenious mechanics that function between this eye and its object merely convey and compute the glance; then, make the image permanent. Similarly, another kind of mechanical focus, no less automatic, is sometimes turned upon an individual that measures the surface reflection to make a quick study, then prints this view to make it an instant archival and nearly impossible to revise.

"You know what they are calling you at the office?" The *Newsweek* photographer is packing up his gear. My image has been fixed on the film of his Nikon. "They call you, 'Son of Spoon River.'"

My reason for writing the book that has caused this photo session was to put down on paper for my children some of the stories my grandfather had told me—the history of his immigration to this country from Ireland and his adventures toward a citizenship never fully granted within the cruel freedom of America.

But to write about Tom Coyne, I would have to write about my grandmother, and to write about my grandparents, I would have to write about their daughter who had left me with them, at the age of one year, to be raised in Kansas City, Missouri. And to write about my mother, I would have to write about my father, Edgar Lee Masters.

The father, then, is only one of the four characters in this family biography, and he is by no means the most important to the narrative—as he was not to my life. Moreover, during the course of the book's composition, the figure of the mother forged a commanding presence in the text as she had done in all of our lives. However, my father was this lawyer-turned-poet who published a book of poems in 1915 that turned the American literary establishment on its head, thereby acquiring a fame that had not been foreseen and a success probably never to be forgiven.

At the same time, to say that his importance in this work was secondary is to shuffle over the hole card I must have hoped to play in this game of chance called publishing. However small his part in the drama might be, it seemed to me his appearance in it might attract some interest in the manuscript. But this didn't happen. My agent refused to offer it, and I circulated the manuscript, mostly on my own, for three years and to every major publishing house, some more than once, until David Godine of Boston finally published it, in 1982, under the title Last Stands: Notes from Memory.

True, it is a difficult book to categorize—always a necessity for the marketing dons of publishing. Was it a biography or a memoir; a novelized autobiography? Also, its narrative was said to be too eccentric, not the usual sequential plotting and with jarring juxtapositions of time and place, startling shifts forward and backward. The staff at Houghton Mifflin; Macmillan; Farrar, Straus & Giroux; Doubleday; Knopf; and on down the line didn't like it. Once published, the same "problems" they had with the manuscript were lavishly praised, even imitated, and the book has been called an "American classic."

But perhaps those editors had been influenced by the portrait of Edgar Lee Masters hanging in their minds—the picture of a one-book author whose damnable luck had exceeded his commonplace gifts, and for whom room was never to be made on William Blake's mountain. And here comes the son, they may have said, daring to put words on paper that allude to this embarrassing figure in American literature. Maybe I should have left the father out of the book altogether? Could I have written the memoir under a pseudonym?

A farmer's son inherits the farm and his husbandry will be evaluated by the jury down at the Grange, comparisons will be drawn between his and his father's management. That he decided to take up agriculture is almost never held against the son. A similar tolerance is extended in other lines of work—coal mining and steel wrangling, the law and medicine, insurance. High-wire acts. Parent and child working at the same task: weaving straw hats, taking up arms, or turning pots—it's an old custom. But in the arts, and especially literature, a peculiar filter puts a harsh vignette around the child who dares to follow a parent into the business of putting ideas and emotions into words on paper. Often, the offspring's work is seen from this angle, his or her modest attempt sometimes found insulting by its very attempt. And it is true, some of us have struck foolish postures before the camera, have made ourselves into curios by dropping the name of a parent to advance our own scribblings. But is this a class picture?

Like all first novelists, I had no say in the biographical material printed on the cover flaps of *The Common Pasture* by Macmillan in 1967. Since then, I've been able to keep my father's name off of subsequent book covers and out of publisher's press releases—save for *Last Stands*. After all, he is a character in the story. But as my virtue frustrated publicists, surely I had to admit the relationship had already been established with the publication of that first novel. The late Granville

Hicks reviewed this book as one of "nine bright beginnings" in the *Saturday Review of Literature*. His complimentary notice singled out the book's compact structure and the style while he identified me as "the son of Edgar Lee Masters who takes as dark a view of human nature as his father."

Now, every writer carries in his kit bag a packet of instant insecurity that can be dissolved by an innocuous comment, or even a casual observation, into a draught of toxic Kool-Aid. Just to reproduce a clear and faithful image of human experience is, almost by definition, impossible (read Mary Shelley), and to even attempt this feat is to raise an insolence that courts eternal punishment. If nothing else, it makes for a chronic case of the jitters. But add to this common doubt the thought that one's work may be scolded or praised because of a single roll in a bed, way in the past, and the ingredients for a stew of paranoia are in the pot.

Some thirty years later, I still wonder if that decent, little book was put into that honored circle of first novelists because Granville Hicks, as literary historian and critic, was amused by its author's parentage. If I have felt that this might have been so—that a special privilege had been extended— surely, the idea must have occurred to others. Let me shoot this from another angle. What if Robert Stone, another one of those "nine bright beginnings" on Hicks's list, had been born of a famous writer—would his fiction be valued any more or any less for it?

Dissatisfaction with one's faux celebrity might have something to do with who happens to be next to you when the shutter clicks. We should be careful of whom we stand near during these moments of record—class reunions, family picnics. Who wants to be fixed for all time, shoulder to shoulder with the classmate who helped Nixon fix the Constitution or with Uncle Jack, the jolly embezzler? But sometimes we are not given the chance to choose our place; we are arranged alphabetically, if you will. So perhaps my complaint is that my father was Edgar Lee Masters, the one-shot author from Chicago. If his name had been Cheever or Van Doren or Hemingway, would I be taking these coy pains with the reader to establish a little distance between him and me? I hope that I would be.

What if his name had been Dumas?

As young Alexander was getting into print, le père wrote him, "You shouldn't sign your name Dumas. My name's too well known, and I can't really add the Elder. I'm too young for that!" But this colossus of French literature (Michelet called him "one of the forces of nature") was clearly a very hard act to follow. He authored over three hundred novels, hundreds of plays, many of which he had adapted from his own novels, such as "The Count of Monte Cristo," or wrote his own versions of "Hamlet" and "Macbeth." The senior Dumas offered to collaborate when young Alexander expressed an interest in writing, but the son turned down the offer. Even so, when Junior published *Camille* in 1848, at the age of twenty-four, salon gossip whispered that the father had written the novel for him.

After all, it was known that father and son shared a mistress or two so why not a plot—especially one that concerned a consumptive courtesan, modeled on an actual woman they both might have bedded? However, the delight with which Paris embraced the appearance of this son following his father overwhelmed such calumny. When the novel became the play "La Dame aux Camelias" and later, with Verdi's help, the opera "La Traviata," Dumas *fils* had named his own path. "My best work, dear boy," his father wrote him, "is you."

The photograph we have of Alexander Dumas, Jr., shows him lounging in a chair, heavy lidded and with a comfortable girth about him that projects his success. But as that photographer (could it have been Nadar?) counted off the seconds it took to fix this image on the gummed paper plate, did he think to himself, "This is the Son of Monte Cristo?" Surely, he did not raise the question with the author of "La Dame aux Camelias."

Virginia Woolf has ably documented the fate of Shakespeare's sister, but she has ignored—for reasons we can only guess at—to mention the playwright's son, the one that survived him. Brother to Hamnet and named for his grandfather, John Shakespeare made a number of appearances as a boy in his father's early plays—assorted babes in arms and pages.

When he landed the role of Beatrice in "Much Ado About Nothing," tongues must have wagged. No account has been found of his performance but all must have agreed that he cost the company very little. Two years later, the plum of Ophelia in "Hamlet" was denied him because his voice had changed—a kind of leveling by the gods that probably gratified the ale klatch down at the Mermaid. So, with or without his father's influence, John's performing days were over. Apparently, he didn't have the presence to do tragedy.

Meanwhile, he had been scribbling little scenes of his own, mostly improvisations and fantastical stuff involving bears and nymphs. Some of these were played out during the intervals of his father's tragedies as the audience bought oranges and milled about. His name has never been attached to these interludes—those that survive—probably because his father was already having trouble with Francis Bacon, who had been bankrolling some of the productions and was even pressing him to have his own name put on some of the plays. Considering all that, the charge of nepotism was something father William surely did not want to deal with. "My name is too well known here in London for you to prosper und'it," the Bard probably wrote his son. "Sign yourself by any other name, your work will be the same."

One source indicates that in 1610 a fringe company in Hempstead produced a play by a certain John Brokespear that was said to be based on a recent essay by Montaigne: It was all about cannibalism in the New World. The play's dark view of human nature may have seemed familiar to some in that suburban audience, and it is even likely that the senior Shakespeare attended opening night, because "The Tempest" appeared the following year. Backstage, during the cast party, father threw arms around son's neck. "Dear boy," he might have said, "you have given me my best work."

The son's play has been lost, perhaps another reason Mrs. Woolf never mentions him, nor did Ben Jonson refer to it in any of his journals, no doubt to save his good friend, Will, further embarrassment. Evidently, Junior went back to Stratford and got into real estate, subsequently to be joined by his father who had burned out after thirty-eight plays, a couple of which he needed John Fletcher's help to finish. Curiously, this ironic twist has escaped mention in even the most scrupulous biography of the Avon master.

So, it can go both ways.

Halfway through high school, it dawned on me that my father was a person of some importance, but from the beginning, this importance was oddly marred. The work on which his fame rested was faulted by some, dismissed by others. A lucky hit. If *Spoon River Anthology* was granted a place in literature at all, that place would be qualified by some as being accidentally won, like the lottery; therefore, unearned. His sudden, unaccountable promotion in 1915 from a lawyer-poetaster, hardly known to Harriet Monroe's Poetry bunch, into a front-rank literary figure raised the mean jealousy of a Sandburg and engendered the undying competitive hatred of a Frost.

Certainly, *Spoon River* stands far above the rest of his work, some fifty or more published novels, books of poetry, and plays, but so does it stand high in the American anthology as well. The metaphorical village he raised on the banks of an Illinois river can even be located on the maps of Poland or Korea or Brazil—pick almost any plate in the atlas, and the aspirations and confusions of its citizenry are a permanent part of the human comedy. That Masters had somehow put this masterpiece together stretched the credulity of the salon wisdom—and still does. It should not have happened to him. Let's see him do it again, the cry went up!

I've always been struck by the similarity between the machine politics I observed my grandmother manipulate as a worker for the Pendergast organization in Kansas City and the kind of associations and tradeoffs that occur in what is sometimes called *po-biz*. You-do-for-me-and-I-do-for-you is standard operating procedure for both institutions, and the figure of an independent is regarded with suspicion in both of these precincts. An individual who has nothing to trade and no outstanding IOUs is never completely accepted by either, certainly never to be trusted.

So probably my father's feelings were hurt. He had expected to be received into that legislature that Shelley had talked about but, instead, he found a membership not much different in kind from the ward heelers of Chicago politics. Here, he thought, he had produced this volume of poems that a lot of people thought were kind of special; yet, far from accepting him, the Sandburgs, the Frosts, the Untermeyers, and the Van Dorens immediately questioned his credentials. He had only one outstanding IOU, to William Marion Reedy who had originally published the poems in his Mirror, and though he might have offered free legal advice—and often did—he had no literary favors to trade any of these new peers. Also, his prairie boy's enthusiasm for the classics must have bored the hell out of them.

On occasion, I would hear him mutter a defense to this charge of being a one-book author, calling up such witnesses as Cervantes and Chaucer, Boccaccio and Whitman. No doubt, the commercial success of *Spoon River Anthology*, as much as its critical acclaim, also contributed to him being put on a different set of scales. So he became bitter and, for some, this reaction was further confirmation of his smallness. He was caught in a bad light and couldn't turn away.

Today's popular entertainment of celebrity-bashing, similar to the bear-baiting of early times, is a way to punish an individual or a group that does not enforce the image our society has of itself, the way it wants to appear. The idea is to distort the camera angle or paste up a picture of these outsiders and offenders that presents a profile which will deserve the establishment's scorn and ridicule. An archival image. The technique is the staple of supermarket tabloids, but to come across the same design in more worthy journals comes as a shock.

Recently, Elizabeth Hardwick had a merry time with my father's history in the *New York Review of Books*. In an essay, ostensibly a review of a new biography of Vachel Lindsay, Ms. Hardwick presented a picture of my father's last half dozen years and death that resembled the farcical helter-skelter of a scene by Feydeau—how my mother supposedly pulled him this way and that, across one state line and another—to fabricate a rather ludricous picture of a period in their lives that, while economically stringent, was actually very serene and comfortable, to be concluded with his death in dignified circumstances not all poets have enjoyed. Hardwick had the chronology wrong, the states wrong, the dates wrong, the circumstances wrong, and the whole package delivered with the saucy verve of the *National Enquirer*.

But was this only sloppy research? Surely, Ms. Hardwick is not unaware of the pitfalls and uncertainties of a poet's life in America, so her paste up of my parent's history is a little puzzling. Could her distortions have been a reflection of that first picture of my father's life and work that the establishment took back in 1915? The editors of the *Review* printed my corrections and Ms. Hardwick, in a somewhat sullen response, admitted to most of her errors and omissions.

But, one last exposure and this one from an architectural angle, if you will. Like Adams's church in New Mexico. On the red sandstone facade of the Hotel Chelsea in New York City are plaques commemorating the different tenancies in this old hostel of various poets, writers, and composers; all are worthy to be so noted. From 1930 until 1944—fourteen years—Edgar Lee Masters lived and worked in rooms on the second floor of the Hotel Chelsea, but his name does not appear on this quaint poets' cornice on West 23rd Street. Not on Blake's mountain, not even on this pile of rock.

Hilary Masters' eighth novel, Home Is the Exile *was published in 1996. His essays and short stories have been published in many journals. Last Stands: Notes from Memory, published in 1982 by David Godine, is a classic and progenitor of the contemporary memoir.*

The Essential Hyphenated Heat-Moon

SCOTT CHISHOLM

SINCE ARRIVING ON THE STAGE OF CREATIVE NONFICTION
with *Blue Highways: A Journey Into America*, William Least Heat-
Moon, born William Lewis Trogdon, continues to dazzle readers with a prose style combining virtuosity of language and
sumptuous detail. Writing in a genre that he describes as the
"literature of place," he sees his work as "an awakening and
connecting" with America. On numerous journeys with him,
in a friendship spanning thirty years, I've watched him take
to the back roads of the nation to satisfy his goal of setting
foot in every county and county seat in every state. "To be
less than fifty miles from everywhere in the lower forty-eight
states" is how he puts it. But who is Heat-Moon? What are
the sources of his content, structure, and style?

His latest opus, *PrairyErth*, marks a giant step in William
Trogdon's literary transformation from Kansas City-born
"white bread" to Native American through the rediscovery of
his Osage heritage and the addition of a hyphen—all part of
an unfolding and redemptive myth. The Heat-Moon name was
conceived by the writer's father as part of his son's childhood
experience in scouting—a way for the father to help his family
connect to its Indian past. Since his father was Heat Moon
and an older half-brother Little Heat Moon, it followed that
William Lewis was naturally "Least" Heat Moon. When he entered college in the early 1960s, he abandoned the name. But
in the early 1980s it became not only a powerful pseudonym

but also a deeply felt means of honoring an all-but-forgotten family past, and, like other aspects of his gritty work, it stems from the earth of his subconscious.

After eight revisions of *Blue Highways* and twelve rejections, he revisited his father's name one night on the loading dock of *The Columbia* (Missouri) *Tribune*, where he worked as a circulation hack, tossing newspaper bundles onto trucks. It was a moment of transforming epiphany. He dashed home and typed William Least Heat Moon on a fresh title page. "That moment changed my life," he says. "I knew then that the book would live, and me with it. It ended the worst twenty years of my life."

But the name was a tongue twister—poison, curse, or allure to promotion types. People ordered *Blue Highways*, the book, "You know, by that new writer, what's-his-Moon." Then there were autographs; Try writing William Least Heat Moon a couple of hundred times a day for months. Tired of being called "Mr. Moon" by admirers and interviewers (he was once referred to as Least-Hot-Meat), and possibly trying to shuck off any implied connection to the Rev. Moon and the "Moonies," he emerges in *PrairyErth* hyphenated as William Least Heat-Moon.

The hyphen makes all the difference. Now lower key, almost lower case, "William" pales and "Least" begins to fade. Like his Osage Indian ancestors, he has completed a vision quest and finally taken his name; nonessentials drop away. "Many tribal Americans believe that a person turns into his name, partakes of its nature in such a way that it is a mold the possessor comes to fill," Heat-Moon writes in *PrairyErth*. The hyphen pairs essentials, completing the last step in his incarnation. Think Crazy Horse, Black Elk, Heat-Moon. Today, he signs his books in a soft bronze ink, two words and the hyphen—Heat-Moon.

In the spring and summer of 1995, he embarked on a trip to cross America by its rivers, from the mouth of the Hudson to the mouth of the Columbia—a journey that he completed in August for a new book. Having ascended and descended the continent on the outflow of its major drainage systems, he plans to write about water, people, and place as only he can. "It's one of three ideas that came to me about the same time in 1974," he claimed at a recent conference for environmental journalists at Robert Redford's Sundance Institute in Utah. *Blue Highways* and *PrairyErth* are the first two.

Although I'm the first to admit that Heat-Moon is secretive about his work, during our travels he never once mentioned any of his three long-standing ideas as having a life as early as 1974. That he was early fascinated by the old blue roads in the Rand McNally Road Atlas, I've no doubt, since he tendered an article to *National Geographic* in 1974 tentatively titled, "Across America on the Blue Roads." Yet he admitted to me that the idea for *Blue Highways* first took shape in his mind much later than 1974, in Nameless, Tennessee, after two weeks on the road.

By early 1983, he was growing anxious about a subject for his second book. I was with him in the Holiday Inn in Rochester, New York, when he hatched a scheme to write text for a less than successful photographic essay, *The Red Couch* (now something of a cult book), hoping it would divert the critics and give him time to think through his next major project— a project that at that time had no firm outline.

The first mention of his intention to focus on "a single place, and go into it deeply," was in the fall of 1983 in Columbia, Missouri, when he described to me the possibilities of "writing about topography in four dimensions," one of which was "time." He was actually describing a tentative structure for what became *PrairyErth*—the same way he'd discovered a structure for *Blue Highways* in the Hopi symbol of emergence.

Similarly, the first time he mentioned his plans to cross America by water was in the winter of 1994, a year after we'd done the lower Mississippi River and four months after we'd taken a trip across the Erie Canal, up the Champlain Canal and down the Hudson River, when it was casually suggested. I outlined a possible route, including a passage through the Great Lakes to Chicago and eventually down the Illinois River to the Mississippi—a plan that he later rejected, substituting the Allegheny and Ohio rivers.

Then, one cold afternoon in mid-January, he called in a fever. "I've got the idea for my new book," he said. "I'm going to cross America by water. It was hats off in the hallways at

Houghton Mifflin." I expect he'd tucked our conversation into his subconscious, reviving it as new.

Recently, he told me that he now considers his yet unwritten "river book" as part of a trilogy, B*lue* H*ighways* and P*rairy-Erth* being the first installments. "On the rivers," he says, "I realized they were part of the same thing."

Whatever the truth about the sources and dates of his ideas, he's written brilliantly about two of them. But the means to that brilliance, especially in his second book, is another matter entirely—and one not clearly understood.

PrairyErth, a critical success but surely a tough read, is light years beyond B*lue* H*ighways*, the ring-around-the-country narrative that first won him fame and followers. He calls this second book, a Kansas prairie memorial, "a deep map, a vertical, rather than horizontal look at one piece of America." That's almost understatement; the book is a heartland core sample drilled from earth's mantle.

Like the love of blue roads that led to B*lue* H*ighways*, the author traces his interest in Kansas' empty spaces to the same childhood fascination for the Rand McNally Road Atlas that he pored over on cross-country trips with his family. His talent is to always see more. "Two-dimensional Rand McNally travelers who see a region as having borders will likely move in only one locality at a time," he writes, "but travelers who perceive a place as part of a deep landscape in slow rotation at the center of a sphere of radiating infinite lines in an indefinite number of directions will move in several regions at once."

Exactly what he means by that seems both as fascinating and as cloudy to me as when he first described it in 1983, but moving in an "indefinite number of directions" is at the heart of the structure and style in *PrairyErth*. The upshot is that Chase County, Kansas, may never have another chronicler of his distinction. Heat-Moon has written its Domesday Book.

In *PrairyErth* the search for a structure was more demanding than the episodic narrative of people, places, and events in B*lue* H*ighways*—a book whose success took even the author by surprise—and the eight-year hiatus before the second book marks a difficult passage in his craft, especially in moving beyond what he saw as a simple and less demanding formula.

Heat-Moon is an ambitious writer. *Blue Highways* is a classic travel book; he reports what he sees in the order in which he sees it with a naturally occurring structure and style to match. *PrairyErth* isn't a classic travel book, if it's a travel book at all; it's a deep, almost organic, journey into fixed place. Encompassing more than the simply episodic, it deals with time in eons, not years, and with the primary elements of an ancient landscape. Form follows function—literary, to be sure, but also more geomorphologic or stratigraphic in intention than *Blue Highways*.

In 1990, six months before *PrairyErth* appeared, I stood with him outside the Premium Ice Cream Shoppe in Logan, Utah. He held a freshly delivered advance copy in his hands, his first look at the book in its proof binding. Heat-Moon asked, "What do you think pleases me most about this cover?" When I didn't respond, he pointed proudly to the line "By the Author of *Blue Highways*." In the dictum of Ezra Pound, he'd made it new.

What many critics and readers fail to appreciate about *PrairyErth* is that Heat-Moon's use of detail is literary geology, a crafting, layer by layer, of the spoken and written sediments of history, natural and animal, upon seven hundred seventy-four square miles of transition zone prairie—a mode that tells as much about the author, his books, and his style as it does about Chase County, Kansas. In his almost total command of detail, he reminds readers of John McPhee, the tireless craftsman and canoeist with whom Heat-Moon once shared a dunking in the chilly March waters of the Oswego River in the Pine Barrens. He dried his camera in McPhee's toaster-oven.

Heat-Moon is a classic digger, the compulsive literary archeologist who uncovers material, centimeter by centimeter, with trowel, brush, and lens. Often he literally is on his knees to capture the moment, the excitement of the spoken or written artifact. His study is frequently strewn with artifacts of his forming prose and, like McPhee, he has a passion for maps. In his search for structure in *PrairyErth*, he spread detailed topographical maps of Chase County across the floor, examining them on hands and knees for days, before unearthing in their twelve crisp quadrangles the pattern for his tracings of tall-grass prairie. Walking Chase County with him on the old Kaw Trail, I asked him about it.

"Quadrangle by quadrangle, I dug into this country—hills, valleys, rivers," he said. "I went at it like an archeologist, like a literary dig. It's what I do best."

Eventually, the controlling structure for "PrairyErth" emerged as a grid-like logo of Chase County's twelve sections, an expanded tic-tac-toe image with a third vertical line added to the frame. Printed at the head of every chapter, each grid contains a black dot, like a compass point, to center the reader's attention on where-in-the-prairie-world Heat-Moon is writing about. His prose becomes a dot-by-dot, step-by-step journey through Chase County where, in his words, we can "take in the numbing distance in small doses and gorge on the little details that beckon."

Heat-Moon's earth-bermed home, in rolling hills above the Missouri River near Columbia, is ordered with other artifacts of his indelible curiosity: books by the thousands in several exceptional collections—American travel and exploration, topography, cartography, natural history, literature, motion pictures, photography. Books are the artifacts of his passions, the sarcophagy, bone, and shard of his need to uncover, record, describe, make clear. In book stores across the country, he doesn't browse: He forages. On a recent trip to Powell's City of Books in Portland, Oregon, I watched as he consumed several shelves of the scarce, rare and hard-to-find, arranging for a shipment to follow him home, including a complete set of nineteenth century U.S. Government Railway Surveys.

Slight-framed (one hundred forty pounds), bearded, in his mid-fifties, looking something like an enlarged Ewok from "Star Wars," he would be easily overlooked if not for the splendor of a magnificent head of silvering hair. Drawn to that, one is next likely to notice his eyes, intense and probing, deep set under a pronounced shelf of bone. A closer look betrays his Osage inheritance in the broad, almost flat forehead and the high coloring of his face. A neat chap, compulsively tidy, he wears only cotton, mostly jeans and crisply laundered open-collared shirts, often layered over with a well-pocketed vest. On literary trips and readings he dresses more upscale, trading the vest for a dun-colored Harris tweed. He prefers sturdy boots, occasionally athletic shoes, but his closet is bare of dress shoes.

Of ties, he has no intimate knowledge. Infrequently, he wears a string tie. Once, in London, I saw him struggle with a tie at the insistence of a waiter at a private club where our host, a former publisher of *Punch*, invited us to dinner. The resulting knot, if it could pass for that, was as thick as Mohammed Ali's fist, and the tie hung like a wide cow's tongue a scant six inches below his Adam's apple. There's a one-of-a-kind photograph of his formal strangulation, so far as I know, the only instance of its kind in Heat-Moon history.

His speech is precise, clipped, economical, and to the point; but this man of many sentences is never superficial. When he puts on frameless reading glasses, he looks less literary than professorial, and he has a way of pursing his lips that gives him a cast of pedantic elegance. Even in jeans and roughouts, he looks oddly formal, even sartorial, like a man about to reinvent spats.

Precise in manner and habits, he keeps lists—of every movie he has seen and how often, of every book he's read and purchased, of every road he's traveled in the United States, of every ferry he's been on, of every lake he's sailed, of every town he's visited. There are other lists, but he keeps those to himself. His journeys are captured in Camp's Notebooks, each containing eighty lined sheets, small enough to fit into a vest pocket. These notebooks—four inches high, three inches wide, link his roads and footsteps.

Like McPhee, he seldom uses a tape recorder. Occasionally, his road talk is spooky. "I took that highway to the sky," he might say, or "That road runs to shadow." His humor is skewed, off-the-wall, often unexpected. Threading through a mangled Alabama landscape where communities look like junked car lots, he says, "Although not widely known, the actual capitol of Alabama is a house trailer."

While Heat-Moon's geologic approach to writing bears similarities to other creative nonfiction writers, including McPhee and Barry Lopez, it owes much to an eccentric individualism that was developing in the early 1960s when we first shared an apartment as graduate students at the University of Missouri. Feisty as a bantam rooster (sudden tempers and equally sudden coolings are characteristic of our relationship), he remains the compulsive note-taker, fully conscious of a finely crafted penmanship that covers each of his pages. That single characteristic—the love of words on a page, the way they fill spaces pleasing to the eye, the feel of pen in hand—is at the heart of his craft and temperament.

But there's a much earlier indicator of his interests: A childhood photo shows him sitting on a potty seat, legs too short to touch the floor, nose in a book. The book is upside down. He's mentioned this photo several times over the years, almost as if it were a kind of early warning. I like to think the child's odd concentration is evident in everything he writes, perhaps a metaphor of sorts for his original and alternative eye on the world. It's as if his craft and talent is to get everything to come out right or right side up—an impulse toward regularity, perfectly ordered in his life and art. All of this enforces, I think, a certain distance.

Twice divorced, he once told me: "I'm a loner and always have been. I find fellow travelers difficult to come by. I write to escape my own limitations—reclusive, hermetic, and hermitic—and to find people who share common interests."

To this day he writes his first two drafts by hand, (books go through eight revisions), arguing that "there's a relationship between hand and brain that can't be duplicated on a computer." Once written in cursive on tan lined paper in brown ink, the copy is transferred to a writing machine of sorts, a primitive Olivetti, part typewriter, part computer, on which he types each page on standard paper. In an era when the written word is imaged, formed, processed, and contained in RAM and gigabyte, and when fifty copies of *PrairyErth* can be stored on one CD-ROM, he seems almost traumatized by the complexity of computers, their programs, their cost. (Last February, he gave up his ancient ghost, finally purchasing a laptop.)

Centering his thrift is a respect for the past and its artifacts—not unusual in a man who still owns the same pair of sunglasses he had in the U.S. Navy in the 1960s and the same pair of battered sneakers he's worn since 1980 through travels and assignments that have taken him twice around the world.

His attachment to things, like words, is archival, not sentimental; Heat-Moon saves everything essential. He is still rankled by the loss of a ballpoint pen he lent me: It was the ballpoint with which he had penned notes for Blue Highways.

Other artifacts of Heat-Moon's metamorphosis are equally enlightening. For example, he describes his doctorate in English literature as "the most useless thing in my life," saying he chose to write on the poet Herrick "only because I could hold his entire corpus between thumb and forefinger." He claims his most useful college degree is a bachelor's in photojournalism which he took post-doc, the results showing up in meditative portraits of American irregulars in Blue Highways. Most of his travels are documented by a sparse photography, balanced frames that extract the essence from scenes, persons, or events, much of it given over to lost Americana. His images reveal the forgotten, forlorn, or off-the-wall—road signs, advertisements, decaying buildings, lunch counters, diners. One Heat-Moon photograph in my possession shows the exterior of the United Bank of Missouri, Tightwad Branch.

"Worth an image," he usually says, braking toward the shoulders, stalking the visual detail.

Unlike his photographs, his notebooks are private, as close to the vest as vest pocket. The notebooks also mirror their owner—small, compact, choked with details. On occasion, he asks me to fill in something overlooked: "What was the name of that restaurant we ate in this morning?" In self-defense, I've taken to using tablets as a way to pass his frequent tests on what I've seen, what I may know, what I will know or won't. When I fail, he worries a detail to death, but he always remembers it in the end. He runs on high-octane curiosity, obsessed by the complexities and images of the unfolding moment. Journeys with him are often electric, like waiting for lightning to strike or what Henry James called "the shock of recognition." What he does with his notes, I've no very clear idea. He says he discards them, but that seems inimical to someone with his compulsive interest in detail. In spite of his denials, I suspect at least some of them are filed, like his photographs, each containing episodes in a continuing saga in which the identity of the main character is still unfolding.

Typical of his talent, he has an astounding memory, precisely recalling events that occurred years ago, reciting with stunning accuracy date, time of day, exact conversation, even inflections in the voice. In fact, he is so precise about recalled details that he is occasionally frightening. Once, driving through that section of Southern Illinois known as Little Egypt, he said, "You see this curve."

"What curve?" The road looked straight as a plank.

"This is the longest curve in Illinois, Bud," he said. "Runs for three miles. Defeats the eye."

The illusion of straight never alters, but the compass on the dash comes round slowly from due south to due east. Although he hasn't been on this road in almost a decade, he knows it like braille. He memorizes country, mile by mile. For this article, I called to ask two details: the name of the river in which he and McPhee were dunked in that sweep of sidling March water and the number of square miles in Chase County, Kansas. "What cats are you letting out of bags?" he demanded, his privacy momentarily threatened. Reassured, he answered in staccato, "Oswego, Seven forty-four."

In truth, I find no difference between the practice of his life and the practice in his books; both entrap essential moments, arrange them, dissect them, reveal the elemental parts, file them away, rearrange them whole in a marvelous prose. Eccentric best defines man and books. In fact, the eccentric detail is what he enjoys best—Dime Box, Texas; "Miss Ginny's Death Book;" the exact number of twigs in a wood rat's nest; a railroad to nowhere; that Bazaar, Kansas, is really bizarre.

One spring, up in Montana near the Canadian border, he confessed to eating America. "Can't help myself," he said, "I'm an addict." He feeds on America and Americana. Whether a pygmy stone here, or a grain of sand there, a portion of the forty-eight contiguous, at least, has passed through him. He tastes all American waters he encounters—rivers, streams, lakes, oceans—and dips his hand to the wrist. Largely vegetarian, he is bent on tasting the cooked flesh of every animal in America, including porcupine, possum, prairie dog, woodchuck and skunk. Admissions like these are as close to sentiment as he ever gets.

But if eccentric detail and uncommon style appeal to readers of Heat-Moon's prose, they also obscure his sources, his literary debts, something he doesn't much talk about. *Blue Highways*, the most easily identifiable, has Steinbeck, Faulkner, and McPhee as immediate antecedents; less obvious are the diaries and journals of eighteenth century Americans crossing the overland trails a century-and-a-half earlier. *PrairyErth* owes a debt to regional and naturalist writers, particularly Gilbert White's "The Natural History of Selborn" (1789), a fact noted by only one reviewer, Paul Theroux.

Yet there are other more telling ghosts in his sources—a debt he owes to his late father. Heat-Moon's obsession with journeys is, in part, a relic of his Anglo-American namesakes, our first true continental wanderers—William Clark and Meriwhether Lewis.

Before transformation and final hyphen, William Lewis Trogdon and I wandered to the gravesites of both explorers, Clark's above the Missouri River in Saint Louis, and Lewis' a few hundred feet from the ruins of Grinder's Tavern in Western Tennessee where he died, mysteriously, on October 11, 1809. Buried in a ramshackle coffin of hewn oak planks, a stone's throw from the Natchez Trace, Lewis' grave lay untended and unmarked for decades, until an aging surveyor pointed out the place. When opened, the grave contained only the upper half of the hero's skeleton. Over it, a remorseful government raised a round stone column upon a base of common fieldstone, its top broken off to denote the stunted life of the "Senior Commander of the Lewis and Clark Expedition and Governor of the Territory of Louisiana."

"Waited forty years for a headstone," Trogdon said. "That's what the white man did to the first man who took the continent's measure." Then, vehemently, "America's not a destination anymore, Bud. It's a moving target—and we do the moving."

What he meant by that, I don't know. Even he confesses to be baffled by it.

One Missouri spring, near his home, we walked upriver beside the "Big Muddy," following the Kansas, Atchison, and Topeka Railroad tracks, searching for a faded Native American moonsign on the bluffs near Boone's Cave, one of a panel of pictographs that Lewis and Clark remarked on during their voyage up the Missouri in 1804. Hundreds were blasted away by railroad engineers. In early afternoon, we found it. Faded by the weathers of two centuries, the ocher and red heat-moon rising looked into us more than we looked at it. The past reached out until the hair on my neck rose.

"A moon at mid-day is a sign," he said, "especially when it carries your name."

If his *Blue Highways* coast-to-coast, border-to-border drift-ings carry with it some subconscious suggestion of his name-sakes, his newly planned water book will almost precisely fol-low their route from the mouth of the Missouri to the Pacific. Whether "white bread," Osage, or halved like his namesake's skeleton, Heat-Moon seems a strangely predestined jour-neyman.

Rarely can you repay him for the pleasure of his prose. Driv-ing deep into Kentucky, before he became hyphenated, I gave him a gem from John Madson's *Where The Sky Began*—an ar-cane term for the land, a piece of remnant geology, a soil-science term that never took in the textbooks, almost a rune. "It's a gift," I told him.

One eye cocked wide with sudden interest. Since he con-fessed that his working title for *Blue Highways* was "The Wind Is Also A Rover," I've taken an interest in his namings, but waiting for me to give up my treasure, he bided his time. I've never known anyone who can wait out a detail with such non-chalance, like a man rolling a cigarette one-handed in a room full of fingerless men. He feigned listening to the engine's slur, casts a glance at a flatland barn, easing the moment.

I spell it out. "P-R-A-I-R-Y-E-R-T-H. It's one word. Prairy-erth."

He didn't respond. His lips moved like he had something solid in his mouth, perhaps a marble rolling around. He sa-vored the word on his tongue for the first time and I swear to God he was trying it out for taste. "Too obscure," he said, spitting it back.

"It's as quirky as you are," I told him.

"Chase County is a transition zone," he says, "part prairie, part plains. Doesn't fit."

"It's perfect. Do you want the word or not? Say so now, or I'll claim it again."

He looked owly, gave me a hard stare. I thought of Paul Theroux's line in "Kingdom By the Sea:" "Writers are painful friends and they are seldom friendly with each other."

"Write it down," he ordered.

So I entered it in his Camp's pocket notebook.

Heat-Moon history and he knew it.

Scott Chisholm lives and writes from the foothills of the Wasatch mountains in Utah. Recent articles, commentary, and fiction have appeared in Creative Nonfiction, Lake Affect, Civilization, Red Herring Mystery Magazine, Edging West, Rough Draft, *and* Western Humanities Review. *He recently completed* Following the Wrong God Home, *a non-Mormon's account of a ninety-one day solo walk across the Mormon trail, and is writing a thriller,* Eye of the Monkey.

The Art of Translation

STEVEN HARVEY

WRITING ESSAYS IS LIKE REALIZING THAT YOU LOVE YOUR wife after all. We sing poems and dream fictions but speak in mere sentences. Sentences are our friends, taken for granted, until one day a few singers and dreamers let go of all that is far away and, watching the face across the kitchen table, see for the first time in years a smile that was there all along, the smile of the girl they married, and learn in lowly prose how to want what they have.

Close your eyes and you can picture a poem as it takes its sinewy shape in the mind. It is seductive and memorable. The personal essay has a shape, too, and a certain loveliness about it, but walk away and try to picture it or describe it to a friend, and you have little more than mousy-brown hair and cute freckles over the nose. Book stores don't even know where to put collections of essays, lumping our shy girls in plain wrappers with how-to books and biographies bearing the slim, the rich, the wild, and the glamorous on their glossy covers.

In the on-going battle to name the genre, I prefer the venerable *personal essay* over other contenders, primarily because it lowers expectations. With *Creative Nonfiction* we are tempted to capitalize and court the grandiose. "This is just not a fiction," the term announces. "It's real! This is not just nonfiction. It's creative!" You open a book of creative nonfiction ready for the best of all possible literary experiences—nothing ahead except disappointment. But with the lowly personal essay, the reader, expecting some dull tract, can be surprised.

The phrase *personal essay* is a pleasant mouthful. *Essay* is appropriately serious, coming from the Latin, *exagium*, meaning to weigh, a reminder that essayists ponder and measure and take stock of the world by weighing their words carefully. It suggests thought, and without a modifier is, probably, a little too austere, conjuring up another word, *examination*, with which it is too often linked, and bringing back memories of dreaded bluebooks. Putting the word *familiar* in front of *essay* is probably a little too cozy, giving a misleading suggestion of safety and shared assumptions, but adding the modifier, *personal*, says that, behind these words, is a human being—a unique recombination of dirt and water and sky.

What they are called matters less than what they do. "Good for what?"—that is my aesthetic. Poetry, of course, is good for nothing, and proud of it, according to W. H. Auden. "Poetry changes nothing," he wrote, and whether he is right or wrong, we know what he means. The reaffirmation of mere beauty is enough. Personal essays, by contrast, are very busy, performing many jobs. They supply information, entertain, and provide flawless and therefore irksome models for millions of college students learning how to write decent prose, but their main business is the expression of the solitary soul in a changing world, a clear and valuable mission.

The personal essay is uniquely positioned for the task. Unlike the ceremonial and communal forms—poetry and drama—the essay came into its own recently, during the Renaissance, and functioned as a vehicle for the voice of the individual. The essay carries on this hard work into our century, which still gives lip service to individualism but no longer believes that any one of us makes much of a difference. The novel, born at the same time, bears this burden as well, but does so by placing the hero among the contending voices of other characters in defining social situations. The personal essay, by contrast, is the lone voice.

The novel—with its party atmosphere—has always been the more popular form, leading envious essayists to ransack the house of fiction. Dialogue, scene, verbal high jinks, narratives, character development, juxtapositions, even fictions are all in the essayist's repertoire of effects. Anything that is good in my essays is true, I like to tell people, and some of the best parts were invented.

And yet, an essay feels very different from a story. Fiction writers hunt for those details which seem striking and memorable. A novelist might describe a character who bolts machine parts and an electric fan to the hood of his car and drives through town. Such choices, whether they come from real life or not, seem made up precisely at the point that they achieve a memorable oddity. "I've got to put that in my next story!"—we suspect the author has said, glad to come upon a detail that we cannot overlook. "Give your character a scar," I once heard Alice Walker tell a group of fiction writers. Essayists, drawn to the mundane rather than the sensational, tend to be suspicious of such scars.

A friend of mine who is an expert on the Romantic poets once told me that when Wordsworth and Coleridge used to walk through the Lake District of England together, they had radically different experiences. Coleridge did not see much around him. Instead, he allowed the landscape to stir his imagination and encourage invention, the walk giving him freedom to look within and examine interior states. Wordsworth, on the other hand, knew the names of wild flowers and trees and noted subtle changes in the landscape and season as he walked, looking outside himself for inspiration. The essayist is more like Wordsworth than Coleridge and the difference can be felt by reading "Tintern Abbey" and "The Rime of the Ancient Mariner" back to back.

It helps to have a dull life. Novelists, dreaming up other lives, can forget the mess they are making of their own as they create strange new worlds to fulfill the yearnings of this one. But personal essayists are never off duty, which makes even simple acts like showering, driving, or sex difficult, if not dangerous. "Much is in little," Horace wrote, and essayists keep the job manageable by thinking for a long, long time about hardly anything at all, an uneventful life allowing the writer to care more about "what is" than "what happens." Desire is the subject of novels—not what I have, but what I want. Capable of glamour and often at odds with the world as God made it, the novel is the prince of prose and apt, at times, to do the devil's business. The essay is the lowly monk of literature quietly going about God's work.

This reverence for the way things usually are marks the essay, though it is not a requirement of the form, and explains the elegiac nature of these works that are recording a present that is continually slipping away, largely unnoticed. Perhaps that is why the form is congenial to the ends of civilizations—when an entire way of life is threatened—and offers a clue for why some of the earliest examples of the personal essay occurred in the Hellenistic period and later at the end of the Roman Empire.

"Getting it right" in fiction means something different than it does in an essay. Fiction tends to myth. It becomes real only as it represents lives on the reader's side of the page. One way to "get it right" in fiction, then, is to make the tale convincing, a plausible sequence of surprises.

Essays begin with something that exists and has meaning before it reaches the page, establishing a different contract between the reader and the writer, a different set of literary obligations. Essays are not arranged by plot, but by anxieties. They don't wonder, "What next?" Instead, like a worried parent, they ask, "Now what?" with a groan. The anxieties are relieved not so much by the telling, like confession, but by the arranging, the way some of us fix a problem at work by cleaning up the desk. "Getting it right" for an essayist means putting events and details into a revealing—a revelatory—relationship with one another. Strolling through the museum of love and change, the essayist rearranges for all to see the treasures we cannot keep.

These differences should not be pushed too hard. Essayists occasionally look up from the turtles and earthworms and moths of everyday life and bring the extraordinary into the lens of their prose, and essays do tell stories. Joan Didion, an exact and exacting essayist, reminded us of the tenacity of the narrative impulse. "We tell stories in order to live," she wrote. But stories and essays are different in one crucial and revealing way, an essential difference inherent in the forms.

The Pandora's box of fiction, unavailable to the personal essayist, is dramatic irony.

The novelist can create a character who speaks in the first person but does not share all—or any—of the author's views. The character becomes that infamous thing, an unreliable narrator, a literary tool that allows the author, as Joyce suggests about Flaubert, to be everywhere in a work and nowhere present at the same time. Novelists—masters of bad faith—often hide behind this device, usually making fun of the character who tells the tale for them, sometimes letting the readers in on the joke, sometimes not. This ironic edge is always present in a first person novel—we are, after all, the last to know the truth about ourselves. Flaubert even perfected a strategy of indirect address, an aping of a character's voice and attitude, which allows the author to create the same effect in third person prose. "Madame Bovary, c'est moi," he wrote. Don't believe it.

So in one famous example the governess telling the tale may blame others for the demise of the children in her care, but we readers, upon whom nothing will be lost, catch the author's wink between the lines and suspect that the governess herself is, in fact, the guilty party. Is the author winking? On Monday, Wednesday, and Friday the governess is guilty as sin and duping us. On Tuesday and Thursday she seems more crazy than sinister and therefore guilty without knowing it. And on Saturday we bemoan our tendency to intellectualize every damn thing, pick up a hard ball and glove, and declare the poor woman innocent. Who knows? The screw turns and turns and turns, endlessly. It's a tricky and sophisticated game, the subject of great debate, and a mountain of literary criticism.

Irony of this kind obviously enriches a text, rendering the simplest tale suddenly subtle and ambiguous, and the writers of personal essays, by the nature of their task, cannot use the technique. Essayists lie and mislead and invent—who doesn't? In all ways except one they remain incorrigibly human and therefore thoroughly unreliable. But there is a lie that they cannot tell with a straight face: They cannot get any aesthetic distance on the narrator. If the essay is personal (and here I leave out some excellent essays, by writers like Swift and Russell Baker, which are not personal in the way I mean), the distinction between author and narrator, by definition, collapses; they see the world eye-to-eye, so to speak. Who you read is what you get.

The personal essayist, by sacrificing the unreliable narrator, removes one tool for complexity from the literary arsenal but suffers no loss. Dramatic irony is the fictional tool that has turned literature in this century into a hall of mirrors. With the author everywhere absent—and God, as Joyce added, paring his fingernails—the reader is left alone in an era of great loneliness. Even when we read masters of these techniques— writers like Nabokov, for instance, in *Pale Fire*—we begin to suspect that literature has been reduced to a game. It may be animated by a great heart, but we sense mainly an absence behind it all—the human being who is speaking the words is so impeccably camouflaged that she or he might as well not be there at all.

In the personal essay, as Thoreau reminded us a century and a half ago in the opening page of Walden, we are stuck with the voice of the author, no intermediary. There are several ways for the writer to offer relief from the inevitable monotone. A mixed diction helps: Aristotle first taught us that, encouraging us to use the whole range of vocabulary that is available to the author's voice. The vulgar requires vulgarity, damn it, and the divine demands all the verbal splendor that the dictionary has to give. Many essayists use quotations as a way of clearing their throats before going on. First-person accounts in novels are often restricted to the speaking voices of the characters, but the first-person voice of the personal essayist can be, without strain, the speaking voice liberated by the reading mind.

A last resort—often required by the essayist whose voice is sounding shrill—is the joke. Out on the limb of a ridiculous proposition or situation, the essayist hands himself a saw. Self-deprecation is the essayist's most convincing tool—the equivalent in writing of comforting others by saying, "You think that's bad?" Such humor is not an evasion or a case of false humility, but a way of making readers feel less alone with their own foibles. And, of course, once we have laughed together, it is easier to talk.

Essayists have an arsenal of techniques like these for modulating, without undermining, the narrator's solo voice, ways of engaging in the dialogue which is the path, Socrates taught us, to wisdom. But that does not mean that the essayist can be, like the novelist, everywhere and nowhere at once in his work. "Here I am," the personal essayist says, like the Old Testament prophets when they were called, trembling, before God, and like the prophets the writer often feels like adding, "Oh Lord." Personal essayists may not have a thesis, a clearly thought out position on the world's imponderables, but they are, at least, willing to stand, come what may, in the same verbal patch as the voice of the essay.

This limitation—the collapse of ironic distance—is chastening for any writer. "Say what you mean and mean what you say," my father used to caution in his firmly tautological way. "Discipline," according to Michel de Montaigne, the father of the personal essay, requires that "one is the same within, by his own volition, as he is outside for fear of the law and what people will say." It is true. In my own case, I have grown to distrust those who talk one way in public and another in private, their pieties in front of others followed by rib-poking obscenities over a beer in a back room. I have grown to distrust myself when I act that way.

The joy in all this is that the reader of the essay is allowed to hear this voice play occasionally with an idea. Ideas haven't fared well in our century, and the prospect for the next century does not seem much better. Poets have, in essence, followed William Carlos Williams in abandoning them. "Not in ideas, but in things," he wrote about poetry, contributing to the impoverishment of the form. Novelists put ideas on the lips of characters they don't trust and say to the reader, in essence, "You decide, I can't." That is why essayists turn the ideas over and over, considering possibilities, allowing for contradictions, aware that the blame will, eventually, fall their way. It is a relief, in fact a privilege, in our age of images and ideologies to follow these solitary minds, these questioning voices willing to offer tentative assertions which they hold as true—

at times even self-evident—in context, a context that the essay, itself, generously supplies.

There is, out there in the world of readers, a longing for a reality behind words. I see it manifested in the tendency to read fiction as biography. Readers study authors' pictures on flaps, looking for clues to the text, trying to invest novels with the authors' real lives. The personal essay goes a long way toward meeting this longing, not because it sticks to reality any more than the novel does—or the poem or the painting, for that matter. But the essayist is stuck with himself or herself, in sickness or health, for richer or poorer, till death—an indicator of the stakes. The essay may not be honest to God or the world, but it had better be honest to a voice.

Being at home in the world—that is the task. Essayists learn to live with what they have and who they are, poking fun at that yakking voice in the head, yes, but respecting it and attending to it as well. Something is always lost in translation, and it is easy to be ironic about what words can't catch. Learning to relax the irony requires an act of generosity, but we do it all the time. If we are generous and lucky when we hear an old tune, we can get past the sappy lyrics to a true emotion. Loving what we have, we find the girl in the wife, or, reversing the metaphor, see the fair-haired boy in the bald man snoring beside his glass of sherry in an easy chair across the room. Creating the possibility for such generosity on the part of readers is the unique work of the personal essay, the by-product of its art, and as it accomplishes this task, as it sets us up for loving all that we will lose, it helps us to be human.

Steven Harvey teaches English at Young Harris College in Georgia. He is the author of two collections of personal essays, Geometry of Lilies *and* Lost in Translation: Personal Essays about Love and Change. *He is also the editor of* In a Dark Wood: Personal Essays by Men about Middle Age.

A Different Kind of Two-Fisted, Two-Breasted Terror
Seymour Krim and Creative Nonfiction

MICHAEL STEPHENS

HAVING RECENTLY WON A NATIONAL AWARD FOR MY OWN creative nonfiction, I wondered what the phrase "creative nonfiction" really meant. The term does not sit well with everyone; some find it pretentious, while others obviously think it ridiculous. Yet it is a phrase that I am comfortable with, and a term I associate with my old literary rabbi, nemesis and mentor, the late Seymour Krim, certainly one of the form's best practitioners. J. R. "Dick" Humphreys coined the expression to describe the course that Seymour Krim was to teach at Columbia University in the late 1970s. Krim wanted a descriptive title for his nonfiction writing workshop that would distinguish the course from a run-of-the-mill journalism or expository writing course, and he had suggested calling it "imaginative nonfiction." Humphreys then suggested the word "creative" making clear to students that it was a creative writing course. I remember because I began to teach in the writing program in 1977 and taught there, on and off, for fourteen years, most of them spent with Humphreys as the director and with Krim as a colleague, But as I noted at a memorial at Columbia that was held for him after he died in 1989, I had known Seymour Krim—much to the surprise of other faculty who knew both of us since the mid-1960s on the Lower East Side. This man might not be the most famous or fashionable practitioner of this prose form, but he was one of its earliest and finest examples.

Seymour Krim and I had a rocky, even combative, relationship. Each begrudgingly admired the other's writing and, occasionally, we were cordial and seemed almost like friends, though he preferred that I be the student and he the teacher, even if our educational nexus was not a traditional one and had been formed a lifetime ago. I first met him when I was twenty years old, and he ran a workshop at St. Mark's in the Bowary Poetry Project in the mid-1960s. Before our fortuitous encounter, I was involved in the poetry workshops given by Joel Oppenheimer, the director of the Poetry Project, and Sam Abrams and Joel Sloman, his assistants; there were also workshops offered by Ted Berrigan, but, for reasons I don't understand today, I had ideological differences with the second and third generation New York School of Poetry writers.

Since I was homeless—that was not the term in those days, so it might be more correct to say I was without a home—I took the liberty of making an extra set of keys when Joel asked me to open the building for him one night while he had one more shot of bourbon and a glass of beer for the road at the R.O.K. Ukrainian Bar up on the block on Second Avenue. With that extra set of keys, I nightly returned to the Old Courthouse after all the workshops ended, and I held court and slept in the room where the writing workshops were held, rolling out a sleeping bag I stashed in the library across the hall and sleeping on the workshop table. Living and crashing in that room is how I met Krim.

It was a wretchedly damp and cold winter night and I came back to the Old Courthouse early, or maybe the prose workshop was running later than usual. At any rate, instead of coming home to a locked building with all its lights out, the door was open, and the workshop room's lights were on, and when I went to investigate, my sleeping quarters were filled with strangers, Krim sitting at the head of the table talking about prose style. It was a meeting of the fiction—it was really a prose—workshop. I sat and listened, telling myself, a poet, that I could write prose better than any of these people. That's how I used to size everything up: I may be a piece of crap but I'm better than any of you. The fact that I had a pocketful of poetry let me think that I wasn't a Bowery bum, although at that point in my life, I did look like a bum, bathing irregularly, broke, without a home, and dreaming a lot of *what if* and *if only* scenarios in my head. What if I become the biggest thing to hit the American literary landscape? They'll be sorry for how badly they treated me. I was never sure who *they* were or just how I was going to become so big. But I sat through the workshop, telling myself that I was going to write a story myself and bring it back to these people next week and show them a thing or two about good writing.

You see, I had this literary hierarchy-after all, I was raised a Catholic and hierarchies came easily to me: In my mind, poetry was king, after which came playwriting, followed by fiction, nonfiction, and then journalism. Poetry was king because it was the highest form of literary expression, and I believed that poets were the arbiters of the soul and, as in the ancient days of Celtic rule, they literally were the kings, just as the *seanachies*, in Ireland had been poet kings. I considered playwriting second best to poetry because it was the grandfather of the form, where Western poetry originated, back in the time of the classical Greek drama and, secretly, I wanted to write a play, too, but I was too shy to approach any theatre people, and then, what would I do if they liked my writing and wanted to develop it? God forbid, but I would have to work with them, and I was too much of a loner to work with anybody. True, I attended these writing workshops on the Lower East Side, but that was for my own benefit as a writer, and I rarely socialized with any of the other writers, and if I did it was always in the context of drinking, either in a bar or at the workshop table, swigging down bottles of cheap wine or quart bottles of beer. So playwriting was out for the time being.

Yet I went back the following week with a story I had written and got typed up on a girlfriend's typewriter, and there I was, a wolf among the prose writers, a spy in their house of love. My story was meant to show how much better a writer I was than anyone else but also to shock them. It was a lyrical piece about a young boy who eats cardboard, but who rationalizes this by explaining that his friend Sappho Milton eats shit. Seymour Krim and the group liked it very much. In fact, Krim was a contributing editor to Evergreen Review at the time, and he took the piece to them for consideration and, while it was not accepted, my first short story that was published was the result of Krim—it was in the Provincetown Review and the story, a talking blues, was called "Red Black & Whitey Greene"—and a few years later, thanks in part to Krim, Evergreen began to publish me with some regularity.

Krim's prose workshop was probably the best writing workshop I ever attended. It was not affiliated with a college or university, and I needed that lack of affiliation to make me want to participate in the experience. I was devoted to my own sense of anarchy besides wanting to be a writer, and I would not have been able to endure any kind of formal writing setting. I had dropped out of a state university after three years so that I wouldn't end up a high school English teacher and, so, footloose and, if not fancy-free, then zoned out and asocial, angry and with a real attitude, amid the love children of the Lower East Side, but also amid the drifters, crooks, con men, drug addicts and pushers, the motorcycle bandits, and the misfits of the world, I could pursue becoming a writer. The workshop was streetwise and informal, like all the workshops at St. Mark's, and it reflected the radical neighborhood in which it was offered—political revolutionaries, drug culture, and edgy street life. I was part of the last group, I guess, though even there my loyalties were shaky. Though I came from a poor family in Brooklyn and farther out on Long Island and had run away from home by the time I was fifteen years old, I continued to exude, even with my filthy clothing and boozy reek and drugged-out eyes, a sense of prep-school rebellion, a false sense of affluence that I think derives from my maternal grandfather, who, when penniless, continued to affect the airs of a wealthy man. I never seemed to come off as a working-class Irish Catholic kid from a large family in anything other than my writing, though I think what interested Krim was that I also had some kind of quality that usually got stated as being tragic-comic Irish, a sense of the ridiculous combined with a more formal sense of life. Thinking about it retrospectively, I affected an air of mystery about where I lived and who I was because I never told any of them that I lived in the workshop room and slept on the workshop table.

Krim had a reputation, not as a fiction writer, but for his essays in a book titled *Views of a Nearsighted Cannoneer*, a '50s underground classic of American prose that would be reissued by Dutton (1968) as a paperback during those years I attended his workshop on the Lower East Side. But try as I might to like him, Krim, in my own street way, always struck me as being kind of square, no matter how hard he tried to be hip and, believe me, his life was nothing if it was not devoted to being the coolest writer who ever lived and, like a lot of people from the Beat era, his own honesty and sincerity—and this man overflowed with both—was vitiated by that ultimately meaningless posture of being cool. Still, I was no dope or mere ingrate with him. And he singlehandedly got me admitted, when I was twenty-one years old, into the Mac-Dowell Colony, because Seymour, ever the worried Jewish mother, was concerned, if I remained on the Lower East Side in the state of booze and drug addiction and without shelter, I would not make it to my twenty-second year and ever write more than the few pages I had already produced. At the beginning of 1968, I left the Lower East Side, St. Mark's Poetry Project, and the workshops there, and took a bus northward to Peterborough, New Hampshire. By the middle of March, the first draft of my first novel already written, I was arrested as the accessory to a drug bust in nearby Keene, New Hampshire, and the MacDowell Colony and I parted ways acrimoniously. Actually, they threw my clothes, manuscripts, and books out into the snow and told me get out of there as quickly as possible and never come back, and when I tried to argue with them that due process had not been served, that they were presuming me guilty before my trial began, I was told, just like in the old Wild West movies, to be out of town by sundown.

During a period in 1968 when I went to San Francisco, I lost touch with Krim, but I did hear, upon my return, of his going first to London for a spell, and then later to Iowa. Years later, I heard how he coined the phrase "creative nonfiction" for a course he taught at Iowa in order to distinguish it from a pedestrian nonfiction course or one in traditional journalism, and how he introduced the course at Columbia. But, of course, that was not true. The course title came into being through Dick Humphreys, director of the writing program, used as a descriptive for Krim's own Wild West, urban wacko kind of creative writing. I suppose that Hunter Thompson's gonzo journalism is the same thing. But creative nonfiction seems so appropriate to Seymour Krim. In that true Krim sense, the phrase was both infelicitous and mellifluous, meaningful and meaningless, a mouthful and just right, a paradigm and an oxymoron, but I would only make those conclusions recently, certainly not during the lifetime of my relationship with him. Creative nonfiction was Krim's thing, I would think, not giving it a second thought, one of his adjuncts of the new journalism, another kind of aberration—I would have called it an abomination in the old days—on the literary battlefront. I was a poet who wound up writing prose, thank you, and that's how I defined myself and how I chose to look at the world, and my interest in Krim's prose developed slowly, phrase by phrase, until it amounted to my reading a full essay, then a couple of them, and, finally today when I look back on this forebear of creative nonfiction, not only with nostalgia and respect, but even a little bit of awe and wonder.

Prior to those encounters with him at Columbia in the late '70s, our paths crossed occasionally in the 1970s at readings I gave at bars in both the Village and East Village, places such as the Tin Palace and Remington's and, once in a while, keeping up with our belligerent natures, we would get into arguments. Usually Krim would complain to me in this nonliterary way of how I had sold out and gone straight—for the life of me I still don't understand what the hell he was talking about since from then to now I've never enjoyed anything like an establishment position and I've never made more than a marginal income from writing or teaching or anything else and, at any rate, my limited amount of teaching never even brought me close to a middle-class existence. What I think he really objected to was the fact that when he met me on the Lower East Side I was a genuine street urchin, an honest-to-God down-and-outer, drunken and disorderly, a fringe personality, slightly dangerous, though mostly comic relief, a ranting lunatic, an angry imbecile, a poetry-writing, prose-spouting thundermouth, a gyrating verbal explosion, a bundle of raw nerve, emaciated, seething, stinking, furious, unsheltered, angry, malcontent, mistreated, malformed, grandiose, and, yes, unpredictable. By the mid-1970s, I was married and had published a few books, one of which derived some literary attention; I was better dressed, fuller in the body, relatively content in marriage, employed, and even somewhat educated now; I bore no resemblance to that mound of emotional confusion and false street-mythologizing from the Lower East Side.

Krim, like so many of the Beats, was a deep romantic and, in those old days on the Lower East Side, I was nothing if not romantic, trying to out-Rimbaud Rimbaud, and now I had become some kind of ordinary citizen of the realm, deeply interested in writing and literature, yes, but no longer concerned with my self-image and how I projected myself upon other people. I had married a Korean opera singer—who knew, at the time, very little about America, and New York literary scenes, and whenever Krim talked to her at these meetings in bars, she didn't respond with the proper enthusiasm to his reminiscences of me as this glorious bum spouting poems and stories. She didn't think I was this refined bit of business either, but my wife wanted to put to rest that old notion of who I was because she rightly saw that that posture had gotten me nowhere quickly.

During my stay in San Francisco in the late '60s, I published my first journalistic piece in *The Village Voice*, a fantasy about the IRA providing guns to the Black Panthers in San Francisco. I recently spent some time in San Francisco, and the details of that time came rushing back into my consciousness, long buried for more than twenty-five years. You see, I didn't think of Krim when I wrote that piece, even though, now, recalling it, I suppose it was a kind of creative nonfiction in that it posed as journalism, though, in fact, it was pure fiction. Of course, the FBI and the IRA didn't think so. Both organizations paid me visits, wanting to know how I knew about these Armalite rifles that the Irish guerrillas provided the Panthers in the Bay Area. I made it up, I told them, it's pure fiction or, if not pure, at least fiction through and through. They left, skeptical, scratching their heads, wondering who the hell I was trying to fool. The IRA was more succinct. They told me that if I blew their cover, they'd blow me away, and I believed them. But it didn't stop me from, time to time, writing journalism, usually when I needed money, and since I played so loose and juicy with facts, I suppose that my journalistic instincts, if not the finished product, had more affinities, with Krim's creative nonfiction than anything else. Yet I did not make that association. I thought of this type of writing not even as writing at all but a kind of easy way to pay the rent, buy cigarettes, and put food on the table. It was like having a newspaper delivery route as a boy, like working at a bookshop, although, better still, I had no boss over me, so it was the best of all worlds, but my devotion to it was so erratic that I didn't even see it in that clear a light, but rather just one of many different ways a freelancer got by in this world. But when Krim wrote and taught about creative nonfiction, he was not just proclaiming this type of writing creative and good, he really meant that it was the best game in town; he believed that the future of American letters would be found in this gap in which facts merged with fictional technique, and the outcome was his hybrid—I don't believe he ever saw it as a bastard form as I did—known as creative nonfiction. And I need to clarify that while I sometimes had a pathetic regard for facts—my rationale was that I was after the right *feelings*—Krim was a first-rate journalist himself, a real professional, something I was not, and so he did not share my slippery notion about facts. I did not really come to terms with facts until I got sober and saw that there was a seam between my imagination and reality, and sometimes it would do a writer well not to blur the two worlds, that such distinctions were necessary, and even good finally in the overall shape of a piece of prose. To Krim, just like all the great creative nonfiction writers such as John McPhee (*Looking for a Ship*), Joan Didion (*Slouching Toward Bethlehem*), Phillip Roth (*Patrimony*), and James Baldwin (*Notes of a Native Son*), facts were what fueled the imagination toward the greater truth. Reality was the great story finally, once facts were acknowledged to be, not so much impediments to the imagination, but rather the touchstones to locate imaginative worlds.

But let me finally crystallize, if for no one but myself, three typical and last encounters with this early master of creative nonfiction, this schlemiel of literary wizards, this dufus of prose bijoux, this old friend and mentor. In the late '70s, married and with a child and out of work, I went back to college to finish up two degrees at City College, then went back to graduate school at Yale—I had been at the School of Drama in 1971–72 as a special student in playwriting mainly because they offered me a full-tuition scholarship that essentially covered all my expenses. But two weeks after returning to graduate school at Yale, Dick Humphreys, whom I did not know yet, asked if I would be interested in teaching an introductory creative writing course for them. It meant that, for two years, once a week, I commuted from New Haven to New York. Thus developed a relationship with Dick—as everyone called J. R. Humphreys—that lasted fourteen years at Columbia until he retired, and continues today outside that academic world. During those Columbia years, a lot of them were spent with Seymour Krim as a colleague. He taught creative nonfiction and, as I said, I never blinked an eye at the genre's name. After all, nonfiction, when you think about it—consider, for instance, non-poetry and non-prose and non-playwriting—is a pretty weird genre name, too, so that creative nonfiction seemed, strangely enough, less odd, maybe because I knew just what Krim meant. He meant, I knew, that type of writing I so often did to make money in journalism; something personal, literary, factual and yet not proscribed by facts; a form as liberated as poetry because it sought to frame the human voice charting experience in the rhythms of paragraphs, which, by then was the writing form of my own poetry—paragraphs and more paragraphs of every form and construction, content and sound. But don't think for a moment that Krim's and my relationship had suddenly become smoother because I honored, if begrudgingly, his beloved writing genre more than I once did, and even practiced it, though I would not realize that fact for a few more years.

What was more typical was to get into some kind of social altercation with him. One such collision happened during a cocktail party Dick Humphreys, and his wife, Peggy, threw for the writing faculty. Krim was drunk and so was I, though my drunkenness was more muted, more fugitive, and he was in one of his roistering moods, loud and confrontational, full of romantic braggadocio, and he confronted me in front of everyone, saying that (this was always his theme with me) I had sold out, that years ago, a little germ on the street of the

Lower East Side, I was far more interesting. Now I had turned into some kind of middle-class parody of what I once was. Of course, he was wrong as usual, but that didn't matter and, like a fool, I took the bait, and we got into a lot of shouting and if I hadn't left, maybe it would have even come to blows. He was the first to apologize; that was the protocol, in fact. He would drop a note, usually a postcard, apologizing for what he said or did, and I would write back or telephone him, saying that it was all right, I apologized too, and that, in fact, I was thankful to him for all the help he gave me early on in my career, but that he had to understand, just because I was married and had a child and taught then at two universities (Columbia and Fordham), I was hardly middle-class because they didn't pay me well enough to be that, and if he reads my writing, he would see that I still maintained the same obsessions and interests that I had when I was a twenty-year-old without a home on the Lower East Side and attended his workshop at St. Mark's in the Bowery.

The worst of these weird encounters with Seymour occurred in the 1980s after I had managed to disappear from everyone's literary consciousness. I think, even though Krim felt that I was a good writer, he thought, too, that I had become more of a teacher than a writer, and that my books were not as interesting to him as they were when I was younger. Though I want to elucidate two more odd encounters with Seymour, I recall, writing this, that we had one lovely meeting. He came down to the West Bank Cafe on 42nd Street, where my play "Our Father" ran on weekends at midnight—no, no, he came to an early show for my play "R & R," about a soldier on leave in a Bangkok whorehouse during the Vietnam War— and, drunk, probably high as a kite on reefer, too, Krim went on and on, staying for the second play, too, about how I had gotten back to writing what God intended for me to do, to make these angry, odd, funny, passionate testaments about big families and working-class people and, before he went off into the night, he embraced me and told me how much he loved me and my work and how we should always be friends, blah blah blah. . . .

It was the kind of social event that drunks experience a thousand times in a lifetime and forget nearly all of them be-

cause upon waking the next day they have forgotten their dec-
larations and feelings and what even propelled them to shout
these things. I could be wrong about this, but I had the feeling
that Krim forgot everything he said when he woke that next
day. Maybe he even had no memory, in a blackout, of being
at the cafe and seeing the plays and telling me how much he
liked both of them (the plays) and me (the playwright). At
any rate, he never mentioned it again. And after that, I did
not see him for quite some time. He drifted away from teaching at Columbia—I think he went off to Israel to teach and
I didn't see him again until he came back after the heart
attack.

I want to place the event I am about to describe after he
saw my play, but I realize now, seeing it replayed in my mind,
that my daughter was still a small child, which would put it
at the beginning of the '80s, after I moved back from New
Haven and was living on 110th Street again. It happened one
late summer morning in front of the building that housed
General Studies at Columbia. My daughter played on the campus in those days, and on hot summer days she liked to play
on the lawn in front of General Studies because it was shaded
and cooler than the rest of the campus. I saw Krim, wearing
a denim shirt and tie with a sport jacket and dungarees, almost a kind of uniform for him, loping toward the building.
He was a big man, even athletic in movement, though this
was only an appearance, because his own creative nonfiction
works belie this observation about his being an athlete; in
fact, he was a classic, unathletic nerd. Still, he was well over
six feet tall and had a big frame, and though his glasses were
formidably thick and a thin cigarillo dangled from his mouth,
he seemed spry and fit, a man alive and purposeful in his
gaze and demeanor, as if he knew where he was going and
that destination was an unimportant one and could not be
brooked. I called his name, and he stopped. He squinted toward me, trying to determine who I was.

Even as he got closer he still could not make me out. I
could see the blankness on his face now.

"Who are you?" he asked.

All my life I have been something of a chameleon, my physical appearance changing from moment to moment, and so

I didn't take offense, at first, at his not knowing me. Besides, we had not seen each other in a couple of years at this point, and I had changed much more than he had. I told him who I was, but the name Michael Stephens did not register any note of familiarity with him. In fact, he was more puzzled, seeming to roll the name around his brain cells. "I'm sorry," he said, "I don't believe I know who you are," and he turned and walked away.

"You son of a bitch!" I shouted after him.

But he was already at the door of General Studies, opened it, and went inside.

That bastard, I thought, I'll never talk to him again. That was the last straw. I didn't need to be involved in that abusive relationship ever again. So I decided to forget about Seymour Krim, I said, that half-baked mediocrity of a prose writer, that prose yenta, that—yes, I said, that fact-happy, yes, that fact-loopy journalist. For that's what he was. He was no creative writer. He was a fact-checking, pencil-pushing newspaper flack. Creative nonfiction, indeed! Creative nonfiction, *my ass*! He *would* write in a genre that defined itself by what it was not, i.e., not fiction, and not straight journalism, it was creative, not in that sense of being imaginative, but in that Hollywood sense of being some ill-defined genre of humanity, the creative talent, the people you paid the cheapest salary to, because, after all, stars were not creative talents, they were stars. Creative talents were the supernumeraries, I thought they were the Seymour Krims of the world. But before I could take this screed much farther, I received a postcard from Krim. And that's when I realized how deeply he had hurt my feelings by the snub. In the postcard, he apologized for his behavior, saying he did not know what happened to his mind, but sometimes it went blank.

My own oldest brother had had, just like Krim did, electroshock treatment in a mental hospital, and I knew that the treatment often messed with one's memory. So I was willing to believe what he said. Perhaps his not recognizing me had less to do with a social one-upmanship than it did with neurological synapses. Krim's essay "The Insanity Bit" was a monumental testament to what happens to the mind under this kind of institutional duress, and to me it was one of his most beautiful and insightful pieces of writing and, yes, a great example of creative nonfiction, an autobiographical outpouring that resembles a personal essay, and yet so rhythmically structured as to bear more resemblance to poetry than prose. The insight came from the nonfiction in the essay on insanity, but the beauty was in that creative part of the writing, its unfathomable rhythmic struts and paragraphical essences. Krim may never have been that cool—in the sense of Miles Davis being the ultimate cool—but there was no writer hipper than he was when the jazz of his prose locked into its syncopations. What Jack Kerouac called spontaneous bop prosody. (I was tempted to say that "Seymour's 'friend' Jack Kerouac said," but as Krim noted in "the Kerouac Legacy," even though he was forever associated with the Beats, especially his championing of them, he only met Kerouac twice and never for more than fifteen minutes, so that their affinities were purely literary, not social or physical.) "The Insanity Bit" is one of the hippest pieces of writing to come out of the latter half of the twentieth century, and decades after it was first published—back in the late '50s,—it still resonates with Krim's ferocious integrity, moral incandescence, intelligence, and emotional honesty, not to mention pure chutzpa to reveal this about himself in prose.

But I am reminded that Krim wrote a couple dozen good essays, enough, I think now, to make him one of the literary immortals he so desperately wanted to be, and thought he had failed miserably at becoming. Failure was the theme running through so much of his best writings, and yet he was able to write about failure with real genius the same way George Orwell wrote about it. In fact, thinking about these two pinnacles of nonfiction writing, they make me realize that in order to write creatively in nonfiction perhaps one needs to be a bit of a failure, that the genre does not lend itself to successes very well. I was reminded of this recently when I read Krims essay "For My Brothers and Sisters in the Failure Business," taken from You & Me (Holt Rinehart & Winston, 1974); I came across it in Phillip Lopate's groundbreaking collection, The Art of the Personal Essay (Anchor Books, 1994), the included essay being a testament, not so much to Krim's failure as his prescience and perseverance, that finally the world was coming to see, a generation removed from his own, that their antecedent went back to fearless writers such as Seymour Krim. As Lopate writes in introductory notes to the essay:

> Ironically, part of Krim's sense of failure came from never having realized his youthful ambition to write big American novels; essay writing seemed to him something of a compromise, a minor art. Had he valued it more highly, he might have realized what a genuine success he was.

Successes don't write creative nonfiction, though. They write big (bloated) novels, plot-infested, mass-appealing, finally onerous behemoths of verbiage and dishonesty. For even though Krim promulgated J. R. Humphreys' term creative nonfiction, I doubt that he would take credit for inventing a form. He was too modest to do that, even when he was being grandiose; his pomposity was more that of someone with low self-esteem, not some high-roller out to let us know what a really grand personage he or she was. And even though he helped to coin the term to delineate what he did among the academic community he suddenly found himself in, Krim never took the time, though he defined many other things in his writing, to define what he meant by the term. But it's easy to trace the progression of his writing to come to an understanding of the term creative nonfiction. He once described new journalism as "the real truth, while whatever everybody else in the newspaper business writes is the official truth."

In other words, nonfiction and journalism had come to mean official truths, while new journalism, or what evolved, academically at least, as creative nonfiction, became the real thing, truth itself. Yet Tom Wolfe and Hunter S. Thompson are not everyone's idea of truth in any shape or form; one might be deemed a literary mercenary and the other a creative fool, a calculated madman. So I think creative nonfiction needs Krim's other literary interest before new journalism to define it, and that was his love and anthologizing of the Beats, that Kerouackian bebop-a-loo-la prose masterpiecing and rhythm-a-neeking, that sense of poetry, where sound makes as much sense as the facts themselves and, in the realm of truth, perhaps the jazz, of prose was the most important ingredient, that ability to convey drifts and meanings by the pulse and beat of the prose.

My own notion of creative nonfiction and Seymour Krim was corroborated by a recent conversation with Dick Humphreys. Especially, he said, what he and Krim meant by creative nonfiction was nonfiction that could be as creative as fiction. "It was writing with emotion," Dick said, "not just writing objectively, in fact, subjective writing was all right." He went on to say that creative nonfiction was prose writing with a voice, voice being the foundation of all creative writing.

Coming upon that highly successful essay on failure in Phillip Lopate's anthology made me think about Krim in ways that I hadn't done for years. Of course, for the longest time I have wanted to write about him and creative nonfiction and have not been able to get the right handle. I suppose seeing the essay in an anthology crystallized some of those feelings I had. I combed the Strand and other used bookstores in New York looking for *Shake It for the World, Smartass*, the only book of his I didn't own. Then I found myself in San Francisco, and in a used bookstore off Union Street I managed to buy a nice copy of the selected essays, *What's This Cat's Story?* (1991). I had two days to kill before the work I had come to do began, and I sat in hotel room reading Krim, and since San Francisco was so closely aligned with the Beats, it was the ideal location to reread my old nemesis and hectoring mentor, my first prose-writing teacher and, oddly enough, one of my literary consciences.

He was a New Yorker, from the Bronx, born in 1922 to a Jewish family. His father died when Seymour was eight, and his mother committed suicide when he was ten. He attended the University of North Carolina, which, before Michael Jordan, was famous for being the alma mater of Thomas Wolfe, one of Krim's early idols, but he soon tired of college and dropped out. When he was in his early thirties, a relative success as an editor and freelancer and staff writer for some fairly prestigious magazines, he had a breakdown and wound up incarcerated for his mental illness. He intended to commit suicide in Newark after he was released, but the sight of an earthy Polish girl dancing brought him back from the cusp of suicide:

> I found the booze and saw a coarse, ignorant Polish girl do such a life-giving, saucy, raucous folk-dance (on the small dance floor to the right of the bar) that I broke into loving sobs like prayers over my drink

which did not keep him from being locked up again, though, until he finally realized, like a lot of other brilliant writers in other eras, that the so-called crazies were not crazy at all. His two great literary loves were the Beats and new journalism. In his lifetime, he published three essay collections, left behind a batch of writings from his younger days and an insanely dense prose exploration too aptly titled "Chaos"—"See, I come from an older America full of a different kind of two-fisted, two-breasted terror"—a harangue without paragraph breaks or even breath pauses, what he thought was his breakthrough prose, though it mostly proved unreadable and unpublishable but for highly selective excerpts. In May 1986 he had a heart attack in Israel while on a Fulbright grant, and when he came back to New York, he grew weaker and sicker. In the end, like his own mother, he was listed as a suicide, though to believe that is to see how misleading words can be when the deeper truth is sought. This was a brave, courageous soldier in the army of literature battling all of life's mediocrities. His death was not a cowardly act, but rather a quietly intelligent one. He had consulted with the Hemlock Society about ending his life. A good friend of his told me that he was neat about it and left notes for the police and then on August 30, 1989, he ended his life, not with a bang or a whimper, but with music on the stereo, though not jazz. I imagine he played something classical because the only times I had ever been to his small neat apartment on East 10th Street, there was marijuana smoke in the air and classical music on the machine.

That was not the last image I had of Seymour, though. I recalled the last time I saw him alive. At a Christmas party for Columbia faculty he got into one of his old-time, demon-from-hell biblical rages at me, once again berating me for my failures, not living up to the potential of my earlier career, and this time, since I was newly sober, he thought it unnatural that a Brooklyn/Irish writer would not—because I could not—drink. The notion that I might die, if I had another drink had nothing to do with it as far as he was concerned. Krim would drink and smoke and blow dope until the end, he said, and so should I, and I ought to get rid of my lace-curtain dreams of being clean and sober and live a little, kid, get out there and make some mischief. Actually, it was not that benign a criticism; this was more primordial, his anger toward me coming from a deeper place inside of him that had nothing to do with me and everything to do with the mortal Seymour Krim. He was less than nine months away from committing suicide, not out of despair, but because he had arrived at the terminus of his life, the existential threshold of this man and writer named Seymour Krim; the heart disease had made this vital man a cripple, incapable of teaching anymore, unable to climb stairs or do anything constructive. His writing career was finished, and yet, thinking back on him now, he really wrote most of his best pieces—though not necessarily all of them—in the 1950s. Now his manner of dress was almost dandyish, quite impeccable and dramatic, the small trademark sideways egg-shaped glasses (the epitome of the late '60s and the hippies) had been replaced by round, Joycean frames, the corduroy replaced by a tweed jacket, the drably colored knit was now a colorful silk tie, and the dungaree jacket was now a fancy overcoat to keep him warm. I was six months sober, just beginning my new life—really just beginning my life for the first time—and he had come to the still point, here at last at land's end. Though he was one of the most generous of teachers, spending his lifetime taking student work, including my own writing, to editors to read; encouraging, nurturing even, at least nurturing if you were odd and out of place and slightly off-center, like he was. The old guy was a benign, annoying, literary cheerleading, badgering, wildly enthusiastic sort of presence in my life, but that evening—as it turned out, the last time I ever saw him—he was in a feckless rage, almost like a rabbinical King Lear raging at the elements and, in this case, the elements being the nature of writing and writers' natures, his own nature being this romantic one that believed that one gives the entire self to a literary art and, finally, it consumes you, then spits you out without a thought to what you did. I always had a much less sentimental view of life and my own writing and, as passionate as I may be or appear to be or become, I always have that Yeatsian colder eye inside of me, assaying everything from the cautious vantage of an artifice, because, being Irish, that's how I see, having read my Joyce as well, and having read him well. Which is not to say that Krim couldn't have a chilling Celtic eye to take in the world.

Sometimes his writing had an oracular chill to it. In one of his 1950s essays on fiction and imaginative writing, he has this to say:

> After Joyce, the intensification of language became a commonplace, until prose writers pored over their words as if they were writing poetry; not because they wanted to show off, but because the exact word (presumably an infection Joyce received from Flaubert and passed into the bloodstream of the English) gave both the fact and beauty at the same time, and the writer's sense of perfection and objective truth could only be satisfied by the higher demonstration of truth which a Joyce had brought into being.

(My God, but everything I loved about this writer can be found in that last sentence—the energy and muscle of the prose, the smartness of the observation, the brilliant turn of phrase, "an infection Joyce received from Flaubert.") But, mostly, instead of being oracular, his prose had a practical edge that belied his hopelessly romantic instincts; this edge was worldly, full of a sense of being in the universe, living a life, not as a Beat, but beat by beat, hour to hour, day to day, week after week, month by month, and, finally, year after year, chronicling the daily progression of the self through an existence. Krim, in countless writing instances, wrote about how fiction failed because it could do nothing more than telling, whereas imaginative writing was all about being. But he did not yet call it creative nonfiction; he said it was "total imaginative writing," and he defined it as "all prose which is revealing or uncovering about the experience of the Self, and then rises to the more intense level of experience we call art, seems by inner intention to have grouped itself together into a specifically modern genre." Seymour went from being a lover of literature of prose fiction to being a lover of the literature of fact; what never changed was his love of prose, and the measure in it, when used effectively, that fathomed the truths of a life in its time. When he finally came to use the term creative nonfiction I think it was just another way—in this case, an academic way—of saying total imaginative writing, the self revealed in writing, but, because of his love of music and his sense of poetry and a never-relinquished love of great literature, this other literature of fact, this imaginative writing he called creative nonfiction, the prose had to be as good as poetry and up to the rigors set down by those former prose masters, writers such as Joyce, Proust, Kafka, and Flaubert.

The upshot of my last encounter with Seymour was yet another postcard apologizing for his behavior, saying I was a good old friend and I should understand the strain of his life, et cetera, et cetera. I did. Because it didn't take a genius to see that the end was at hand. In less than nine months, he would be dead. When he died, I pulled out a manila folder I had of a few letters I saved; two full letters and one fragment. The latter was written from Israel, just before the heart attack, and was a classical Krim letter whose style was not unlike his essays themselves, deeply intelligent, thoughtful, witty, kvetching, admonishing, patriarchal, meekly bullying, and full of love. Here is the opening of one letter from the late 1970s, shortly after I published an experimental prose work called "Still Life" (Kroesen Books, 1978). He writes:

> I hope I'm right in thinking that I've earned the privilege of speaking utterly straight to you about writing, since I copped your cherry as it were; you were a prose virgin until our old Workshop, and accident led to my intriguing you with the possibilities of prose, which made for a conjunction that can never actually die. I'll always be a shadow conscience for your work, even when you're a hell of a lot better and more acclaimed writer than myself. I think you know just what I mean, without my trying to stretch or impose on the implications.

It was written on yellow typing paper, neatly typed with only a few errors, all of them corrected, and went on to chide, castigate, plead, and warn me about being too indulgent a writer, too show-off a writer, too much a writer who wrote his writing for writing's sake. For Chrissakes, he was right, of course.

People are more interesting to me than ideas, which I think is both the fault and virtue of working as a journalist. I have tried to write about my old friend and mentor Seymour Krim first and about creative nonfiction second. As I write this I don't think he was the founder or father or grandfather of creative nonfiction, though I think he was one of its best practitioners. He did not coin the term "creative nonfiction"—I now know Dick Humphreys did—but he was the thing itself. To me, he was a great prose writer, a true stylist and, just as important as the facts in this type of writing, is the honesty a writer brings to the form, and Seymour was nothing if he was not honest. "Ask for a White Cadillac," his account of going up to Harlem to get laid, may anger blacks and make whites shake their heads and say, "What a fool," about this man, but no one can doubt the veracity of the piece, and no one would condemn its honesty and, after all, our sexual desires, our erotic appetites, are not particularly social or socialized behaviors; they are enacted in the dark, privately, unfettered of social disapproval, and a good prose writer strips down in the same way, walking naked before the reader.

What all of this prosing over Krim and—with apologies to my dear old friend Dick Humphreys—this Mickey Mouse of a phrase associated with him is really about is debt-paying and acknowledgment, about creating continuity, of continuance of the craft no matter under what name it comes by; it's about gratitude. A prose by any other name would smell just as sweet as this creative nonfiction thing, Seymour. But this was your baby, old friend. That's the point. Though Krim always saw me alternately as this smoldering belligerent street kid with enormous talent for writing prose or this sellout little Irish bastard who betrayed my Lower East Side instincts by going off to college and getting three degrees, and then having the balls to show up at Columbia to teach creative writing for fourteen years, I think he saw me as the creative personnel and himself as a kind of cigar-chomping talent scout, the agent, the flack, the public relations man. He would have shit in his literary pajamas to learn, post-mortem, that after he turned to dust, I turned to nonfiction instead of fiction. I know what Seymour would do because I knew Seymour, and I know what he always did. At first, he would get pissed off at me, tell me that I'm ruining my God-given talents by writing this book about Korea or this book for essays about fighting, writing, and drinking, and then, shortly thereafter, I'd receive a letter on yellow paper, neatly typed, beautifully written, offering me a sensational blurb for the book, and telling me what a fine writer I am and how wrong it was of him to tell me that I was losing my talent and, always genuinely modest finally, he would make some unflattering comparison about his own writing and mine, and end by saying that we ought to get together before both of us got too old. With all the pessimism in his work, he finally was the great optimist. He was less Sartre and more Whitman, the self he sang was only the existential one on the surface; underneath it all, the self he explored was of the barbaric yawp, of the bespectacled prose-drunk nonfiction genius kicking out the jams.

Prose is what first made us acquaintances and is what cemented the relationship, allowing the peaks and valleys to be ironed out into a sort of friendship despite my reservations with the word *friendship* as I've defined our relationship here; prose is what it is all about, for him, for me, for all of us— as Krim himself might put it—in the writing game; prose is what keeps me alive and what drove that crazy old fart Krim to the brink of madness in its pursuit. Old nearsighted cannoneer, dear old smartass, once titled a book *You & Me*, which I took to be a kind of Sonny and Cher title, Seymour's coming into the age of the Beatles, though he would forever be associated with the '50s, not rock-n-roll, but Jack Kerouac and Allen Ginsburg, the Beats, and the jazz of the city, the classical music of his tiny crib on 10th Street. The Symphony Sid of prose, the endless commentator, observer, the inside outsider, the outside insider, the slightly stoned-out and out-of-it Ralph Waldo of our mid-century, only beyond the pale, outside the normal ken of the establishment. Finally, he was more an American Walter Benjamin than anything else—and how can one pay a higher compliment to a prose writer—a brilliant prose stylist, a wandering Jew, a friend to geniuses, a philosopher in journalists clothing. Call it creative nonfiction. I call it Krim.

Michael Stephen's book, Green Dreams, Essays Under the Influence of the Irish, *published in 1994 by the University of Georgia Press, won the Associated Writing Programs Award for Creative Nonfiction. He also wrote* The Brooklyn Book of the Dead, *University of Georgia Press, 1994, and* Our Father, *a play. He teaches at Emerson College.*

Darcy Frey
Reaching New Heights

TRACY MARX

IN HIS UNADULTERATED PURSUIT OF A GOOD STORY, Darcy Frey ends up writing about large issues—the politics of life and death, as doctors in a newborn intensive care unit debate over the viability of a tiny life barely ready to exist outside the womb; the fight against the cultural inequities of race and class, as witness to the bullying of an innocent homeless woman by an onslaught of suburban police; the precarious safety of us all, as in a moment of terror that is all too frequent, an air traffic controller's radar scope goes suddenly black—and the true stakes of lives built around sports in his first book, *The Last Shot: City Streets, Basketball Dreams*. Named a *New York Times* Notable Book of the Year, *The Last Shot* is a powerful account of hopes dependent on basketball, set in the context of four young, inner-city athletes at a crucial moment when, as Frey writes, "Never in their lives would they be in possession of so little and on the brink of so much."

Frey's articles have made the pages and covers of such major publications as *Harper's*, *Rolling Stone*, *Sports Illustrated*, and also *The New York Times Magazine*, for which he is a contributing writer. To date, he has received a National Magazine Award— a Livingston Award, given annually to three journalists under the age of thirty five—and a Sigma Delta Chi Award from the Society of Professional Journalists, in addition to the success of *The Last Shot*. As a result, one might expect Frey's list of publications to be much longer than it is, perhaps because his writing conveys a certain expertise, a confident yet unobtrusive voice that suggests a longer track record. His early success is a testament not only to his skill and perseverance, but also to his admitted good fortune in connecting with distinguished editors along the way, including former *Atlantic Monthly* editor Richard Todd, known for discovering and nurturing such talented writers as Pulitzer Prize-winner Tracy Kidder, Mark Kramer, and novelist Ward Just.

Until I meet him, my knowledge of Darcy Frey, beside the facts that he is white and male, is limited exclusively to his work and its provocative images. Certainly, I've been affected by what I've read: His exposure of the stunning chaos at the Federal Aviation Administration will forever influence my travel plans, and I have developed an uncharacteristic interest in college basketball that has friends confused. One might easily wonder what kind of path has informed Frey's ability to penetrate the stressful conditions that are so often at the heart of his work.

Curiosity notwithstanding, I approach Frey's neighborhood on Manhattan's Upper West Side with some ambivalence about this business of mind-probing, demanding answers to what are the sometimes inexplicable mysteries of creation. I'm consoled however, by the kind of writer Frey appears to be—exposing, questioning, a truth-seeker himself. And I wonder, too, what kind of face is worn by the ambition his accomplishments must require.

Frey has situated himself in one of the quieter, more homogeneous areas of the city, a neighborhood that is home to many of Manhattan's community of artists and writers, with convenient access to theatres and museums. His building is nestled between the pedestrian activity of a main avenue at one end and the Hudson River not far off on the other. His apartment lies above street level, somewhat removed from the chaos below, and at a safer distance from the urgency and conflict he is so often obliged to put himself in the midst of.

Just as I expected, Darcy Frey is none of what I expected. There is no sign of aviator goggles, or a scuba suit poised for his next adventure, no wild profusion of facial hair. Nor is he a bespectacled, scholarly type, surrounded by a disarray of books and papers. The face of ambition, it turns out, bears friendly green eyes, sandy hair of a respectable length, and an easy-going, personable manner. He could easily be taken for a graduate student, or one of his neighborhood's yuppie fathers, with a baby strapped to his chest.

After sharing my ambivalence with him, Frey assures me that he is happy to discuss his work, although he makes the distinction between discussing completed work and work in progress, acknowledging the vulnerable nature of the latter. "It's definitely harder to talk about work in progress because it feels so tenuous that it's even happening, and to talk about it sometimes scares me because I'm afraid that whatever access I might have to the words I need is going to vanish if I discuss it too much. But talking about done work is different."

That established, I wonder if he can trace his relationship to writing, perhaps illustrate how he came to be a nonfiction writer. Frey worked on his high school and college newspapers. While in college, he noticed something called literary journalism, or creative nonfiction. "I took a seminar in which I read 'the greats,' John McPhee, Joan Didion, Tom Wolfe, Tracy Kidder, and it was really then that I started to think, that's the kind of writing that I would love to be able to do." Upon graduation, faced with a choice between going the newspaper route or the magazine route, Frey chose magazines, sensing a greater potential to work on longer narratives, to focus more on writing and sentences. "Magazine and book writing both give wonderful opportunities to work with story and narrative, using scenes as the building blocks rather than simply constructing from quotes and facts, and also allowing for analysis and use of language to convey different states of emotion."

After college, Frey worked at *American Lawyer*, an investigative magazine about the legal business. He stayed for three years and learned an "incredible" amount about reporting from editor Steven Brill, the man since responsible for revolutionizing media coverage of the legal system with his creation of Court T.V. "It was an amazing place because you could write magazine stories, but they had to be reported like investigative newspaper accounts. I always had in my mind this idea of a kind of writing that sounded different than most consumer magazine writing, that shaped stories around narrative, and paid close attention to language, mood, atmosphere, scene-setting. Obviously, the *New Yorker* was one place that was doing that, but another place I discovered was a little magazine published in western Massachusetts called the *New England Monthly.*"

It was while on assignment for *American Lawyer* that Frey happened upon a *New England Monthly* article about a Connecticut town, titled "Darien: The Town as Country Club," written by Richard Todd. Frey recalls the article as "one of the most astonishing pieces of nonfiction I'd ever read, and I decided I had to go work at this magazine because they would publish this kind of stuff." *The New England Monthly* piece, Frey explains, was about "how exclusive, and white, and privileged, and racist, the town was—but it was written with this deft, light, understated touch—it was an exposé, but done with the most gorgeous language. I was just completely blown away by it."

In 1988 Frey joined *New England Monthly* as an editor. "The kicker to the story is that Richard Todd was the executive editor at the magazine, and so I got to know him." And, just as Frey had anticipated, the experience proved invaluable. "In the same way that *American Lawyer* taught me the principles of thorough reporting, editing and writing for *New England Monthly* helped me really figure out how to be a writer. Those were the twin training grounds for me, and also working at a place that took so much care with language. Even the bits of unsigned 'house' copy that filled the front of the magazine were written with the most extraordinary care."

While on staff at *New England Monthly*, Frey wrote "The Big Empty," a piece he cites as being a turning point for him as a writer, and ultimately, in the later decision to work on his book. In the piece, Frey profiles the town of Stamford, Connecticut, the economic and racial stratification caused by its era of urban renewal, and the consequences for its residents—in particular, the murder of one homeless woman who lived and died over the course of Frey's reporting. "That was the first time I started to write in a way that sounded like me. Everything until then kind of sounded like I was trying to sound like somebody else, but with that story, I thought, I can kind of understand what it means now to recognize the sound of your own voice. It was the longest thing I'd ever written and so I was able to really concentrate on things like narrative and story line, and I was able to, for the first time, tell a story kind of from beginning to end. I discovered that I actually liked telling stories. It was very exciting—rather than just getting a quick snapshot of something in an article, I was able to build slowly, whether it was the sense of the city, the woman, or the pessimism." The piece was completed just as *New England Monthly*, "one of those great magazines that flourished editorially but not financially," folded, and was instead published in *Rolling Stone* magazine in 1991. But it was the experience of finding his voice, and working with a sympathetic editor, that served as the impetus for Frey's eventual decision to write a book.

After six years of magazine staff work, Frey's instincts told him it was time to return to New York, and to break out on his own as a writer. A stint at *Harper's* magazine as a temporary substitute for an on-leave editor provided the right transition. It also was Frey's last full-time job. Soon after leaving Harper's to begin life as a freelancer, he formulated the proposal for *The Last Shot*.

Frey is quick to point out his good fortune on the career path. "I've been blessed with magazine and book editors who never pulled me back from using creative elements in my writing, and I feel really blessed that these editors have wanted stories to have an individual voice. One of the things that editors have done for me, that I haven't been able to do for myself, is to be more journalistic, to give a framework to whatever story I'm working with that resonates to the questions and curiosities the general reader might have—which I think of as journalistic endeavor rather than purely creative writing. And when you can balance journalistic aspirations in terms of explaining, investigating, exposing to the reader, and you can do it in a narrative, creative, character-driven way, then that's what I aspire to—to have enough reporting that it feels like a true piece of journalism, but to do it in as vivid a way as possible, so if I can, I am making the reading experience as vivid and exciting as I can make it."

The rest of the "kicker" to Frey's story is that while at *New England Monthly*, Richard Todd retained his position as book editor at Houghton Mifflin publishers, and it was for him that Frey wrote *The Last Shot*.

The story behind the realization of *The Last Shot* is not only one of the transformation of an idea, but of a writer's vision, his relationship to his material, and his voice in it.

"What do you mean?" Corey, a key character in the book, says. "No one reads books anymore."

"Then why is Darcy writing about us?"

" 'Cause he just wants to write," Corey replies on my behalf. "I know what that's like."

"Then he's a fool," Stephon, another important character, concludes.

from *The Last Shot*

In *The Last Shot*, Frey chronicles a period in the lives of four teenage basketball stars whose chances to emerge from a legacy of poverty as independent, successful adults, hinges not merely on their athletic prowess, but on their ability to navigate the tough conditions of ghetto life, a disadvantaged educational system, and a National College Athletic Association (NCAA) system whose rules "seem designed to foil them." The book may be seen as the fullest representation of Frey's skill and appreciation for fine reportage and fundamentals of story. It also shares with his previous works not only an element of social conscience, but a subtle sense of rooting for the underdog. It contains, as one reviewer put it, "just the right amount of outrage."

I wonder if, on some level, caring and writing have become related for Frey. His answer however, is an unflinching *no*. "I think it's extremely dangerous to write with some sort of agenda of social good. If there is some social good that comes out of a piece of writing, that's wonderful, one always hopes for that. But in terms of having that as a goal, I actually stay away from that. I think I gravitate towards stories because they are good stories, because they are opportunities for telling a good story." His opinion clear, Frey does however, acknowledge the link I've suggested:

I do see this similarity between some of the pieces I've written and the book. I guess it's that I like writing about non-famous people, and they are usually in some sort of stressful or difficult situation. And there is also a common theme of individuals working in a system that sometimes gives them a lot of problems—whether it's inner-city basketball players dealing with an exploitative college athletic system, or a homeless woman dealing with a political system in her hometown that conspires to keep her on the street, or two young parents who get pulled into this very complicated medical and moral situation that they are totally ill-prepared for; and even the air-traffic controller story, which is basically about hard-working men in a system set up by the FAA that's kind of destroying them. So it's funny, either I just gravitate toward those story ideas, or, in the situation in which I find myself, that's what my eye alights on, and I kind of draw that out of it. But, yes, I seem to be interested in individuals working in a system of inequity.

Despite the basketball context, Frey always had aspirations that *The Last Shot* would be more than a "sports book." With his storyteller's sensibility, and a hint of the screenwriter clearly at work, he considered various alternatives for a place to set his urban America idea—a playground, a particular city block, spending a year at a housing project. "Then I thought playground, basketball, a school—it ended up being a fairly conventional idea—hanging out with a sports team. But I got to it very slowly, wondering about the best setting so I could have a group of characters, a finite period of time. With a team I'd get to hang out with kids, which is fun, but there is also the natural drama of the games and practices, and the school year."

At Coney Island, New York's Abraham Lincoln High School, Frey found everything he was looking for—characters, setting, drama, and most important, Corey Johnson, Stephon Marbury, Tchaka Shipp, and Russell Thomas (not his real name). "First I met the whole basketball team, and then the four kids, who I loved right away—their difference from each other, the way they played off each other in interesting ways—and Coney Island is an amazing neighborhood, so rich in atmosphere and history, and so removed from the rest of New York, it seemed like the perfect place." Frey's announcement to the young athletes that he planned to spend a year in their company and write a book, was greeted with overwhelming enthusiasm.

Over the course of his reporting, Frey was a daily presence in the lives of the four young men, at school, home, practice, with girlfriends and friends, accompanying them to summer basketball camps, often taking long road trips with them in his small Toyota. As a "white, middle-class, outsider," the comfortable relationship forged between Frey and the four African American teenagers raises interest in his own background, and in the process by which he was able to gain entry into their world.

Like the history of his writing career, information about Frey's background comes from him quickly. He spent the first several years of his life in the Fordham Road area of the Bronx, New York, before his family moved to Yonkers. His mother is a teacher at The Fieldston School in the Bronx, a private prep school that Frey attended, and his father used to run a rare book firm in Manhattan. Frey attended Ohio's Oberlin College, but has always lived in New York, except for the two years spent on staff at out-of-state magazines. Despite the differences between Frey and his subjects, it took little effort for him to gain their trust. And though he admits to having been geared for a fair amount of suspicion and wariness, any friction he experienced over the course of his research did not come from the athletes.

It was really amazing and wonderful how well and quickly we established a way of being together. One reason was probably the sheer amount of time I spent with them. And the long road trips gave me an opportunity to get to know them in a very relaxed kind of way. I never had to 'interview' them in any conventional sense. It was what I call 'hang around reporting,' where I'm really just watching and observing, getting their interactions with other people and letting people reveal themselves slowly, rather than asking a series of questions and waiting for answers. And I think it was the right strategy for these kids—that we got to know each other, over time, and I can make sense of who they are. And my wanting to spend all this time with them didn't strike them as odd either, because in New York City, star basketball players are used to a fair amount of attention, mostly from reporters and recruiters, which was probably helpful.

Frey also admits that he was initially quite fearful of the Coney Island neighborhood, where, unlike in the integrated high school, he was virtually the only white person. "At the beginning I felt lost and intimidated, but once I got to know the four kids, they were incredibly welcoming to me, and then I was basically in their company." It seemed that conditions for the project couldn't have been better.

With five months of research time left in his one year plan, however, the wintry decline of activity on Coney Island's streets and basketball courts portrayed in the book ironically coincided with the decline of Frey's access to his story. Fear and suspicion on the part of some of the parents, as well as interference by the NCAA banning Frey from accompanying the boys on their college campus recruiting visits, ultimately severed their communication, and brought the book to a halt. For Frey, the turn of events only further illustrated the machinations of a manipulative basketball establishment, and its effects on the families caught up in its practices.

With his reporting interrupted before the boys had chosen their colleges, and before the season and school year were over, Frey had no official ending to his book. He describes the period as a time of incredible frustration, depression, and panic. "I thought the book was finished, over, wasn't going to work." And the combination of having the book fall apart and losing the company of the kids made it especially trying. "I went through a sort of post-partum depression, because for nine months I'd had only one mission in life, which was to get in my car, drive to Coney Island, and spend time with these kids. I was basically lost. I didn't know what to do with myself, or my material."

His book project abandoned, Frey realized however, that he at least had enough material for a magazine piece. He approached the editors at *Harper's* at an opportune moment when the magazine was starting its "Folio" section, a quarterly segment devoted to longer works. He credits the guidance of the *Harper's* editors in writing the award-winning article, enabling him to envision the project as a book once again.

"They really pushed me to give the piece a real beginning, middle, and end, and to use my obstacles as a reporter as part of the story. I'd thought it would be a third person, omnisciently told story that was going to have no reference to me, but then I realized, no, some of the most interesting discoveries came about because of the obstacles, and, if used, would be wonderful material." Thereby "stumbling into the investigative part of it," a year after deciding to kill the project, Frey called his book editor.

"I really thought I was going to be writing this kind of book about victory, about kids triumphing over their circumstances and environment, and I had this picture that it would end on graduation day, and the kids would throw their mortarboard hats into the air and go off to the college of their dreams. But the more time I spent in Coney Island with these kids and recruiters, the more I realized I was really writing a book one hundred eighty degrees opposite of what I thought, which was basically about how circumstances and environment triumph over the best efforts of kids. So it became an investigative book almost by accident, because I kind of stumbled upon this story that was much more complicated and exploitative than I had thought when I started. I had to let my old assumptions for the book fall away, and then it became a very different book, and more personal in some ways—not just because I put myself in it, but also because I got into some of those delicate relationships that I'd formed with the kids and their families, and the friction of all of that. When that stuff was happening, I wasn't thinking that it was 'book stuff,' I thought it was just conversations telling me that the book wasn't working. In terms of the writing, I had to figure out a way to write in the first person that didn't impede the story itself, to always be there, but kind of transparently there, so that the reader could see through me to the kids, which is the point of the book. And that was hard for me."

Difficult as it may have been, Frey's accomplishment is evident, not only in the praise both the Harper's piece and the book have received, but more importantly, in Frey's own satisfaction with the work. It's a relief to learn that this dedicated writer wouldn't change a thing, including the complications he deems "an odd piece of fortune."

Predictably, comparisons abound between *The Last Shot* and the documentary film "Hoop Dreams," which was released about a month after the book's publication. Even the front jacket of Frey's book boasts a *Newsweek* quote naming it a "worthy literary companion," to the film. Frey likes the film and agrees that it is eerily similar, although "the book is more opinionated, while the film is told very dispassionately and seemingly impersonally, is more hands-off. But maybe it draws the same conclusions about the system these kids are in."

Though one might get the feeling that he would succeed at whatever he pursued, Frey seems uniquely qualified for his chosen field. When I wonder if he ever loses interest in a subject or tires of research, he tells me that "the issue is usually how do I tear myself away from the reporting and start writing. I always get so drawn into the research that I've never had to manufacture a way to be interested." And while some writers with a narrower range of interests would be less receptive to working for *American Lawyer*, or, during a dry spell, the guide for the Arts & Entertainment channel, Frey acknowledges that his openness to a wide range of subjects is a great benefit to this career. Like the gifted young athletes in his book, who learned basketball through observation, the scrutiny of their neighborhood's elders and by playing the game, Frey seems to be a natural. Yet he doesn't consider himself an "artist," but rather, "a journalist who pays attention to writing style," reserving the term for the great novelists and nonfiction writers of "another league."

I wonder too, about the impact of the attention his book has drawn to him. The real impact, he tells me, is the luxury of being able to choose his projects more selectively, and to have more room to write them, time to devote to the research, and the later attention to writing craft to which he is so clearly devoted.

Just when it seems to me that Frey's path has become deservedly smoother, I learn that his current project is a book about the last two years of his father's life, and the ways families deal with terminal and chronic illness. Our conversation has looped back to the tenuous issue of work in progress, and this time on a sensitive subject in which I assume Frey will have to make an appearance. But I sense I will have to wait to find out. There is little doubt that Frey will meet whatever challenges lay ahead, that he will continue to, as Doris Lessing writes, "strengthen the power of that 'other eye,' which we can use to judge ourselves." And if he manages to accomplish some greater good in the process, so much the better.

Tracy Marx is a Writer-in-the-College at the Eugene Lang College of the New School for Social Research and works at a New York City publishing house. She is also pursuing her M.A. in creative writing at The City College of New York.

Like a Flower of Feathers or a Winged Branch

ELLEN GILCHRIST

THIS IS PEDRO CALDERON DE LA BARCA'S DESCRIPTION of a bluebird. I read this one morning in a doctor's office and have thought of it daily ever since. Every time I see a bird or a branch of leaves or a flower I think of it.

This is the job of writing, to carve indelible metaphors into the mind of a reader. *Can't you see,* the writer must tell the reader. It is all one thing. Look outside yourself and see that we are all fashioned of the same forms, the seven basic forms of crystals. Look outside yourself. Look at me.

If that is the task, how can the writer achieve it? I think it is like building a wall. Let us suppose that the beginning writer is a man living alone on a piece of land. He wants to build a wall to keep other people from coming onto his land, but he has no tools or knowledge. All he knows is that he wishes to construct a barrier. He collects what he finds lying around, leaves and fallen branches. He stacks these things up. The first wind blows them away.

He finds stones and begins to make piles of them, but they are heavy and cumbersome and in short supply so he soon gives that up. Then he travels to the next piece of land and finds a man who is making bricks out of clay and stacking them up. Our man likes that idea. He goes home and makes a wall of clay bricks, but the spring rains melt the bricks and the wall tumbles.

He meets a third man who is making bricks and letting

them dry in the sun before he stacks them up. Our man is very excited by this idea. He goes home and works twice as hard as before. He doesn't care how hard it is to do, now he will make a wall that will hold.

As he works day after day and week after week fashioning the bricks and setting them out in the sun to dry, he begins to imagine a wall so beautiful that other men will come to see it and marvel at its beauty. He begins to make each brick exactly the same size, with sides carefully trimmed. He notices the clay from the banks of his creek makes more beautifully colored bricks than the clay near his campfire. He begins to make long trips to bring back this thicker, redder clay. Now he doesn't like the sun-colored bricks he made to begin with. He discards them. He is excited. He has lost his sense of time. He barely remembers to eat. He is going to make the most beautiful wall in the kingdom, the longest and the tallest and the most beautiful. Every day he gets up and works on the wall. He is a happy man. He has forgotten why he is building a wall. He has forgotten that he thought there was something that needed walling in or walling out. He is an artist with a plan and materials and skills. He has become a builder.

My life as a writer has been like that man making that wall. I have forgotten what I wanted from this work. I have never liked celebrity or having people ask me questions. Aside from being paid so I can go on writing, there is nothing the outside world gives me in exchange for my writing that is of value to me. I do not take pleasure in other people's praise, and I don't believe their criticism.

I love to make up characters and make things happen to them and then make them strong enough to survive their problems and go on to happy times. "Happy trails to you," I say to my characters at the end of my stories. I nearly always let my characters have happy endings because I wish that for myself and for my readers. I don't want to send my readers to bed with sad or malignant endings.

Pedro Calderon de la Barca lived in Spain in tragic times. His father was a tyrant, and the only woman he ever loved died in childbirth. She died giving birth to Calderon's illegitimate child. Because of these things Calderon was forced to have a tragic view of life. He was concerned with guilt. He believed that a man can be responsible through his own wrongdoing for the wrongdoing of another. That the greatest sinner is also the most sinned against. These are deeply tragic beliefs, and yet the poetry with which Calderon expressed these beliefs was so beautiful that it has lasted all these years.

Like a flower of feathers or a winged branch. That is what we want to write. But first we must learn to make a wall. We must find what materials are available to us, and we must learn to shape them, and we must forget what we were doing it for. If you get lonely, and it is lonely work, invoke the spirits of past artists to stand by you and teach you by their examples. Today, for me, it is Don Pedro Calderon de la Barca, poet and playwright, born January 17, 1600, Madrid, Spain, died, May 25, 1681, Madrid.

Ellen Gilchrist lives in a stone and glass house built into the east-facing side of a hill in the Ozark Mountains. She reads and writes all day and is currently rereading the works of John McPhee and worrying about the curve of binding energy. She has three grown sons and eight grandchildren. She has published fourteen books. Her latest book is The Courts of Love.

Nonfiction in First Person, Without Apology

NATALIA RACHEL SINGER

IN HIS INTRODUCTION TO THE 1989 *THE BEST AMERICAN Essays*, Geoffrey Wolff tells a story about how, in writing an essay on "King Lear" as a young boarding school boy, he could not help but narrate some of his own misunderstandings with his Duke of Deception father to illustrate his sympathy with Cordelia. Wolff's teacher wrote the customary "Who cares?" in red ink on his essay, insisting, as we were all taught, that when one writes nonfiction, it is necessary to "take facts in, quietly manipulate them behind an opaque scrim, and display them as though the arranger never arranged." Reading Wolff's story made me think of my childhood in Cleveland, and my decision, at the ripe age of five, to devote my life to becoming a writer. I remember thinking, as I watched my parents' marriage dissolve, and I stayed up late staring out the window at the oak tree in the yard and listening to the cranes at the city dump two blocks away scoop up crushed aluminum, that if I could record *this*: parents fighting, squirrels crunching acorns, garbage sorted like bad memories—that if I could find words to make sense of my own life—I could write anything. But in the neighborhood I grew up in, to be a writer meant to be a dead English novelist, like Charles Dickens. It simply wasn't done. Some people had heard of Ernest Hemingway, but you had to know something about fishing and bullfighting. Women writers usually went mad or changed their names to George. I wanted to continue to be a female person, and I wanted to tell "the truth." I wanted to explore "real life." Mine, at least for starters. I would have liked to have written my memoirs, but only famous people wrote their memoirs. To my teachers, writing about "real life" meant only one thing, and I was tracked early on to write for newspapers.

By the time I got to high school I was writing most of the feature stories on our school paper. I was often asked to go after "difficult and sensitive" subjects which required intimate self-disclosures from the interviewees. My portfolio is filled with family tales of woe and grief. Picture me at fifteen, asking a laid-off worker from the Acorn Chemical Corporation plant, the father of eight, what it feels like now that his house has just burned down and all of his family's possessions have been destroyed. Imagine me interviewing the pastor's wife after her son, who was in my homeroom on the rare days he showed up, has just fatally overdosed on windowpane. It is no wonder that I was soon nicknamed "The Sob Story Queen."

I did not know that I would someday decide I had exploited the people I wrote about. It never occurred to me to question why these stories did not satisfy my burning desire to write, or why, after writing them quickly and easily, I would hop on the back of Gary Pritchik's big black motorcycle and ride to the river where we tried again and again, beneath the blinking yellow factory lights, to set the Cuyahoga on fire. As a highschooler, I did not aim to achieve High Art; I wanted to pile up enough extra-curricular activities on my record to get into a decent college as far away from Cleveland as possible.

When I was asked to write a feature story on a friend of mine named Sharon who was suffering from Lupus, I realized that I was getting uncomfortable with this form of writing. I did it anyway, and the story won me a major journalism prize in Ohio, plus a scholarship to the Medill School of Journalism at Northwestern University, but it cost me a friend. After I wrote the story, Sharon and I simply never felt comfortable with one another again. It was as though, as Native Americans once said about their photographers, that I had stolen her soul. What interests me now about this incident is that out of all the people who might have written the article, I was truly the most familiar with Sharon's "before-and-after story," because I knew her body like I knew my own. Sharon and I had gone on our first diet together back in eighth grade. We had taken each other's measurements week after week and finally, one spring morning, had pronounced each other beautiful. We had coached each other on what to expect from boys. None of that was in the story because my hard-nosed editor would have written "Who cares?" across the front with his favorite grease pencil. Sharon remained other and her situation was simply tragic. Stripped of the noisy, meddling, "I," the writer whose observations affect and interact with and ultimately bring life to the observed, Sharon as subject was now reduced to an object; she was not that living, wisecracking teen-age girl with whom I'd once compared bellies and thighs.

Our first year in journalism school we had to take a course called Basic Writing; 50 percent of our grade was based on our final feature story which would be read in front of the class. I had not written a feature since the one I wrote on Sharon, and I was gun-shy. I searched the campus desperately for story ideas until one day, in the middle of Sex Role Socialization Class, my professor told us about a fascinating woman she'd met at a party the night before who was a preschool teacher by day, and madam for the most elite massage parlor in Chicago by night. This was before the time when we began to have suspicions about some of our preschool teachers. The madam—whose name I've since forgotten but it was something very unexotic, like Doris—would be coming to the next class, and was eager to talk to any of us in private.

The next Saturday the madam drove out to Evanston in her beat-up orange Opal and sat across from me in my dorm room beneath my Arthur Rackham poster of Alice in Wonderland, eating the cookies and milk I'd bought at the campus snack shop. She reminded me of Mama Cass turned bombshell in her flowing Indian skirts and her low-cut blouse with the shiny red heart she'd lipsticked onto her considerable cleavage. When she laughed her whole body shook, and the heart bobbed up and down like a fish. Outside the window there were kids playing Frisbee while she told me everything I wanted to know, and more. Finally, after we'd talked for hours, she picked up my stuffed koala bear with its N.U. garter belt looped around its waist like a goofy satin hoola hoop, and she set it down again on top of the tape recorder. "You aren't going to get the real story inside your sweet little ivory tower over here," she said. "If you really want to know your material, you have to spend a day at 'the house.'"

"The house" was not as seedy as I'd imagined. The "waiting area" was furnished discreetly with beige couches and chairs, Impressionist prints, potted plants, and a stereo that was playing the Brandenburg Concertos. I would have thought I was in an upscale dentist's office if not for the two women posing at the window in fancy lingerie. One of these women told me that before she'd started hooking six months before she'd only slept with one man in her life, her abusive ex-husband. She was twenty-seven. She looked at me with anger, imagining condemnation in my eyes. The other woman was eighteen, just my age, and I took to her immediately. Both were black, although the madam assured me that the massage parlor was a veritable melting pot of colors and Chicago neighborhoods, and that white girls who looked like junior varsity cheerleaders were in high demand.

As the madam had promised, the house catered to men's fantasies, and women were hired on the basis of whether or not they fit a "type." There was also a room full of costumes and make-up which could have serviced a theatre's full repertory season, from "MacBeth" to "A Streetcar Named Desire." My new friend, the eighteen-year-old, was six feet tall, and she'd been hired to deal specifically with men who needed women to be big. Her most frequent client was a prosecuting attorney who happened to be nearly seven feet tall. When he appeared socially with his wife, who was not quite five feet, people called them Mutt and Jeff. When the prosecutor visited the house, his lady for hire donned boxing gloves, duked it out with him in their imaginary ring, and knocked him down. Afterwards he would leap up unharmed, take off his gloves and hers, measure all seventy-two inches of her against the bedroom door with a yardstick, and then promptly carry her to bed, a redeemed slugger.

Then there was the pediatric prof at the medical school who wrote medical books by day and kinky fairy tales at night. The management required its women to be eighteen-and-over but they had no trouble finding voting-age gals who looked undeveloped, ponytailed, and girly-girlish enough to play Little Red Riding Hood to his Big Bad Wolf in those alliterative scripts he brought with him. And then there was the tax accountant necrophiliac.

The only client I talked to was the priest, who went there every Sunday after church and stayed all day. He loved to bake for his women and today he brought a loaf of bread which we all broke together and washed down with Diet Pepsi instead of wine. He was a lonely, inarticulate man with a voice that sighed instead of sang, and I could not imagine him inspiring fervor and faith from behind his pulpit. Nor, for that matter, could I—or did I want to—picture him naked and panting with one of these women, but that's exactly what I ultimately saw. Just as I was getting ready to leave, the twenty-seven-year-old insisted that if I were a true journalist and not a princess from the suburbs that I'd complete my research from behind the bedroom door. Before I could think about it I was in the same room with them, watching, notebook in hand, while they oiled, massaged, and stroked the priest to transcendence, all "on the house."

That night, tucked safely inside my dorm room, I began to wade through all this rich material. Immediately I was pressed with many writerly problems. How was I to deal with point of view? Whose story was it? The working women's? The clients'? My original goal had been to profile the madam, but she was swiftly being eclipsed by the prosecutor, the pediatrician, the necrophiliac, and the priest, who were all far stranger than she was. How much of the dirt should I put in? What should I leave to the imagination? What about what I'd seen with my own eyes inside that room?

I finally chose to make the place and its strange characters the subject of my article, and to do this I took myself entirely out of the story. I wrote it as though I were a bug on the wall watching a typical day in the house, but I tried to use the voice of the madam as much as I could.

As it turned out, the teaching assistant took me aside later and told me he thought I could publish it in *The Chicago Reader*. Other students in the class had interviewed the Chicago journalists they hoped to line up internships with for the summer and he and the prof were thankful that I'd gone for something with "grit." There was only one problem, he said, and that was the style. It was simply too literary. If I cut out all the adjectives, he said, I would be on my way to becoming a journalist.

I turned down his generous offer, as flattered as I was, because I'd promised the women I wouldn't publish the piece. Now that I look back, it seems that there were other reasons why I didn't want to sell this story to the *Reader*. One was that I wasn't interested in developing the dry, "just the facts" style that the t.a. thought I needed to master in order to become a valid journalist. The other reason was that the real story for me was not, as everyone supposed, that respectable professional men can be sleazy but simply that an eighteen-year-old girl/woman with Arthur Rackham posters and a stuffed koala bear with a Northwestern garter belt had been in this place and talked to these people and seen what she'd seen, and that she had somehow been changed by having told this story. My problem, in 1976, was that I didn't know of a journalistic form that would allow me to tell it the way it wanted to be told; those new literary journalists were not yet being taught. But neither, I discovered when I switched into creative writing, could it be told in a poem or short story.

Poetry writing was a two-quarter sequence taught by a woman who was writing her doctoral dissertation on the Modernist poets. Each week she had us read several volumes of the poet of the week—Eliot, Pound, Moore, Bogan, Stevens, Williams, and others—and then write two poems, the first a "pastiche" for which we obviously stole not only the poet's technical bag of tricks but his or her material as well, and the other an "imitation" for which we borrowed a technique but still tried to write our own poem. By the end of the first semester, whatever "voice" we'd all had before had been consumed by the tones and postures of our Modernist mentors. We would call each other on the phone and say, "How do you write a poem?"

The summer after that workshop I went to Wesleyan College and attended my first writers' conference. My workshop teacher read my poems and was kind enough to point out the origins of each line in my work. "That's from Shakespeare's Sonnet 18," he said, "and that's from 'Love Song of J. Alfred

Prufrock,' " and "that's one of Louise Bogan's metaphors for depression. Where are you in these poems?"

A year or so later I went to one of my old poetry teacher's readings. She closed with a poem about the town where she'd grown up, which was somewhere—I couldn't believe it—in the South. I'd always assumed, given her diction, that she'd spent much of her life in English boarding schools. Maybe she had. Then it dawned on me. On a certain level, my teacher's aspirations to literary academia may have been spawned by a profound self-hatred. As mine had. Along with the dreams of countless other girl-women I knew skulking around misera-bly in the library. If my teacher had exerted so much energy trying to transform herself from the "down home" girl to the Oxford poet scholar, then how could she help me go deep into myself to find my authentic voice and material and story? I signed up for fiction writing and hoped for the best.

The fiction writing class was taught by a tall, trim, blue-jeaned, very hip late-thirtyish fellow who was nicknamed "The Marlboro Man" by the circle of female students who had crushes on him. He had a slight Western twang and wore cow-boy boots. When he came to our parties he smoked pot with us and told humorous anecdotes about the famous writers he'd met. His class was entertaining and lively. We got to write about subjects closer to our own life, but there was still a lot of stigma against being "self-indulgent" and "autobiographi-cal." Style was more important than content—you had to be slick and exude a certain daring razzmatazz. You couldn't be political or direct. Processing personal experience was only okay if you applied heavy irony. Think of the times. It was now 1978, and people everywhere were trying to numb their pain from the previous decade by wearing shiny half-buttoned shirts and jumping into vats of hot water with near-strangers to the beat of the Bee Gees.

Although there was some lip service paid to original voice and place in my writing training, the fashionable voices were usually male back then: Bellow, Nabokov, Gass, excerpts from Pynchon, and a smattering of Ishmael Reed for color. I felt pressure to rev up my narrative engine, just as, when the Carver school made the grade soon thereafter, I felt pressure to edit everything back out except for the name brand products. And as far as place was concerned, it seemed to me you had only two choices. You could write about rural New England, of course, or you could write about the gritty "mean streets" of a Chicago, L.A., or New York. But what about a place as modest and chintzy as Cleveland, nicknamed "The Mistake by the Lake?" When I looked out the window I saw not Mt. Monadnock, not the pushers at the subway, but a few scrappy trees and a mechanical crane devouring crushed cars. I wrote stories, back then, set in places I'd never been, like Paris and Barcelona and San Francisco, because, it seemed, my own eyes had never seen anything worth mentioning.

I've heard that when Annie Dillard first began writing what became *Pilgrim at Tinker Creek*, she intended to set it in Acadia National Park in Maine and write it in third person, in the voice of a fifty-year-old male academic metaphysician. After a time she realized that she didn't know Acadia the way she knew her home in Virginia, but it took a great deal of coaxing on the part of an enlightened editor to get her to write it in her own young female voice. This book, published just a year before I started college, points to a problem that women and people of color have always had in this country. Many of us have gotten one too many "Who cares?" written in red ink on our work. I think it is very common for the writer, especially the student writer, to approach a writing project with the feeling I am not worthy, as I am, with what I know now, to tell this story as I see it in my own words. To be an authority on this subject I have to hide behind the voice of someone else, perhaps someone whiter, with more Y chromosomes; to sound like I've been around I have to be from New York, or London, or Paris, or a charming old farm in New England with a ghost in the apple orchard who recites Robert Frost.

It was not until I was nearly thirty—just as memoir and the whole genre of creative nonfiction began to flower—that the stories from my life I'd tried to disguise and romanticize in fiction came exploding, honestly and urgently, onto the page. As a writer, a teacher, and a reader myself, I have come to see that today's readers are hungering for I-as-eye-witness truth, perhaps because we live in an age where it is now commonly known that our political leaders are liars and thieves. People are choosing to learn about Vietnamese war brides, the years of Stalin, and the American 1950s not from the so-called expert historians or the ruling patriarchs who led from inside their offices, but from *real* people whose solitary landscapes and single voices have a power that illuminates the larger humanity we all share—which makes, as the short story once did, the strange familiar and the familiar strange.

Just as readers are hungry to learn the truth in a language that is more lively than they find in the daily papers, our students yearn to tell their own truths and to come to understand themselves and their connection to the world better in the process. Creative nonfiction is a genre in which student writers can use their authentic voices and make no bones about their presence in the work. They can write about places they know well. They can feel that what they have seen with their own eyes is of literary value, and of human value to others.

It is my belief that education should be a nourishing place for the heart and soul as well as the mind, and it should build confidence, not destroy it. How do we help our students draw on their own resources, not just their acquired knowledge? The teaching of creative nonfiction can validate the students' current lives, and strengthen their writing skills. Nonfiction writing in first person teaches the young writer to sharpen her powers of observation and use of memory, to hone his specificity and finesse for naming concrete things, and to create an honest, living voice. For the student writer, the permission to write about something he or she passionately cares about is what motivates that writer to go the extra mile to make the prose vivid and clear, rather than flat, empty, and vague. To write first-person nonfiction well, one must make contact with what Brenda Ueland calls "our True Self, the very Center, for . . . here lies all originality, talent, honor, truthfulness, courage, and cheerfulness."

I suspect that had courses in creative nonfiction been available to me back in Cleveland, I could have saved myself about fifteen years' worth of writing mistakes.

Perhaps one day when encouraging a student to seek her "True Self" in nonfiction prose is a basic component of writing pedagogy and not some retrograde 1960s concept, it will be customary to write "Why do you care about this?" on student essays, instead of "Who cares?" Perhaps helping our students search for "the very Center" right from the start will save them several years of writing mistakes. Whereas William Gass, in his introduction to In *the Heart of the Heart of Country* advises the aspiring young fiction writer always to "wait five years," the young nonfiction writer who has found his or her voice can often master a particular piece of memoir well enough to create something worthwhile and even publishable right now.

Natalia Rachel Singer is an associate professor of English at St. Lawrence University where she teaches, among other things, writing courses in creative nonfiction. This essay appeared in the first issue of Creative Nonfiction *and was reprinted in* The Best Writing on Writing, Volume 1, *and the* Essayist at Work *issue of* Creative Nonfiction, Issue 6. *Her work, both fiction and nonfiction, has appeared in a number of places including* Ms., Harper's, Redbook, The North American Review, *and* Confrontation.

Excavations

LISA KNOPP

Among my daily papers which I bestow on the public, there are some which are written with regularity and method and others that run out into the wildness of those compositions which go by the name of essays. As for the first, I have the whole scheme of the discourse in my mind, before I set pen to paper. In the other kinds of writing, it is sufficient that I have several thoughts on the subject, without troubling myself to range them in such order that they may seem to grow out of one another and be disposed under the proper heads. —Joseph Addison, Spectator, No. 476 (Friday, Sept. 4, 1712)

IT WAS A WALK THAT HAD ALREADY YIELDED PLENTY. I HAD ventured far enough from the road to stand on the shore of a lake of ferns, each cupped heavenward like a satellite dish. I'd weighted my cardigan pockets with flinty gray-and-white striped rocks. I'd sloshed through a soggy ditch beneath eight-foot-tall reeds—part cattail, part tasseled corn—where I found the frogs I'd been hearing. I'd studied grasshoppers that bore little resemblance to the green hoppers I'd chased in Iowa meadows as a child and held in my clasped palms until they spit tobacco. Vermont grasshoppers are black, gold, brown, and winged, and I couldn't persuade them to spit for anything.

But then, on the gravel shoulder, I found a dun, mouse-like creature, dead, curled in a fetal position. It was a mouse with a snout, but no mere pig's snout: This was a proboscis with a flair. It was piggish with two nostrils near the center, but from the outer rim sprouted fingers of pink flesh like the spokes of a rimless wheel, the petals of a sunflower or the tentacles of a branching idea.

This was too much to trust to my memory, so, I broke my rule of leaving wild things—even dead wild things—at peace, rolled the corpse onto a Kleenex with a twig, and carried it home. Once there, I laid it on my desk and sketched its fabulous nose in my notebook. Then I sketched its entirety with words: "A dun, mouse-like creature, dead, curled in a fetal position. . . ."

Since I hadn't anticipated the need for a spade or shovel when I packed for my week and a half in Vermont, once my notebook was full, I flushed the creature down the toilet—the most respectable burial I could give under the circumstances.

For nature essayists, the subjects for our excavations fall at our feet like bread rained from heaven. A dead opossum. A flushed pheasant. An approaching cloud of mayflies. Bare branches studded with white-headed eagles. Consequently, when I was stopped short by a dead mole on the road, I knew I would write about her, though I wasn't yet sure what I would write. Yet other gifts presented me with an angle, a handle, a purpose as soon as I beheld them. While driving back to Nebraska from Vermont, for instance, I was startled by a great blue heron standing stock still near a farm pond in the midst of a moving landscape so close to Interstate 80 that I questioned my own ability to see and name. In September, I only had eyes for flaming groves of sumac and spent all autumn reading and writing about their border existence while carrying sprigs of dried purple berries in my buttonhole. Next, two failed attempts at autobiographical essays which, above all, reminded me why I need to write about other living things than myself (more timely and timeless; less self-indulgent; more downright interesting). Then, one January morning, it happened. I woke up as I always do with the desire to write, but on this day I had no subject matter. No circle of hell could be worse. So, I resurrected the mole.

Still, I wasn't ready to write since I hadn't a slant on my subject. Though I was a half a continent, a half a year away from that August afternoon when I found the mole's body, I was no closer, no further from making an essay about it than I had been. I knew if I didn't find some way to write about it, I'd turn its now warm body over and over in my mind in the middle of the night, fretting myself sleepless until I found an angle, a handle, a purpose. So, I did the next best thing to writing about the star-nosed mole: I went to the library and read about it.

Most of the facts I read—and the metaphors I glimpsed—pertained to the Condylura cristata's two farthest ends: the tip of its blooming nose and what I discovered to be its not–so–rat-like tail. I learned that its nose (which I had not noted in such fine detail) was comprised exactly and always (barring accidents) of twenty-two pink flesh rays or tentacles, one-quarter to one-half inch long. These are arranged symmetrically, eleven on each side, the two topmost rays held rigidly forward while the others move continually in the mole's search for food. Once it nabs a succulent earthworm with its shovel feet, it removes all distractions by retracting its rays so it can work, chewing down the length of the worm as if it were spaghetti. A nose with manners.

While mole experts Terry Yates and Richard Pedersen claim the exact function of the nasal rays isn't yet known, it's apparent that this nose, like the weird snout of the anteater, the tapir, or the elephant is a highly specialized sensory device. Each of the twenty-two rays, in fact, is covered with papillae (David Van Vleck saw fifteen to twenty on just the base of a single ray under low magnification), and each papilla bears one to three sensory organs named after T. Eimer, the German scientist who "discovered" them in 1871. This means that the mole's pointed nose isn't an earthmover as we might expect (the feet do that), but a sensitive instrument that directs the forepaws in their work. The nose, then, is a locator of the mole's prey and its position in the world.

Almost as interesting as the mole's remarkable nose is its tail. In August, it looks like that of a rat or mouse: a long whip about half the length of the creature's body from tentacle tip to tail base. But in the winter or early spring, that tail is quite a different story. Then, it is constricted near the base, swollen with stored fat near the middle like that of a snake who's just swallowed a small animal. Most swollen tails are as big around as a No. 2 lead pencil, some are as large in cross-section as a dime and, curiously, some tails never swell.

Apparently, moles use the stored fat during breeding season or other times when their food intake cannot meet their energy requirements. Eadie and Hamilton learned that the great majority of star-nosed moles of both sexes had swollen tails prior to and during the breeding season, but once the season was over, their tails were rat-like again. In addition to acting as a portable pantry, this tail functions as an antenna of sorts. In his study of the European mole, Godet states that the characteristically erect tail acts as an organ of touch, maintaining contact with the roof of the tunnels rather like the overhead pickup of an electric train.

Some other noteworthy facts about Condylura cristata. Weight: three ounces. Length: six inches. Habits: diurnal, nocturnal, active year round. Preferred habitat: damp, boggy soil near streams or in swamps and meadows in New England and southeastern Canada. Food: insects, worms, small fish, vegetable matter. Tunnels: deep and permanent where nests are built; shallow surface runways where food is gotten. Breeding: one litter per year of two to five molelets (my own terminology, I believe). Since other small mammals produce three to four litters per year, the mole's low replacement rate suggests few predators: an occasional hawk, owl, skunk, fox, coyote, snake, raccoon, cat, dog, big fish or golf course owner.

Joseph Wood Krutch says that to the essayist, a fact is "at best a peg to hang something on." A typewritten page-and-a-half of facts about the secret life of the mole only takes me a little closer to an essay about it. Now I have pegs. But what shall I hang upon them?

Some facts are so taut and humming, I could hang onto their tails and be carried into the heart of an essay. Consider this simple fact from Victor H. Cahalane: "Few people have ever seen a mole." Not exactly an earth-moving revelation until I add it to the following list: Few people have ever seen a miracle, the heart of darkness, an exploding star, or birds mating in mid-air. Therein lies the focus and the motive for an essay about a mole: why and how those of us who have witnessed the extraordinary should communicate our experience to those who haven't.

Julian of Norwich, an essayist of sorts, received sixteen "shewings" or revelations of divine love during her thirtieth year while on what she and others believed to be her death-bed. Julian survived, but had no other revelations and so spent the rest of her anchored days writing and revising the substance of that one extraordinary night: " . . . and truly charity urgeth me to tell you of it," she confessed. The nature essayist's reason for witnessing is often more mundane than soul salvation. Michel Guillaume Jean de Crèvecoeur, for instance, observed two snakes engaged in mortal battle, their necks wrapped twice around each other's, their tails lashed around hemp stalks to obtain greater leverage so it appeared that the two stalks were playing tug-of-war with the twined reptiles. Crèvecoeur felt compelled to relate the anecdote simply because the circumstances were "as true as they are singular."

Another fact, another promise of an essay: "Relatively speaking," write Yates and Pedersen, "little is known scientifically of these mammals. . . . Moles are probably the least understood major component of the North American mammalian fauna." Even though we've lost our hankering for moleskin caps and purses, even though tiny baked moles don't grace our tables as do tiny baked quails, and never do moles make good house pets, rarely living a year in captivity and requiring dirt and worms and all, nonetheless we should be interested in any creature capable of moving our foundation. Because moles sometimes eat what we've planted or move the soil away from it, we've devoted more attention to their eating habits and how best to exterminate them from our lawns than any other aspect of their biology. Still, there's more to the mole than what it does and does not eat.

This assertion leads me to speculate about how much else is so unstudied. Once I read that approximately seven hundred arachnid species have yet to be discovered. Initially, my fascination with this statistic lay in that so much remained to be named in a world chin deep in nouns—common, proper, colloquial, scientific, vulgar, euphemistic, and so forth. But then, I began wondering how such a fantastic and unsubstantiated figure was reached. In other words, how could anyone even roughly estimate the breadth of what she does not know? Do experts in all fields—archaeology, astronomy, linguistics, music—possess similar statistics about their respective unknowns?

If the mole is so unstudied, I suspect there is an entire essay on the curious few who have made it their life work. T. Eimer, for instance, the first known to have studied the star-nosed mole's *schnauze*. Or W. R. Eadie, who researched everything from skin gland activity and pelage differences to male accessory reproductive glands and unique prostatic secretions. What type of passion and audacity does such life work demand? A little biography could reveal a lot not only about those who study moles, but about any naturalist with an all-consuming passion. After all, I suppose the moody, aristocratic John James Audubon is wilder and rarer than any of the birds and mammals whose biographies he wrote. Second-generation violaphile, Viola Brainerd Baird, scaling Mount Olympus in search of a rare violet species or raising hybrids to maturity with her father Ezra Brainerd (husband of Frances Viola) delights me more than any of the careful paintings and descriptions in her *Wild Violets of North America* (University of Chicago Press, 1985). So, too, Charles Darwin's final work, *The Formation of Vegetable Mould, Through the Actions of Worms, With Observation of Their Habits*, leaves me more intrigued with the habits of this particular scientist (he shined a bull-lantern in the worms' eyes to determine if they could see; he chewed a plug of tobacco near their noses to test their sense of smell; he placed their earth-filled pots on his piano and banged away to see if they could hear) than it does about the humus-creating annelids. Darwin suspected that readers would be much more interested in his theory that humans "descended" than they would be in how worms had formed the rich topsoil in which humans planted their crops and so, in an addendum to his autobiography, he apologized: "This is a subject of small importance; and I know not whether it will interest any reader, but it has interested me." An essay about those who shun the popular and profitable for that of seemingly small importance is an essay I want to write; it is an essay I want to read.

Though little is known of the mole, the few passionate researchers who have excavated its hidden life have provided enough facts to refute widely held misconceptions. (If these assumptions cloud our ability to see the mole as it really is, then this essay could be another meditation on the same, earlier fact: "Few people have ever seen a mole.") "Looking at the mole, we would expect the animal to be rather slow and somewhat methodical," observed Richard Headstrom. "But surprisingly, the speed with which it can tunnel through the earth is almost incredible." Headstrom reports that the star-nosed mole has been clocked tunneling a distance of two hundred thirty-five feet in a single night. How much else do we incorrectly assume about the mole? (At this point, I expect an essay full of appearances and realities.) For instance, I expected the mole to wear a ratty, mangy coat living in dirt and leaf litter nests the way it does, but I've observed that its coat is velvety soft, the hairs lying smoothly and willingly in either direction. While I would expect it to be nearly deaf since its outer ear is all but invisible, the structure of the middle and inner ear are relatively large; therefore, its hearing may be quite keen. Neither is the mole mute. Godfrey and Crowcroft report that moles emit at least two sounds distinguishable by the human ear: "a soft twittering made when feeding or exploring, and loud squeaks made singly or in succession when fighting." Because the mole's nasal passages are longer than those in most other animals, we would expect its snout to be extraordinarily sensitive, able to smell an earthworm at fifty paces, but it is not. The nose is sensitive, but as a feeler, not as a sniffer. Finally, because the mole has few predators to escape and breeds so seldom (once a year, three-year life span), we might expect it to sleep its life away since there is so little to stay awake for. But in truth, the mole works around the clock, snatching sleep only occasionally. Because the mole works so much and because it has such a fast metabolism, it must eat one-third to one-half its body weight in food each day just to stay alive. Imagine how many waking hours it would require for an average-sized woman to eat forty to sixty pounds of food per day. So, too, the mole. At this point, my essay about appearances and realities could take a sharp, argumentative turn and persuade the reader to elect the industrious, sensitive, unassuming mole as our national symbol instead of the lazy, thieving fish vulture.

The same topic of appearance and reality approached from another direction: how different mammalogists reach different conclusions about similar data. In 1927, Fred Stevens of Ithaca, New York, presented William John Hamilton, Jr., of Cornell University with a male and female Condylura (the female was not pregnant) which Stevens had taken from the same minnow trap. Hamilton offered two interpretations for the presence of two moles in the same place: either they were together for an early courtship prior to mating or they exhibited a tendency for companionship. Hamilton places more weight on the latter, concluding that the star-nosed mole is not only gregarious, but colonial. Cahalane's position is more moderate: While no mole will ever win a congeniality award, the star-nosed and hairy-tailed are more tolerant of their kind than are other mole species. Moreover, it is not uncommon for them to use a community system of runways. Yates and Pedersen agree that moles may be found together, but believe this curiosity relates more to food supply than to need for companionship. Similarly, Leonard Lee Rue III portrays the star-nosed as a recluse. "Although this species is more sociable than the common mole, most moles lead a solitary existence. Only rarely are several moles found inhabiting the same tunnel, and these usually are females and their young of the year. The female does not tolerate the male after breeding, but raises her family by herself." Colonial? Together out of necessity? Hermits? I am curious about how the mammalogist's own attitudes towards companionship and solitude influence his reading of the mole's behavior. "What we observe is not nature itself," says Werner Heisenberg, "but nature exposed to our method of questioning." What questions were each of these scientists asking about the mole? What questions am I asking about the mole and those who study it?

At this point, I pause to reread what I've written. I am struck by my own metaphorical loose ends. In paragraph five, I state that the mole is like the subject of an essay ("For nature essayists, the subjects for our excavations fall at our feet like bread rained from heaven"), which is to say that our subjects are at the same time sought, uncovered, and sometimes brought forth; prayed for, waited upon, and sometimes received. The metaphor is accurate if you don't think too long about where moles come from. A few paragraphs later, I suggest that the movement of moles and essayists in their search for prey or their way in the world are each guided by a felt or intuitive sense. A few pages later, I say that the essayist's method is like the method of those who devote themselves to studying the homely form of the mole instead of something more glamorous (wolves, cranes, whales) involving more exciting methods of discovery (dog-sleds, blinds, wet suits) in exotic parts of the globe (Siberia, Japan, California). Not all mammalogists, not all essayists have to leave home to find their subject matter: Just this week, I've seen three common Eastern moles within blocks of my house.

Too, I am struck by my reliance on metaphor to reveal the act of essaying. But this is fitting. Trying to capture the essay or the act of essaying in words is like "trying to catch a fish in the open hand," says Elizabeth Hardwick. The essay is too protean, too slippery, too edgeless for definitions and parameters. The only recourse is to capture it partially through metaphors or, better, to demonstrate essaying in an essay that doubles back on itself, self-consciously reflecting on the method that produced it.

Which leads me to my next topic: an essay whose sole subject is form, an essay about preliminaries. The star-nosed mole introduces itself fringed nose first, typically tubular body next, and barometric tail last. Other creaturely introductions include: hard, toothless seed case crackers; fatty, velvety, neighing muzzles; rooting, rip-snorting snouts; twitching, pink buttons; neat reptilian pin pricks; sharp-pointed blood suckers. Like the introduction to an essay, noses usually proceed the body even if only by a nose. Like any first impression, they can be deceptive (the remainder of the star-nosed mole is quite dull compared to its elaborate fanfare). Just as an introduction only positions the essayist for her excavations, the dinner guests for the meat of the conversation, the mole's nose only locates the place where the feet will begin digging. My essay about introductions would not only explain their similarity to noses, but would itself be a series of positionings. An essay that is pure preface. An essay that introduces nothing. An essay, like this one, that never leaves the ground.

If the mole's nose is like an introduction, perhaps the body of the mole's work is like the body of the essayist's work. (Or different than.) An extended analogy could shed light on the dark burrowings of both. Again, the facts speak. While excavating, the mole uses every last hair and muscle. It turns its body forty-five degrees to the right if it is pushing dirt with its left forepaw, forty-five degrees to the left if it is pushing dirt with its right spade. Thus, it creates a back and forth spiraling motion like that of an electric borer. Nature essayist Richard Rhodes identifies the spiral rather than the circle or line as the movement of the essay itself and, for this reason, he says the essay is the most extemporaneous written form and, by definition, always unfinished.

Just as snow plowed from the road has to go someplace, so, too, the shoveled earth. When constructing deep tunnels, the mole throws the loosened soil under and back, then uses its hind feet to kick it to the rear. When a load has accumulated, it literally somersaults, then pushes the dirt ahead until it spills out forming the mountain we call a molehill. From the upstairs window we can imagine or deduce the process that produced the pattern just as surely as the best essays bear hints of the process that produced them. But when the mole tunnels near the surface, evidence remains that leaves nothing to the imagination—soft raised ridges wrinkle the lawn or pasture. One reading tells it all.

The essay's path is cut not with big clawed feet, but through "the act of thinking things out, feeling and finding a way; it is the mind in the marvels and miseries of its making, in the work of the imagination, the search for form," as William Gass explains. The essayist's cutting claws are also the words she chooses. In *The Writing Life*, Annie Dillard observes: "The line of words is a miner's pick, a woodcarver's gouge, a surgeon's probe. You wield it, and it digs a path you follow. Soon you find yourself in a new territory . . . You make the path boldly and follow it fearfully. You go where the path leads. . . ."

Not so different from the way the mole works. "Apparently, it digs wherever fancy or food takes it without thought of any definite plan, so that ultimately it ends up with an intricate

system of many-branched tunnels," Headstrom observes. Zo-
ologist David Van Vleck terms it the "hit-or-miss path of the
mole." While a rare essayist such as John McPhee cuts a certain path ("I want to get the structural problems out of the
way first, so I can get to what matters more . . . the story
. . ."), most essayists set out "with no predetermined path
or destination, no particular aim in mind, save the discovery
of reality," according to R. Lane Kauffmann in his essay on
the essayist's methods. Most essayists, then, in their search
for form, use what Walter Pater called an "un-methodical
method."

Finally, there is a sharp contrast between the world where
excavations take place and the world one finds upon re-emer-
gence. "Once well underground," reports the Mole in *The Wind
and the Willows*, "you know exactly where you are. Nothing can
happen to you, and nothing can get at you. You're entirely
your own master, and you don't have to consult anybody or
mind what they say. Things go on all the same overhead and
you let 'em, and don't bother about 'em. When you want to, up
you go, and there the things are, waiting for you." Predators,
weather, shadows, nesting materials, and nosy mammalogists. The essayist opens the door of her study to find hungry
children, dirty laundry, a ringing telephone, and an empty
bank account.

Nature's other gifts present a single focus or one focus
sharper and more engaging than the rest as soon as I per-
ceived them. The mole, however, is too full of essay-worthy
possibilities. More coats than pegs to hang them on. Too
many directions in which I could dig my path. So many slants,
I can't handle my subject. Too many tricks in this bag. With
a little more time, a little more paper, and someone to tend
the children just a little longer, I'd have a dozen more angles.
But enough is enough. All these speculations have brought
me no nearer to an essay about the mole than when I began.

"I do not see the whole of anything," Michel de Montaigne
assures me. "Of a hundred members and faces that each thing
has, I take one, sometimes only to pick it, sometimes to brush
the surface, sometimes to pinch it to the bone." For Montaigne, it was a matter of picking a course and following it,

accepting that some paths must remain untraveled, some members and faces, undeveloped. So, too, for me. If I've come this far, I have selected a path and pursued it. But whose furry surface have I brushed? What creature have I tried to pinch to the bone?

I examine my own meanderings. I walk beside raised ridges. I remember how my excavations connect one mountain to the next. From this distance I see that what appeared to be an essay about the mole in reality was—from the papillae on each tentacle to the tip of the sleek tail to each clod of earth moved—an essay about essaying.

Lisa Knopp lives with her son and daughter in Carbondale, Illinois, where she teaches creative nonfiction at Southern Illinois University. Her book, Field of Vision, from which "Excavations" is taken, was published in 1996 by the University of Iowa Press. A new collection of essays, titled Small Things, is under review.

Sacred Visualization
A Profile of
Terry Tempest Williams

BRENDA MILLER

I FIRST MET TERRY TEMPEST WILLIAMS AT THE ANNUAL Thoreau conference in Missoula, Montana. It was a spring day in 1990. I sat on a gray folding chair in small room at the Missoula Holiday Inn, along with fifteen other students, as we waited for the workshop on environmental writing to begin. I knew that outside purple phlox bloomed along the banks of the Clark Fork River, and trout hovered below the surface of the fast-running water. I knew the cottonwoods were in bloom, and I thought it paradoxical that writers so enamored of nature should be inside a windowless basement on such a beautiful day. But then Terry Tempest Williams strode into the conference room, and the natural world seemed to breeze in with her—in the flash of her eyes, in the glow of her wind-burned cheeks, in her calm authority and self-respect. She sat down in the chair next to mine and, before saying a word, she brought a clay whistle the shape of a turtle to her lips. She blew three pure, high notes and allowed the sounds to die away into the charged silence of the room.

In this way, Williams brought a roomful of restless people into the present moment, ready to listen, to write, to act. Only later, after reading her books, did I realize this as a gesture she repeats continually in her writing persona as well. She writes books and essays based on her personal history, transforming that history through a language of poetry, faith, and the human heart.

The next day, at the conference luncheon, Williams read "the Clan of One-Breasted Women," an essay which eventually became the epilogue to her book-length memoir *Refuge: An Unnatural History of Family and Place* (Pantheon, 1991). As she read about the seven women in her family who had died from ovarian and breast cancer, as she indicted the U.S. government for its above-ground nuclear testing in the Nevada and Utah deserts, her voice shook with rage and sorrow. "One by one, I have watched the women in my family die common, heroic deaths," she read to the packed crowd in the hotel auditorium. "I cared for them, bathed their scarred bodies, and kept their secrets. I watched beautiful women become bald as Cytoxan, Cisplatin, and Adriamycin were injected into their veins. I held their foreheads as they vomited green-black bile, and I shot them with morphine when the pain became inhuman."

Williams paused, looking up from her text to make eye contact with her audience. No one in the room moved, all of us holding our breaths in stunned silence. "The price of obedience has become too high," Williams said.

As a Mormon woman who has lived in Utah all her life, Williams' outspokenness, and her desire to tell stories that "bypass rhetoric" in search of the truth, transgress the rules of behavior sanctioned by the Church of Jesus Christ of Latter Day Saints' orthodoxy. Identified as a "hellraiser" by Mother Jones, and a "visionary" by Utne Reader, Williams challenges the status quo, and at the same time emphasizes her fierce loyalty to those aspects of life—nature, family, and community—proved worthy of it.

At a recent benefit reading, Katharine Coles, a local novelist and poet, introduced Williams by saying her writing "has introduced the landscape of Utah into the lyrical imagination of the nation. Her work explores what it means to be fully adult—politically, familially, and erotically—in the human and natural world. Terry has used her work to build her readers pathways of language . . . a constant reminder that we are linked morally, physically, and spiritually to the world we live in."

Williams is naturalist-in-residence at the Museum of Natural History at the University of Utah, and her intimate connection to wild nature, and her fierce desire to protect these lands, fuels her writing. In one of her early works, *Coyote's Canyon* (Peregrine Smith, 1989), Williams leads her readers to imagine the red rock as a living organism that bleeds if cut open. She then asks us to perform the gesture that elucidates the visceral connection Williams feels with the Utah landscape: "Pull out your pocketknife, open the blade, and run it across your burnished arms. If you draw blood, you are human. If you draw wet sand that dries quickly, then you will know you have become part of the desert."

Williams' relationship with the land demands that kind of reciprocity. Her stance as a writer and as a woman demands the willingness to be transformed through close attention and unapologetic love. It asks for a thin skin that absorbs pain, pleasure, joy and sorrow in equal measure from a life lived in close proximity nature.

In Coyote's Canyon, Williams interspersed short, personal essays with fictional accounts similar in tone and structure to the Navajo legends she explored in her first book, *Pieces of White Shell: A Journey to Navajo Land* (Charles Scribner's Sons, 1984). But whether fictional or personal, Williams' project is to tell the truth by telling a story, and the role of storyteller is not a responsibility to be taken lightly. "A story is never random," she writes in her epilogue to the book. "It must be framed with fierce attention, trust, and affection. . . . Story is a sacred visualization."

She tells her own story not as a cautionary tale, or even as confession, but as a way of healing rifts both within herself and within society. In *Refuge*, Williams integrated two stories: one a personal narrative about her mother dying of ovarian cancer, the other a chronicle of the rise of the Great Salt Lake that threatened to decimate bird populations at the Bear River Migratory Bird Refuge. In a recent conversation at her Emigration Canyon home, Williams told me she always writes her books in response to a personal question, and the question for this book was: "How do I take refuge in change?" She finds this refuge by remaining present with her family, and by trying to communicate directly with the landscape. In one section of the narrative she asks, "How do we correspond with the land when paper and ink won't do?" She responds to her own question by initiating bodily contact with the world: "I can drum my heart beat back into the Earth, beating, hearts beating, my hands on the Earth . . ." While many environmental writers, such as Edward Abbey and John Muir, question their abilities to adequately represent the landscape to other human beings, Williams seeks to express her humanness back to nature itself, and she does so through her own body. She "co-responds" with the earth, an active engagement that signals die dissolution of boundaries between self and other, between self and nature, so fundamental to her artistic and personal epiphanies.

Williams' latest work, *Desert Quartet: An Erotic Landscape* (Pantheon, 1995), takes up that flesh-to-flesh correspondence, and carries it one step further. This book was written out of the question: "What would it mean to make love to the land? "It is a short work, comprised of four sections: Earth, Air, Fire, and Water, and the text is interwoven with color drawings by sixty-four-year-old Mary Frank, an artist from New York City. In *Desert Quartet*, Williams pays attention to the elemental qualities inherent in nature in order to understand, in her words, "what it means to be human." For example, in the section "Earth," Williams writes: "The palms of my hands search for a pulse in die rocks . . . The arousal of my breath rises in me like music, like love, as the possessive muscles between my legs tighten and release." The physicality of Williams' work is not new; she has always been exploring the erotics of place, both in description and in her fierce desire to protect the lands she loves. "I write the personal landscape. It's my life experience," she said. We are so afraid of the erotic. We've relegated it to the level of the pornographic, which in my mind is all about the voyeur, when erotic in the pure sense is all about engagement, reciprocity, fusion."

The dividing line between eroticism and pornography, for Williams, is determined by the stance of the observer. "Huge portions of our population are in that state of disengagement, of numbness, the state of being a voyeur," Williams said. "We've become a nation of spectators. Look at the enormous attention given to the O. J. Simpson case, or the huge amount of money we pay to our athletes, it's all about being a spectator. What's even more frightening to me is that we become voyeurs with an opinion, based on superficialities. So again it comes back to the notion of the land and direct contact. We're losing contact with the natural world, we're losing our frame of reference as human beings connected to place."

Williams believes that Desert Quartet was born the moment her mother died in her bed at home, with Williams at her side. "Everything we had shared in our lives came together in that moment of trust," Williams said. "And in that sense it was very erotic. Shockingly so. So that as we were breathing together, as she was breathing herself in to the next world, I was able to accompany her almost as a midwife. It was that absolute focus on breath, and the only thing I had to compare it to was making love. And that was startling to me."

Williams was also strongly influenced by her reading of the French feminist theorist Helene Cixous. She remembers that when she read "women must learn to write out of the body," she recognized the force of that position at once. "I just went, boom, exactly. Because we read so much that's all in the mind, and that's just another way to sever us from our sources. So, in Desert Quartet, I wanted to experiment, I wanted to play with language, I wanted to see what it would be like to write out of the body, to write out of the bones."

Even for Williams, whose work often risks sentimentality in order to close the distance between author and subject, the form and language of Desert Quartet was risky, not only for a Mormon woman expressing her sexuality, but for a writer hoping to be comprehended. "It doesn't make sense, in a linear way," she admitted. "I wanted a reader to feel it before they understood it. To feel it through their faith, to feel it emotionally before they understood it intellectually. And that maybe to understand it intellectually is beside the point. In the same way that when we're in love, it's not about the intellect. It is about the body. It's about chemistry, it's blood, it's fluid.

"But that introduces chaos. Anyone who's been in love knows that chaos is at the heart of love, and it's a huge risk, you don't know where it will take you. So I think about what it means to live and love with a broken heart. But it's worth the risk, because if we don't, then we live our lives in an impoverished state, disconnected from anything that is real. We become numb, which in my mind is one step from death."

The evocation of the erotic, for Williams, is also one way of returning the populace to an awareness of what is at stake in the political battles for public lands in the West. Williams serves on the board of the Southern Utah Wilderness Alliance, a grassroots organization dedicated to counteracting exploitative wilderness measures put forth by the republican Utah delegation. With the photographer Stephen Trimble, she compiled a booklet titled *Testimony: Writers of the West Speak on Behalf of Utah Wilderness*. This collection of essays, stories, and poems by prominent authors now sits on the desks of lawmakers in Congress, serving as written testimony to the economic, spiritual, and emotional values of wilderness.

The eroticism of *Desert Quartet* brings a sense of urgency to these slow-moving political issues. "Adrienne Rich makes that linkage," Williams said, "to feel love so deeply it compels one into action. Love is never passive."

Williams considers her vision essentially female, in that she doesn't strive to categorize and limit the possibilities of either the landscape or human beings. "We can learn to make peace with our contradictory nature as women," she said. "I think that's always been a hard thing for me, that we can be both fierce and compassionate at once. That we can be absolutely calm and chaotic in the same moment. Nothing is as it appears." Williams has been influenced in her work by the canonical figures of environmental writing, most notably Edward Abby and Wallace Stegner, but her personal writing models tend to be women such as as Emily Dickinson, Rachel Carson, Virginia Woolf, and Adrienne Rich. "Those female voices move me most and challenge me most," she said. "They challenge me stay true to what we know as women."

At the age of forty, Williams is the matriarch of her family. As she writes in *Refuge*, seven women in her family have died of cancer, and her doctor has told her that "it's not a question of if, but when" she'll contract the disease as well. She considers herself, and the others living in Utah during the 1950s and '60s, "downwinders," and as such the urgency to tell her story increases. For the fiftieth anniversary of the bombing of Hiroshima, Williams traveled to Japan to meet with survivors of the attack. She read to them from "The Clan of One-Breasted Women," but such forthright honesty and revelation overwhelmed the Japanese audience, who have been conditioned to silence. They could not respond at first, but gradually their own personal stories emerged in oblique ways. In an article about the trip titled "A Downwinder in Hiroshima," Williams wrote: "I think about how each individual story is carried like a wound, like a talisman, how much we need to hear the truth of one another's lives. . . . The Japanese have a word, *aware*, which speaks to both the beauty and pain of our lives, that sorrow is not a grief one forgets or recovers from but is a burning, searing illumination of love for the delicacy and strength of our relations."

When I asked her if she's afraid of death, Williams grew quiet, looking past me through the window into her garden. "I am fearful," she finally said. "It's very painful. Death is not an abstraction for me. I learned this early on. When my mother was diagnosed with cancer, she was thirty eight, and I was fifteen. And I remember it was like a big plastic dome that had been shielding me, shielding us, had suddenly shattered. There was nothing to count on. Or the only thing to count on was the day at hand. It's all we have. It's all any of us has." She looked back at me, her eyes intent on my face. "As my grandmother said, 'Just go with it.' We don't really have a choice anyway, so we might as well just go with it. It sounds too simple to be true, but it is."

She then recited from memory some lines from the title piece of her essay collection *An Unspoken Hunger: Stories from the Field* (Pantheon, 1994): ". . . eating avocados with sharp silver blades, risking the blood of our tongues repeatedly." That sharp edge, where beauty coexists with the possibility of pain and injury, is where most of her writing occurs, even the physical act of the work itself. Williams writes in the basement of her home, and often she finds herself resisting the trek downstairs. "It's because writing asks so much of us. I mean who really wants to go downstairs to the Chair of Pain every day? But what choice do we have? Once you lose yourself in that process of alchemy, you don't have a choice, you have to keep going." Once she gets going on a piece though, she becomes energized by the routine. "I love revision," she said. "Writing is always a process. It's against my nature to have these words on a piece of paper, so fixed and static. You change every time you come to it. And every reader brings something to the page. That's the sorcery of literature."

When she's deeply immersed in a project, Williams will often go to her family's cabin in rural Wyoming on a writing retreat. Once there, she's "underground" and inaccessible. Those days are the most ritualistic for her in terms of walking, dreaming, bathing, reading, and writing. In her daily life she has her days to herself, and her routine might include taking care of her two grandfathers (who are in their nineties), working at the museum, traveling for her environmental work, or visiting with her nieces and goddaughters. She's married to Brooke Williams, also a writer and environmental activist. "When he comes home we have dinner and that sacred time together. And I'll tell you, we've been married twenty years and it's been my greatest blessing. It's what provides stability. I think Brook and I share a vision of the world, so there isn't tension. We're both very committed, but we go about it in different ways." Brooke works with rural communities to help them develop a viable economic future in relationship to wild places.

She characterizes Brooke's work as "more on the ground" than her own, though she sees her writing as being of use in other ways. "It becomes pragmatic," she said. She believes a letter to the editor, a letter to one's senator, an article for a magazine, are all ways writers can, and should, be of use. "To simply tell it straight, that's where our language does the most good. To be a witness. To be of witness." And once a writer initiates the process of representation, she not only becomes accountable to the reading public, she also learns more about the experience which originally spurred the writing act. "It's not all the internal story, it's the external story. You engage in a relationship with the reader, that you don't have when you're writing. You come to know the story in a more whole way."

In her essay "The Wild Card," Williams wrestles with "the obligations of a public life and the spiritual necessity for a private one. Am I an activist or an artist? Do I stay home or do I speak out? . . . When Edward Abbey calls for the artist to be a critic of his or her society, do we live on the page or do we live in the world?" Williams has chosen both avenues, deciding her life would be incomplete without both a passionate engagement with community and the artistic rendering of the personal stories which emerge from commitment to place. If you live in Utah, you see Terry Tempest Williams' name come up everywhere: as the featured reader at a benefit auction for Writers at Work (a local writing conference); as a contributor to *The Crossroads Anthology*, a collection of local work whose sales will benefit poverty relief organizations; as a participant in "Watershed, Writers, Nature, and Community," a conference sponsored by Poet Laureate Robert Hass in Washington, DC; and as one of the keynote speakers at the inaugural Stegner Center Symposium on the campus of the University of Utah.

The last time I saw Terry Tempest Williams was at this symposium, titled "The Native Home of Hope: Community, Ecology and the West." At this conference, writers, activists, lawyers, and politicians from across the United States gathered together to hammer out the ideological issues surrounding the management of public lands in the West, and they did so in honor of the late Wallace Stegner, constantly quoting his work as proverb and oracle. At the conference dinner, Williams didn't look much different than she had six years ago in that small room in Missoula—the same intense green eyes, the same wild black hair, the same composure and undivided attention. At any moment I expected her to pull a clay whistle from her pocket and bring it to her lips.

But instead she told a story. She described an incident that happened many years ago when she and the environmental lawyer Charles Wilkinson took to Wallace Stegner a written statement that protested the policies of the Bush administration. They wanted Stegner's input and editorial advice. "We were very nervous," Williams said. "Especially about the writing." She read the statement aloud to him, a document which, in abstract language, called for awareness and a healing of the damage already done to the land. "We looked at Wally," Williams continued. "He started to laugh, and he said, 'That's it? That's all?'" He then proceeded to take apart each political act against the environment with such force, such charisma, such depth, such aplomb, that it was a truly humiliating moment."

Williams paused for a moment. Then, her voice shaking, she said, "Wally's questions created a standard against which I now write. I'll often hear Wally's voice saying, 'That's it? That's all?' I feel his hand on my shoulder, his voice saying 'Take it further, be bold, be brave.' I find his questions the most compelling and instructive."

Brenda Miller is a Doctoral student in creative writing at the University of Utah. She received a Pushcart Prize for an essay that originally appeared in The Georgia Review, *and her work has appeared or is forthcoming in* Prairie Schooner, Willow Springs, Yoga Journal, Seattle Magazine *and* Seattle Weekly. *She is currently at work on a collection of essays titled* A Thousand Buddhas," *and a memoir.*

Phillip Lopate
New York Storyteller

MELINDA COREY

ON THE DAY I MET PHILLIP LOPATE, HIS CAR HAD BEEN TOWED. "I was in an alternate-side zone, but it used to be an eleven o'clock . . ."—lingo for New York's street-parking system that requires residents to move cars two to three times per week or face towing. "They just changed [the signs] because they're tearing up the street. . . . It seems unfair but it takes so much time to appeal it in court that I probably just should swallow it." Having just seen my car towed in the same neighborhood for the same reasons, I agreed.

I talked with Lopate at his new home, a century-old Brooklyn brownstone, in a not-so-gentrified neighborhood known as Carroll Gardens. Our mutual community is generally genteel and welcoming, particularly by Brooklyn standards. In the days when Al Capone was married at a nearby Catholic church, the place was called South Brooklyn; in the 1960s, real estate mavens rechristened it Carroll Gardens, for the deep European flower beds in the front yards. Now, despite some gentrification, Carroll Gardens retains its Italian working-class roots. Retirees line the Off-Track Betting parlor or cappuccino stands marked "Members Only." Over the past twenty years, the neighborhood has become popular for artists and writers. "We really tried to stay in Manhattan," said Lopate, "but we would have needed a million dollars to get the space we wanted. . . . We looked for one day in Brooklyn. As soon as I moved back I loved it. . . . I'm a Brooklyn boy, but I came back to a much better neighborhood than I lived in when I was a kid. So it was as though I died and moved to heaven."

Born in Queens, raised in Brooklyn, Lopate graduated from Columbia University, a natural stop for city-bred intellectuals. For more than a decade, he taught creative writing in the Manhattan public schools, part of a Teachers and Writers Collaborative Program on the arts. The experience served as the subject for his first nonfiction book, *Being With Children*. Despite his outerborough ties, his first two essay collections, *Bachelorhood* and *Against Joie de Vivre*, established him as a Manhattanite, loyal to its adult amusement arcade life of temporary connections, writ light ("The Greek Coffee Shop") or dark ("Suicide of a Schoolteacher"). Much more than painting a portrait of a city, Lopate offers the experience of city life through its people. In large part, they are not the likely subjects of glossy magazine profiles; they are family, acquaintances, colleagues. In every case, they are part of a story Lopate wants to tell—about his parents' marriage ("Willy"), a female friend ("Osao"), his child's recent birth ("Delivering Lily," *Creative Nonfiction* 5). "Underneath everything," he says, "I'm a storyteller." Lopate speaks deliberately, urgently, and quietly, with a familiar New Yorker's self-assurance that despite the city's distractions, these ideas deserve to, and will, be heard. He has the compact shape and slightly worried expression produced by the weight of urban living. His attire bespeaks the same intense ease: The soft cream, and black cottons, wools, and linens suggest intimacy with Soho, Barney's, and the 92nd Street Y—someone completely at home in the city. To those who fear snowblowers and wrinkle-free blends, it is reassuring.

On the first floor of his roomy brownstone, Lopate introduces me to his wife, graphic designer Cheryl Cipriani (she designed his book, *The Art of the Personal Essay*), and his wavy-haired toddler Lily. He and I turn upstairs to the spacious room transformed into what Lopate calls the "study of my dreams." The light walls are lined with custom-built bookcases filled with comfortably worn hardcovers and trade paperbacks. We sit in armchairs near the fireplace, surrounded by family photos, antique children's toys, and a tin with the cremated remains of Lopate's father. A laptop sits atop a long, uncluttered table flanked by picture windows. "I don't look out the windows," says Lopate of the prewriting exercise deemed expendable since daughter Lily was born, and talk of the writer's saw of habits begins. The family cat, Newman, sits on my lap as I take notes.

"I generally wake up at about quarter to eight," he continues, "and go upstairs to where Lily is and take care of her for a few hours. Then I try to get some work done." Has Lily affected his writing habits in other ways? "I have to work in a much more concentrated way," he says. "Since the baby was born, I have slivers of time and sometimes it's an hour-and-a-half or sometimes even forty minutes . . . There's no such thing as courting the muse—the second I get to myself I have to start to work . . . I've trained myself to think on my feet." Does he think about writing while playing with Lily? He answers immediately, "No. I think my brain has turned to mush now when I'm taking care of Lily." When does he work out writing problems? "A good time is when I first wake up and I'm not quite awake. I can submit questions to my half-sleeping mind and will often come up with answers, whereas if I'm trying to do the same thing at midday, it's hard to hold a gun to my head and say, 'Think, Think!' "

Still, despite the commanding presence of a child, Lopate concludes, "If anything, I've written a lot during this last year [since Lily was born]. I think it's been a salvation to go to another place and try to assert authority, to think about issues, to try to be smart. It's so different from trying to take your cues from a baby. A baby requires reactive intelligence," he continues. "It's like dancing with a partner who's directing the show." But the balance of home and work suits Lopate. Aside from teaching at Hofstra University (on Long Island), he remains in New York City. "I've never gone to a writers' colony," he says. "I write at home, where I can see my friends afterward or just walk the street and drain out with familiar sights. I guess in that way I'm a very domestic creature."

Like many essayists, Lopate took a circuitous route to the form. "I don't know of any seventeen-year-old kids who want to grow up and become essayists. It doesn't have the status or the glamour, as E. B. White said. . . . Poetry has its cachet as the empress of the arts and the novel has a kind of machismo—it's big and it attempts to define a whole society. I remember first reading Montaigne in Humanities at Columbia and I said, 'Why is this guy in with all these other great writers? What's so special about him?' Now of course Montaigne is probably the most important writer for me, but when I was eighteen, the lack of crisis and epiphany—the very equilibrium that Montaigne represented—was something that couldn't appeal to my adolescent sensibility."

While in college, Lopate came to know the essay through first person narratives. "I loved the sound of confessional first person prose—'Notes from Underground,' 'The Good Soldier,' 'My Last Duchess,' Gide's 'L'Immoraliste.' " In particular, he admired "chatterbox writers" like Jack Kerouac, Walt Whitman, and Virginia Woolf. "I never was drawn to minimalists," he says. "I always liked a sense of capaciousness, a sense of amplitude [such as] Whitman represented, of walking around in his thoughts. I have to confess that when I read Hemingway in college it was all I could do to keep from simply attacking him when I wrote the paper. I didn't have a Hemingwayesque bone in my body."

Also influencing his appreciation of the essay was his early affection for the unreliable narrator. "I liked a kind of cheekiness, a quality of mischief. And I saw it in Fielding and Sterne, in Diderot, in Dostoyevsky, and in Gogol. . . . I didn't like the idea of being good; I liked the idea of being bad. So Nietzsche was a writer to whom I was very drawn because he seemed to be giving permission to wicked thoughts. . . . [His writing also] has the sense of mini-essays. The epigrammatic is something I learned from Nietzsche."

The influence of these writers shows in his early novels. "I was very interested when I was younger in the conversation and dynamics of conversation and my first novel, which never got published, was all conversation practically—it was about the way people talk to each other."

The transition to essays seemed natural for Lopate in part because he has defined the essay (in his introduction to *The Art of the Personal Essay*) as a conversational form. "It's a conversation between the essayist and reader," he says, "and it also often partakes of a conversational flavor just in the way that turns of phrase are used to make it informal." His training in the novel has helped him to use conversation widely, including taking the liberty of recreating dialogue when necessary. As an example, I asked how he remembered the landlady's ample riffs in the essay, "Never Live Above Your Landlord." He said, "in some cases, I write them in my diary right after it happens. A lot of conversations in my books are not 100 percent accurate, they're recreated; certainly I have no recall about conversations that took place twenty years ago. . . . If I had just been a nonfiction writer, I think I'd be different."

Lopate's response fits what seems to be his interest in psychological, rather than literal, truth. His essays may vary in structure, from the traditionally seamless and ruminative "My Drawer" to the complex and surprising "Anticipation of 'La Notte': The Heroic Age of Moviegoing," but the focus remains on human sensibility—how people feel, think, and act. It also fits his analysis of his essay writing process as "following a feeling," a pursuit that began when he was writing novels. "It wasn't so much that I was caught up in a story as I was trying to capture a certain mood and stay in that mood. . . . When I wrote 'The Rug Merchant,' I was trying to imitate a mood that I got from Japanese literature and Japanese movies, a kind of in-dwelling mood. When I wrote 'Confessions of Summer,' I was at first at least paying homage to [twentieth century Italian poet and novelist Cesare] Pavese and that kind of melancholy urban mood that I got from his work."

But Lopate always comes back to the need for a story. "Just because I'm an essayist doesn't mean I'm not a storyteller," he says. "I think my essays have a strong sense of narrative. I need a story, even if it is no more of a story than the conflict in my thoughts between two positions."

Because the conflict is a driving force behind his essays, it makes sense that he is at least as concerned with the process of writing an essay as with its perfect outcome on paper. "There's a very tricky essay in the new book ("Memories of Greenwich Village: A Meander" in *Portrait of My Body*), about these two writers, Anatole Broyard and Leonard Michaels, and Greenwich Village, and it gave me no end of trouble. . . . I showed it to a friend of mine and she pointed to one section and said, 'Well, that's the heart of your piece. You should cut out all the rest and just make a much shorter piece.' And I thought, well yes, that's the way she writes and that's what she would do and that makes perfect sense but it's not the way I write. I'd rather write a flawed piece that at least attempts to connect these strands than just something that cuts to the chase. . . . I'm allowing the reader the option to read things that I myself don't think are perfect but I still think they're interesting. Sometimes we don't arrive at this epiphany."

Earlier in the afternoon, Lopate raised the fundamental challenge of the personal essay when he discussed his essay, "My Drawer." "I realized when I was writing it that I was just moving from one subject to another and saying what I could and trying to be amusing, but I was aware in that essay of a need to deepen somehow and this has always seemed to me an important goal of essay writing. You can't just stay at the same level, you have to take the essay down to another place, another level of self-investigation, self-examination. A lot of times when I read things that look like personal essays in magazines they stay at the same level of inquiry that occurs at the beginning. They don't raise the ante of risk as they're going along. I have to do that . . . because in addition to writing these things to be effective literary statements I also am using them as a kind of self-investigation. I want to find out something. They're genuine investigations, they're essays in the Montaignian sense."

He cites the essay, "Samson and Delilah and the Kids" as an example of his attempts to probe more deeply with the personal essay. A commissioned piece, it could easily have duplicated material he had written on his family, but he says, "I wanted another way of doing it. I wanted to move from Cecil B. De Mille to the opera to my mother and father to meditations on power and sexuality. I wanted different tones. It's always been a dream of mine to have different tones in the same piece, and sometimes those tones are moods, like something funny, something sad, something whimsical, sometimes reflective and sometimes they're actually linguistic tones, like slang and high, almost archaic language. The idea is that we have these many different dictions inside us and we have street talk, we have academic talk, we have the way we would talk if we were giving testimony to the court."

But the aim of uniting so many ideas and voices was difficult and time consuming. "I learned to work with fragments leading to a whole," he says, "and I wasn't sure that it would ever coalesce. I kept writing and writing—I must have written one hundred pages. I overwrote that piece so much . . . I wrote everything I could think about and then two weeks before I had to hand it in, I was really getting desperate. I sat down with all the notes and passages on the floor and . . . made three piles—one was 'keep,' one was 'throw out,' and the other one was 'maybe'. . . . and I started cutting and pasting and making transitions. But the essay incorporates doubts in it. It says, 'What do I mean by this, what does all this have to do with anything, when is this going to cohere?' That's the suspense of it. You have to provide answers, not just ask questions."

Lopate's pursuit of psychological truth has distinguished his work. "I've always felt my strongest interest to be psychology. That's why images are not what matters to me most. What matters to me is the way people relate to each other and the way they deal with their own neuroses or whatever."

In eschewing the imagistic, Lopate believes he is countering a tendency that limits much of current prose. "Some writers," he says, "move from image to image and their writing is an archipelago of images. . . . It irritates me a little—this jumping from image to image—because it feels a little precious to me." Does it have anything to do with the popularity of film? "That's an interesting question," he says. "No. I guess because I'm such a movie lover, I don't. I think there are fashions within writing."

More troubling to the state of the essay is the effect of what Lopate calls "the erosion of authority" on the personal essay. He laments "the disappearance of a kind of natural encyclopedic, dilettantish authority . . . someone who could talk about anything and assert authority." Mary McCarthy, Edmund Wilson, James Baldwin, and Paul Goodman are among those "easy, cultivated persons" who once carried such authority. Over the years, he says, academics in part popularized the specialization of authority, stripping the generalist of importance. In place of the authority of the human is the image, which, Lopate says, has come to take authority because "the person can no longer claim that authority." In the absence of this easy authority, there are targeted types of authority, often revealed in books about personal shortcomings, dysfunctions, addictions, and disabilities. Books about sexual addiction, alcoholism and the like make for "a kind of shorthand for identity," says Lopate, which makes the books easy to market. "One thing that fascinates me is that there are so many memoirs now by people who are only in their late twenties and early thirties." One reason for this, he believes, is that "a lot of young writers who are getting M.F.A.s in poetry and fiction, particularly fiction, would rather be writing autobiography. . . . So they write all these autobiographical short stories and then they want to write a book and they don't have quite enough experience. . . . So they write a memoir which focuses on their parents and themselves or some burning problem which has to do with ethnicity or disability . . . and it becomes a way to write a first book."

Lopate feels the essay is suffering the effects of its "blandification" throughout much of the century. In the 1930s and 1940s, he says, readers began to see the essay as a "kind of whimsical moth," the kind of work best represented by "E. B. White at his worst—fey, and associated with a kind of marginalized gentility." Although Baldwin, McCarthy, and others revived the form in the 1950s, it has since retired to its marginalized position—a position so shaky that it lacks its own section in most book stores.

To fight the continued marginalization of the essay, Lopate will be editing a new essay annual. Developed at Doubleday/Anchor (his publisher) in partial response to the success of the *Best American Essays* series, it will be "very, very different," offering "less of an establishment feeling" and "more of a continental feeling." While *Best American Essays* often focuses on established sources and sometimes includes examples of literary journalism, Lopate's new annual will "have more newcomers, some foreigners, even pieces that haven't appeared in a magazine at all." He concludes, "I just want to open up the windows and let in a little more fresh air."

This desire to explore the boundaries of the personal essay extends to Lopate's own work as well, even though, he admits, "it's hard to make yourself improve and write better in an environment which seems insufficiently conscious of the form." In his latest collection, *Portrait of My Body*, his essays center on the concerns of middle age and "the kinds of questions that you face when you're not working out of youthful enthusiasm." His aims, he said, were largely different in his first collection, *Bachelorhood*, which was "a kind of enchanting book, in the sense that it was popular and deservedly so. . . . It didn't take itself seriously as an exploration of a form, in part because it was actually combined with poems and stories." It also sold New York City, in pieces about "walking and moving in the city and getting into and out of situations." With his second collection, *Against Joie de Vivre*, he experimented widely with the form, pushing it far past the "six-page whimsical meditation." Its structure of five big essays connected by smaller pieces gained "a lot of respect from other writers" as well as review attention. It also left Lopate thinking about how he could challenge himself for his next collection: "I pushed this form pretty far and I wonder how much further I can push it. . . . This is as good as I can do, I can't do better than this. . . . What's left to do?"

The problem of challenging oneself in a "self-cannibalizing," mildly respected form, Lopate says, is compounded by the absence of a community of essayists. "I don't find essayists egging each other on to do more. A lot of my friends are actually novelists who have gotten intrigued with writing essays [Max Apple, Lynne Sharon Schwartz, Rosellen Brown], . . . but the essayists themselves, I may be out of the loop and they may be having wonderful discussions in which they're inciting each other, but I don't think so. I think it's like the moment in the biography of Montgomery Clift [by Patricia Bosworth] when Clift was in seclusion and had been banged up, and Marlon Brando, who wasn't even a friend of Clift's, came to visit him and said, 'You have to get back to acting because I need you. I need somebody to compete with, I need somebody to bounce off of.'"

Still, Lopate says, "You have to keep challenging yourself."

At present, some general challenges include "length and the desire to synthesize," and being more honest. For the former two aims, he cites Montaigne's later essays and Woolf's *A Room of One's Own* as guides; for the latter, he turns inward. "I don't want to confess just for the sake of confessing. I've found it's sometimes hard for me to be accurate about my virtues, . . . to [know] the degree to which I am a good friend, a good husband, a decent citizen." How could you write so thoughtfully about people if you did not care about humanity? I ask. "Well," he says, "that's the intent, that through the thoughtfulness you'll get to something that's fair, that's just."

Two and one-half hours have passed; evening is on. It is time to return to the life that feeds the essays, to family and our respective young daughters. The thought of my daughter Martha leads me to ask my final question: In the introduction to *The Art of the Personal Essay*, you say that the "wisest thing an author can do is to mine his obsessions." What are yours today? As with all my other questions, Lopate was pensive and deliberate: "I'm not sure what my present obsessions are. I just finished a book in which I realized afterward that I was obsessed with the themes of solipsism and detachment. I saw solipsism as the down side of the lively personal voice. . . . I [was also] interested in the limits of sympathy and the fact that people know the vocabulary of sympathy, they know the vocabulary of wisdom, but that doesn't mean that they really feel it or can do it . . . I'm interested in the disjunction between knowing what is mature and not being able to be mature. I don't want to present myself as more mature than I am. . . . I feel as though I more or less tried to trick myself into maturity by getting married and having a baby, but is it really going to make me mature? . . . I now understand a little more what it means to accept responsibility. And this is finally what I want to do, accept responsibility for my actions, for my flaws, for my family, for the possibility to feel as if I could find some way to redress some of the wrongs of the world. . . . I think about just trying to understand what I call the catastrophe of one's personality—you know, trying to understand that and to try to be a human being. I think that's my obsession—to try to be a human being, not to assume I am a human being."

Melinda Corey's articles and essays have appeared in the New York Times Book Review, Poets & Writers, Kirkus Reviews, and Turnstiles, among other periodicals. With her husband, George Ochowa, she has written several popular reference books, including The Encyclopedia of the Victorian World (Henry Holt, 1996), The Dictionary of Film Quotations (Crown, 1995), and four titles in the New York Public Library "Book of Answers" series (1990–94). She holds an M.F.A. in nonfiction from Columbia University.

Not Interviewing Frank Sinatra

GAY TALESE

AS ONE WHO WAS IDENTIFIED IN THE 1960S WITH THE POPU-larization of a literary genre known best as *The New Journalism*—an innovation of uncertain origin that appeared prominently in *Esquire, Harper's, The New Yorker*, and other magazines, and was practiced by such writers as Norman Mailer and Lillian Ross, John McPhee, Tom Wolfe, and the later Truman Capote—I now find myself cheerlessly conceding that those impressive pieces of the past (exhaustively researched, creatively organized, distinctive in style and attitude) are now increasingly rare, victimized in part by the reluctance of to-day's magazine editors to subsidize the escalating financial cost of such efforts, and diminished also by the inclination of so many younger magazine writers to save time and energy by conducting interviews with the use of that expedient but somewhat benumbing literary device, the tape recorder.

I myself have been interviewed by writers carrying recorders, and as I sit answering their questions, I see them half-listening, nodding pleasantly, and relaxing in the knowledge that the little wheels are rolling. But what they are getting from me (and I assume from other people they talk to) is not the insight that comes from deep probing and perceptive analysis and old-fashioned legwork; it is rather the first-draft drift of my mind, a once-over-lightly dialogue that—while perhaps semiautomatic of a society permeated by fast-food computerized bottom-line impersonalized workmanship—

too frequently reduces the once-artful craft of magazine writing to the level of talk radio on paper.

Far from decrying this trend, most editors tacitly approve of it, because a taped interview that is faithfully transcribed can protect the periodical from those interviewees who might later claim that they had been damagingly misquoted—accusations that, in these times of impulsive litigation and soaring legal fees, cause much anxiety, and sometimes timidity, among even the most independent and courageous of editors.

Another reason editors are accepting of the tape recorder is that it enables them to obtain publishable articles from the influx of facile freelancers at pay rates below what would be expected and deserved by writers of more deliberation and commitment. With one or two interviews and a few hours of tape, a relatively inexperienced journalist today can produce a three-thousand-word article that relies heavily on direct quotation and (depending largely on the promotional value of the subject at the newsstand) will gain a writer's fee of anywhere from approximately five hundred to slightly more than two thousand—which is fair payment, considering the time and skill involved, but it is less than what was being paid for articles of similar length and topicality when I began writing for some of these same magazines more than a quarter of a century ago.

In those days, however, the contemporary writers I admired usually devoted weeks and months to research and organization, writing and rewriting, before our articles were considered worthy of occupying the magazine space that today is filled by many of our successors in one tenth the time. And in the past, too, magazines seemed more liberal than now about research expenses.

During the winter of 1965 I recall being sent to Los Angeles by *Esquire* for an interview with Frank Sinatra, which the singer's publicist had arranged earlier with the magazine's editor. But after I had checked into the Beverly Wilshire, had reserved a rental car in the hotel garage, and had spent the evening of my arrival in a spacious room digesting a thick pack of background material on Sinatra, along with an equally thick steak accompanied by a fine bottle of California burgundy, I received a call from Sinatra's office saying that my scheduled interview the next afternoon would not take place.

Mr. Sinatra was very upset by the latest headlines in the press about his alleged Mafia connections, the caller explained, adding that Mr. Sinatra was also suffering from a head cold that threatened to postpone a recording date later in the week at a studio where I had hoped to observe the singer at work. Perhaps when Mr. Sinatra was feeling better, the caller went on, and perhaps if I would also submit my interview to the Sinatra office prior to its publication in Es-*quire*, an interview could be rescheduled.

After commiserating about Mr. Sinatra's cold and the news items about the Mafia, I politely explained that I was obliged to honor my editor's right to being the first judge of my work; but I did ask if I might telephone the Sinatra office later in the week on the chance that his health and spirits might then be so improved that he would grant me a brief visit. I could call, Sinatra's representative said, but he could promise nothing.

For the rest of the week, after apprising Harold Hayes, the E*squire* editor, of the situation, I arranged to interview a few actors and musicians, studio executives and record producers, restaurant owners and female acquaintances who had known Sinatra in one way or another through the years. From most of these people I got something: a tiny nugget of information here, a bit of color there, small pieces for a large mosaic that I hoped would reflect the man who for decades had commanded the spotlight and had cast long shadows across the fickle industry of entertainment and the American consciousness.

As I proceeded with my interviews—taking people out each day to lunch and dinner while amassing expenses that, including my hotel room and car, exceeded one thousand three hundred dollars after the first week—I rarely, if ever, removed a pen and pad from my pocket, and I certainly would not have considered using a tape recorder had I owned one. To have done so would have possibly inhibited these individuals' candor, or would have otherwise altered the relaxed, trusting, and forthcoming atmosphere that I believe was encouraged by my seemingly less assiduous research manner and the promise that, however retentive I considered my memory to be, I would not identifiably attribute or quote anything told me without first checking back with the source for confirmation and clarification.

Quoting people verbatim, to be sure, has rarely blended well with my narrative style of writing or with my wish to observe and describe people actively engaged in ordinary but revealing situations rather than to confine them to a room and present them in the passive posture of a monologist. Since my earliest days in journalism, I was far less interested in the exact words that came out of people's mouths than in the essence of their meaning. More important than what people say is what they think, even though the latter may initially be difficult for them to articulate and may require much pondering and reworking within the interviewee's mind—which is what I gently try to prod and stimulate as I query, interrelate, and identify with my subjects as I personally accompany them whenever possible, be it on their errands, their appointments, their aimless peregrinations before dinner or after work. Wherever it is, I try physically to be there in my role as a curious confidant, a trustworthy fellow traveler searching into their interior, seeking to discover, clarify, and finally to describe in words (my words) what they personify and how they think.

There are times, however, when I do take notes. Occasionally there is a remark that one hears—a turn of phrase, a special word, a personal revelation conveyed in an inimitable style—that should be put on paper at once lest part of it be forgotten. That is when I may take out a notepad and say, "That's wonderful! Let me get that down just as you said it;" and the person, usually flattered, not only repeats it but expands upon it. On such occasions there can emerge a heightened spirit of cooperation, almost of collaboration, as the person interviewed recognizes that he has contributed something that the writer appreciates to the point of wanting to preserve it in print.

At other times I make notes unobserved by the interviewee—such as during those interruptions in our talks when the person has temporarily left the room, thus allowing me moments in which to jot down what I believe to be the relevant parts of our conversation. I also occasionally make notes immediately after the interview is completed, when things are still very fresh in mind. Then, later in the evening, before I go to bed, I sit at my typewriter and describe in detail (sometimes filling four or five pages, single-spaced) my recollections of what I had seen and heard that day—a chronicle to which I constantly add pages with each passing day of the entire period of research.

This chronicle is kept in an ever-expanding series of cardboard folders containing such data as the places where I and my sources had breakfast, lunch, and dinner (restaurant receipts enclosed to document my expenses); the exact time, length, locale, and subject matter of every interview; together with the agreed-upon conditions of each meeting (i.e., am I free to identify the source, or am I obliged to contact that individual later for clarification and/or clearance?). And the pages of the chronicle also include my personal impressions of the people I interviewed, their mannerisms and physical description, my assessment of their credibility, and much about my own private feelings and concerns as I work my way through each day—an intimate addendum that now, after thirty years of habit, is of use to a somewhat autobiographical book I am writing; but the original intent of such admissive writing was self-clarification, reaffirming my own voice on paper after hours of concentrated listening to others, and also, not infrequently, the venting of some of the frustration I felt when my research appeared to be going badly, as it certainly did in the winter of 1965 when I was unable to meet face to face with Frank Sinatra.

After trying without success to reschedule the Sinatra interview during my second week in Los Angeles (I was told that he still had a cold), I continued to meet with people who were variously employed in some of Sinatra's many business enterprises—his record company, his film company, his real estate operation, his missile parts firm, his airplane hangar—and I also saw people who were more personally associated with the singer, such as his overshadowed son, his favorite haberdasher in Beverly Hills, one of his bodyguards (an ex-pro lineman), and a little gray-haired lady who traveled with Sinatra around the country tours, carrying in a satchel his sixty hairpieces.

From such people I collected an assortment of facts and comments, but what I gained at first from these interviews was no particular insight or eloquent summation of Sinatra's stature; it was rather the awareness that so many of these people, who lived and worked in so many separate places, were united in the knowledge that Frank Sinatra had a cold. When I would allude to this in conversations, citing it as the reason my interview with him was being postponed, they would nod and say yes, they were aware of his cold, and they also knew from their contacts within Sinatra's inner circle that he was a more difficult man to be around when his throat was sore and his nose was running. Some of the musicians and studio technicians were delayed from working in his recording studio because of the cold, while others among his personal staff of seventy-five were not only sensitive to the effects of his ailment but they revealed examples of how volatile and short-tempered he had been all week because he was unable to meet his singing standards. And one evening in my hotel, I wrote in the chronicle:

> . . . it is a few nights before Sinatra's recording session, but his voice is weak, sore and uncertain. Sinatra is ill. He is a victim of an ailment so common that most people would consider it trivial. But when it gets to Sinatra it can plunge him into a state of anguish, deep depression, pain, even rage. Frank Sinatra has a cold.
>
> Sinatra with a cold is Picasso without paint. Ferrari without fuel—only worse. For the common cold robs Sinatra of that uninsurable jewel, his voice, cutting into the core of his confidence, and it affects not only his own psyche but also seems to cause a kind of psychosomatic nasal drip within dozens of people who work for him, drink with him, love him, depend on him for their own welfare and stability.
>
> A Sinatra with a cold can, in a small way, send vibrations through the entertainment industry and beyond as surely as a President of the United States, suddenly sick, can shake the national economy. . .

The next morning I received a call from Frank Sinatra's public relations director.

"I hear you're all over town seeing Frank's friends, taking Frank's friends to dinner," he began, almost accusingly.

"I'm working," I said. "How's Frank's cold?" (We were suddenly on a familiar basis.)

"Much better, but he still won't talk to you. But you can come with me tomorrow afternoon to a television taping if you'd like. Frank's going to try to tape part of his NBC special. . . . Be outside your hotel at three. I'll pick you up."

I suspected that Sinatra's publicist wanted to keep a closer eye on me, but I was nonetheless pleased to be invited to the taping of the first segment of the one-hour special that NBC-TV was scheduled to air in two weeks, titled *Sinatra—The Man and His Music.*

On the following afternoon, promptly and politely, I was picked up in a Mercedes convertible driven by Sinatra's dapper publicist, a square-jawed man with reddish hair and a deep tan who wore a three-piece gabardine suit that I favorably commented upon soon after getting into the car—prompting him to acknowledge, with a certain satisfaction, that he had obtained it at a special price from Frank's favorite haberdasher. As we drove, our conversation remained amiably centered around such subjects as clothes, sports, and the weather until we arrived at the NBC building and pulled into a white concrete parking lot in which there were about thirty other Mercedes convertibles as well as a number of limousines in which were slumped blackcapped drivers trying to sleep.

Entering the building, I followed the publicist through the corridor into an enormous studio dominated by a white stage and white walls and dozens of lamps and lights dangling everywhere I looked. The place resembled a gigantic operating room. Gathered in one corner of the room behind the stage, awaiting the appearance of Sinatra, were about one-hundred people—camera crews, technical advisers, Budweiser admen, attractive young women, Sinatra's bodyguards and hangers-on, and also the director of the show, a sandy-haired, cordial man named Dwight Hemion, whom I had known from New York because we had daughters who were preschool playmates. As I stood chatting with Hemion, and overhearing conversations all around me, and listening to the forty-three musicians, sitting in tuxedos on the bandstand, warming up their instruments, my mind was racing with ideas and impressions; and I would have liked to have taken out my notepad for a second or two. But I knew better.

And yet after two hours in the studio—during which time Sinatra's publicist never left my side, even when I went to the bathroom—I was able to recall later that night precise details about what I had seen and heard at the taping and in my hotel I wrote in the chronicle:

> Frank finally arrived on stage, wearing a high-necked yellow pullover, and even from my distant vantage point his face looked pale, his eyes seemed watery. He cleared his throat a few times. Then the musicians, who had been sitting stiffly and silently in their seats ever since Frank had joined them on the platform, began to play the opening song, "Don't Worry about Me." Then Frank sang through the whole song—a rehearsal prior to taping—and his voice sounded fine to me, and it apparently sounded fine to him, too, because after the rehearsal he suddenly wanted to get it on tape.
>
> He looked up toward the director, Dwight Hemion, who sat in the glass-enclosed control booth overlooking the stage, and he yelled: "Why don't we tape this mother?"
>
> Some people laughed in the background, and Frank stood there tapping a foot, waiting for some response from Hemion.
>
> "Why don't we tape this mother?" Sinatra repeated, louder, but Hemion just sat up there with his headset around his ears, flanked by other men also wearing headsets, staring down at a table of knobs or something. Frank stood fidgeting on the white stage, glaring up at the booth, and finally the production stage manager—a man who stood to the left of Sinatra, and also wore a headset—repeated Frank's words exactly into his line to the control room: "Why don't we tape this mother?"
>
> Maybe Hemion's switch was off up there, I don't know, and it was hard to see Hemion's face because of the obscuring reflections the lights made against the glass booth. But by this time Sinatra is clutching and stretching his yellow pullover out of shape and screaming up at Hemion: "Why don't we put on a coat and tie, and tape this. . ."
>
> "Okay, Frank," Hemion cut in calmly, having apparently not been plugged into Sinatra's tantrum, "would you mind going back over. . ."
>
> "Yes I would mind going back!" Sinatra snapped. "When

we stop doing things around here the way we did them in 1950 maybe we. . ."

. . . Although Dwight Hemion later managed to calm Sinatra down, and in time to successfully tape the first song and a few others, Sinatra's voice became increasingly raspy as the show progressed—and on two occasions it cracked completely, causing Sinatra such anguish that in a fitful moment he decided to scrub the whole day's session. "Forget it, just forget it!" he told Hemion. "You're wasting your time. What you got there," he continued, nodding to the singing image of himself on the TV monitor, "is a man with a cold."

There was hardly a sound heard in the studio for a moment or two, except for the clacking heels of Sinatra as he left the stage and disappeared. Then the musicians put aside their instruments, and everybody else slowly turned toward the exit . . . In the car, coming back to the hotel, Frank's publicist said they'd try to retape the show within the week, he'd let me know when. He also said that in a few weeks he was going to Las Vegas for the Patterson-Clay heavyweight fight (Frank & friends would be there to watch it), and if I wanted to go he'd book me a room at the Sands and we could fly together. Sure, I said . . . but to myself I'm thinking: How long will Esquire continue to pay my expenses? By the end of this week, I'll have spent more than three thousand dollars, have not yet talked to Sinatra, and, at the rate we're going, it's possible I never will . . .

Before going to bed that night, I telephoned Harold Hayes in New York, briefed him on all that was happening and not happening, and expressed concern about the expenses.

"Don't worry about the expenses as long as you're getting something out there," he said. "Are you getting something?"

"I'm getting something," I said, "but I don't exactly know what it is."

"Then stay out here until you find out."

I stayed another three weeks, ran up expenses close to five thousand dollars, returned to New York, and then took another six weeks to organize and write a fifty-five-page article that was largely drawn from a two-hundred-page chronicle that represented interviews with more than one hundred people and described Sinatra in such places as a bar in Beverly Hills (where he got into a fight), a casino in Las Vegas (where he lost a small fortune at blackjack), and the NBC studio in

Burbank (where, after recovering from the cold, he retaped the show and sang beautifully).

The *Esquire* editors titled the piece "Frank Sinatra Has a Cold," and it appeared in the April 1966 issue. It remains in print today in a Dell paperback collection of mine called *Fame and Obscurity*. While I was never given the opportunity to sit down and speak alone with Frank Sinatra, this fact is perhaps one of the strengths of the article. What could he or *would* he have said (being among the most guarded of public figures) that would have revealed him better than an observing writer watching him in action, seeing him in stressful situations, listening and lingering along the sidelines of his life?

This method of lingering and careful listening and describing scenes that offer insight into the individuals's character and personality—a method that a generation ago came to be called *The New Journalism*—was, at its best, really fortified by the *old journalism's* principles of tireless legwork and fidelity to factual accuracy. As time-consuming and financially costly as it was, it was this research that marked my Sinatra piece and dozens of other magazine articles that I published during the 1960s—and there were other writers during this period who were doing even more research than I was, particularly at *The New Yorker*, one of the few publications that could afford, and today still chooses to afford, the high cost of sending writers out on the road and allowing them whatever time it takes to write with depth and understanding about people and places. Among the writers of my generation at *The New Yorker* who personify this dedication to roadwork are Calvin Trillin and the aforementioned John McPhee; and the most recent example of it at *Esquire* was the piece about the former baseball star Ted Williams, written by Richard Ben Cramer, an old-fashioned legman of thirty-six whose keen capacity to *listen* has obviously not been dulled or otherwise corrupted by the plastic ear of a tape recorder.

But such examples in magazines are, as I mentioned earlier, becoming more and more rare in the 1980s and 1990s, especially among freelancers. The best of the nonfiction writers today—those unaffiliated with such solvent institutions as *The New Yorker*—are either having their research expenses underwritten by the book industry (and are excerpting parts of their books in magazines), or they are best-selling writers who can afford to do a well researched magazine piece if they fancy the subject, or they are writers whose financial support comes mainly from faculty salaries and foundation grants. And what this latter group of writers are publishing today, mainly in modestly remunerative literary periodicals, are pieces that tell us more about themselves than about other people. They are opinioned pieces of intellectual or cultural content, or articles that are decidedly reflective and personal, and not dependent on costly time and travel. They are works researched out of a writer's own recollections. They are close to a writer's heart and place of dwelling. The road has become too expensive. The writer is home.

Gay Talese is the author of the recently acclaimed bestseller Unto the Sons *(1992), a historical memoir spanning two world wars and possessing what Norman Mailer called "the sweep and the detail of a grand nineteenth-century novel," Talese's earlier best-sellers dealt with the history and influence of* The New York Times (The Kingdom and the Power, Bantam, *1970), the inside story of a Mafia family (*Honor Thy Father, World Publications, *1971), and the changing moral values of America between World War II and the era before AIDS (*Thy Neighbor's Wife, Doubleday, *1980). His other works include* The Bridge, New York—A Serendipiter's Journey, *and a collection of his articles, principally from the pages of* Esquire *magazine (where he was credited by Tom Wolfe with the creation of an inventive form of nonfiction writing called "The New Journalism"), called "Fame and Obscurity" (World Publications, 1970). Born in Ocean City, New Jersey, Talese graduated from the University of Alabama in 1949; after two years in the military, he began a ten-year career on the staff of* The New York Times. *He is currently working on a sequel to* Unto The Sons *(Knopf, 1992) and has recently completed, with Professor Barbara Lounsbery of the University of Northern Iowa, a textbook and anthology for students of nonfiction titled* The Literature of Reality *(1996).*

A Conversation with Diane Ackerman

KATHLEEN VESLANY

WHEN THE MAN BEHIND THE CONCIERGE DESK CALLS OUT
my name, I look up to see a phone receiver being waved in
my direction.

"Kathleen, it's Diane. I'll be there, but I'm a little distance
away. Could I trouble you to wait for another ten minutes or
so?"

The voice on the phone is louder and fuller than a whisper,
but with the same throaty earnestness about it. It's a voice
that fits remarkably well with the type of poetry and prose
Diane Ackerman writes: clear, confident, precise. Its tone is,
at the same time, intimate and authoritative. Her s's are
sharp, her vowels deep, and the interrogative lift of "Could I
trouble you" is poised so politely that I could forget the word,
"No."

Of course I will wait. Fifteen minutes later, we meet in the
lobby and she suggests that we talk in an empty lounge
nearby.

Ackerman is dressed casually in matching turquoise pants
and shirt, pink socks and white tennis shoes. She is on the
small side; lean and shorter than average, but not short. She
looks younger than her forty-six years. As we settle ourselves,
she discusses her work on the upcoming PBS series based on
her best-selling book, A Natural History of the Senses. The series
will consist of five parts, one for the physiological and cultural
exploration of each sense. Ackerman has been involved in ev-

ery step of the project, from fund raising to writing the treatment to narrating the script. This afternoon, she plans to fly
to California and continue work on the series.

Almost as soon as the tape recorder is placed on the glass
table between us, she picks it up and holds it like a mi-
crophone—"I'll just keep this here for you, I think it'll make
your life a little easier," she offers—and there it remains,
below her moderately lined eyelids, below her wide, bright
mouth.

We begin with a sort of verbal time line: starting with her
childhood in Waukegan, Illinois, and Allentown, Pennsylvania, then on to her year at Boston University, in the late '60s.
She tells of her transfer to Pennsylvania State University
where a computer error declared her major to be English and
she accepted the mistake as fate. We move through the degrees from Cornell University; M.F.A., M.A., Ph.D., rattled off
as they were achieved, in rapid succession. From there, she
taught at the University of Pittsburgh, Washington University,
New York University, Cornell, and Columbia.

When we arrive in the present, I ask if she hears much from
her readers and she does, a great deal. Particularly in response to A *Natural History of the Senses* and *The Moon by Whale
Light*, readers have written to share their experiences with the
woman who seems so willing to give of her own.

Ackerman's voice lifts a bit, as in a grateful flutter, when
telling of one woman who wrote to say "that if I ever wondered
whom I was writing my nature essays for, it was for her, and
that she was in my pocket whenever I was traveling. I can't
tell you how much that thought touches me."

Part of her gratitude may stem from the shame she felt
about her writing as a young girl, when neither her creativity
nor her expression of it were encouraged. In the introduction
to *The Moon by Whale Light*, Ackerman recalls crossing rooms
without touching the floor, by hopping from banister to door-
knob (to see if it could be done). She worried neighbors by
talking to herself, she was reprimanded for coloring trees that
weren't green, she proposed experiments to determine
whether people could fly, she imagined that the dark fruits in
a nearby plum orchard were really bats.

"I was ashamed because I had a secret world. Children are

the biggest conformists: They don't want to be different, they want to be like their chums."

Her recourse was to continue writing on her own, somewhat secretly. It was not until she met her partner, novelist Paul West, that encouragement came. Ackerman studied English literature at Penn State under West, who tutored her informally in prose writing for nearly ten years.

When Ackerman began to publish her work in graduate school and get some response to it, she was stunned. "It was amazing to me that people would actually praise me for and enjoy what I was most ashamed of for so many years of my life. It made me part of a community spread out in time and in country: a community of writers, some of whom were dead—some of whom I felt closest to were dead." Such feelings of kinship extended to John Donne, Colette, Lucretius, Boethius, Virginia Woolf, Rilke, and Proust.

At this point, something jars me and I remind myself out loud that I should be taking notes. I have been so soothed by Ackerman's voice, so caught up in the careful way she selects each word, that I need to remember to write things down. That her voluminous hair, as curly and long as it is black, is held back on both sides by gold barrettes. That her eyes are dark and the corners of her lips lift slightly, drawing her mouth toward a constant smile. That below her throat there is a butterfly pendant with green and blue wings, held by a thin, gold chain.

I saw Ackerman for the first time at a reading she gave some months ago in Pittsburgh. Behind the lectern on a sparse stage, Ackerman read from her journal about her education, from a piece about the capabilities of poetry and from an excerpt of *The Moon by Whale Light* in which she recalls watching a mother whale with her baby off the coast of Patagonia. Then, an excerpt from her latest book, *A Natural History of Love*, about the feelings people hold for their pets. She finished with a cluster of poems.

Her delivery remained distinct, deliberate, and animated as she deftly moved between genres, the narrative blending with the lyrical and resulting in an evening that would please the fans of her poetry as much as those of her prose. During moments of dialogue, her eyebrows would lift when she smiled and the audience laughed on cue. Ackerman's language, coupled with her voice and gestures, allowed her to create a distinct intimacy in a room filled with nearly five hundred people.

After the reading, in response to a question from the eager audience, Ackerman shared the fantasy she has clung to since youth in which she alone would be a dozen or more people living different lives, all at one time. And while "Twilight of the Tenderfoot" afforded time on a New Mexican ranch, "On Extended Wings" showed the author as a pilot, and "The Moon by Whale Light" took her into caves, swamps, and icy waters, these experiences are separate and temporal. The impossibility that makes hers a fantasy is that the dozen lives feed back simultaneously into one sensibility—Ackerman wants to feel them all, at the same moment. She'd like to be a construction worker. She'd like the wealth of a lifetime on a ranch. The diverse and prolific body of her work suggests a woman intent on getting as close to such a sensory montage as she can.

Since her first book of poetry, *The Planets: A Cosmic Pastoral* was published in 1976, Ackerman's readers have acquired a taste for her style and interests, through poems that consider planets, comets, rockets, and the map of constellations. Her second collection of poetry, *Wife of Light*, shows the writer's "miscellaneous muse" by touching on such subjects as aliens, St. Augustine, George Sand, and the Atlantic moonfish. Her first work of nonfiction, the Western memoir, tracks her own initiation into cattle ranching and the cowboy lifestyle and was followed by a third volume of poetry, *Lady Faustus*. Following her second memoir, "On Extended Wings," this time about flying, and a play, "Reverse Thunder," came an expansive flurry of work. *A Natural History of the Senses*, *Jaguar of Sweet Laughter* and *The Moon by Whale Light* came on the heels of one another and were written in tandem, over a period of nearly four years.

If a poem, as Ackerman has said, "knows about illusion and magic, how to glorify what is not glorious, how to bankrupt what is," her prose is equally cognizant. And so the prosody and imagery of Ackerman's poetry seem to bleed into and feed from the immersion and precision of her nonfiction. The result is a hybrid of sorts that combines the sensual with the scientific, the lyrical with the cerebral, and finds that one informs the other.

The reviews are favorable, for the most part, to Ackerman's "valuable" projects and to her diligence as a writer who "leaves no stone (or adjective) unturned in her search for material." Her poetry has been praised for its rich imagery, exploratory nature, and its broad range in voice and mood—as has her prose for the author's willingness to have "endured the various discomforts gamely, asked some good questions, hungered after improbable experiences on behalf of her readers and herself, and absorbed an incredible quantity of sensory detail." Still, sometimes those compliments run in the same reviews that question her "structural finesse," find her "not obtrusive," and suggest that "A poet ought to be more careful."

While Ackerman is encouraged that "99 percent of the reviews are very positive," she tries not to pay attention to either of the extremes. "There are always a few reviewers with special biases, who are envious or competitive, or philosophically opposed to your book. And there are those who just don't like you and review you, not your book." Such responses are "nasty, but unavoidable" and Ackerman tries to move beyond the whole lot and return to her writing.

Ackerman's work is the frequent subject of reviews. Her work, particularly her prose, is reviewed in a broad spectrum of publications, from the *National Catholic Reporter* to *Vogue* to *New Statesmen & Society*. If some charge that Ackerman may be "a bit too proprietary, too much of a hostess" who finds "too many things ravishing," others assert that it is "a pleasure to journey in her company." PBS seems to agree, as does *People Weekly*, which ran a three-page profile on the writer in 1991 subtitled, "Writer Diane Ackerman once groped a gator for art's sake." The phrase refers to a chapter in *The Moon by Whale Light*, in which Ackerman determines the sex of an alligator. Above the article's headline, there is a photo of Ackerman lying on her side, propped up on one elbow, with her spare hand stroking the neck of a penguin standing inches away.

Perhaps it's the range and scope of Ackerman's subjects

that inspire so many venues. Perhaps it is Ackerman herself, who maintains a strong presence in her work. In A *Natural History of the Senses*, she offers many of her own habits, preferences, and perceptions to anchor the abstract and scientific overview. Discussing the symbolism of hair, Ackerman includes the story of teasing her hair in the '50s, to which her father commented, "Teased? You've driven it insane." Explaining the pharmacology of chocolate, the writer confesses to her own urge to fly to a Parisian restaurant where the cocoa has a chocolate bar melted in each cup. Speaking of how hard it is to describe a smell, Ackerman takes her own stab at it, offering that violets smell something like burnt sugar cubes dipped in lemon.

The reader learns that Ackerman begins most days by picking a bouquet from her garden; that when she visited Istanbul, the mosques seemed to carve up the sky; and, among other things, what it felt like when her legs were waxed. In *Twilight of the Tenderfoot*, the reader meets Ackerman on the front cover, sitting on a horse, in a yellow shirt, jeans, purple chaps and a cowboy hat crowning her long mane of hair. She holds the reins firmly in her hands. She is distinctively within her work—as a journalist, poet, sensory cartographer. Her vantage point is the filter through which the reader sees. As one reviewer wrote, Ackerman harbors "a willingness to use herself as a medium."

Because Ackerman weaves so much of her daily life into her studies of the sensory and natural worlds, I wonder whether she is always thinking like a writer, if the process of mining from personal experience and memory for her art ever slows or stops.

"I don't ever worry about 'thinking like a writer,'" she answers quickly. "If you were to ask me, 'Do I think like a poet?' then the answer is, 'Yes.'

"What I mean is that even though I write an enormous amount of prose, much more prose than I do poetry, the source of my creativity is in poetry. I think that when you read the prose of Rilke, you can tell that a poet wrote it. And probably when you read my prose, you can tell that a poet wrote it because my concerns are a poet's concerns. Even though there are a lot of wonderful novelists concerned with the human condition, that's something that has seduced poets, especially.

"When I write prose, I don't fret about the prose rhythm of the whole chapter. I don't think in large structures like that, although I know fiction writers who do. I understand the general architecture of the book—I outline the book so I do know what I'm going to be writing. But I write it tiny piece by tiny piece and worry about how each word will fit. I think that my structures are smaller."

"Do you see things that poetry can let you do that prose can't, or vice versa?" I ask, "or are the two so closely connected for you that . . ."

"Actually, I'm going to back up a second to the last question," she tells me with a laugh. I laugh, too, though feeling a bit sheepish for having interrupted. I tell myself to pay closer attention to her pace, to the deep breaths she takes that signal more explanation to come.

After fully explaining that she has a poet's attitude when writing, as well as "a naturalist's affectionate curiosity," she moves us forward by rephrasing my question when she is ready for it.

"Okay, so now the next question: 'Are there things that can be done in prose writing that can't be done in poetry?'" she asks herself. "Well, in some cases," Ackerman begins, "I don't have to choose.

"The senses book includes a lot of embedded poems. For one reason or another, they didn't work for me as poems, but I realized that they were extremely relevant to what I was writing about in prose and I just set them out as prose and extrapolated a little bit and worked with them, finessed them. I did the same thing in The Moon by Whale Light. So, the edge of poetry, the perimeter of poetry and prose is blurred in my mind.

"And there are different kinds of prose that I write for different circumstances," she continues. "These days, few glossy magazines print poetry or even poetic prose. So, when I am commissioned to write a magazine essay, I know what is required of me. I also don't want to betray myself as a literary writer, so I try to work out a balance—something that will fulfill me creatively and also satisfy the restrictions of whatever magazine I'm working for."

The first rule Ackerman uses to resolve that criterion is to accept only commissions that overlap with the particular book she is working on. The second is to remind herself that however her essays appear in a magazine, she can do what she wants with them when they appear in a book. That [final] version, she hopes, will endure.

For *The Moon by Whale Light*, a book of four essays originally published in *The New Yorker*, Ackerman sailed around Antarctica to study penguins, sat on top of an alligator, and swam within arm's length of a whale. When these chapters first appeared in the magazine, "it made sense in that context to write them in the first person present," she explains, "so that the reader was with me in the field and didn't know what was going to happen around the next paragraph, or indeed, even if the writer would live or die. That's the advantage of writing in the first person present. But, when it came to putting pieces together in a book, well these were all things that had happened to me. They needed a certain kind of distancing; it made sense for many reasons to put them into the past tense."

While we're on the subject of narrative choices, I ask Ackerman how she decides to let herself enter a scene or share a memory.

"Readers tell me that my books are very intimate and that they feel they know me from reading my books. I love hearing that. I want to have a personal connection with them, but I also know that it's a controlled intimacy," she laughs. "I only put in what I want to risk putting in. All writers reveal and conceal a lot of themselves in their books. Very often, I meet writers whose work I admire and discover that they are only too human. In some cases, tragically malicious and awkward people. They're just normal people. The writing, the art, was the best that they could rise to in very privileged moments. I'm sure that's true for me also."

She stops talking and it's hard to tell if she's waiting for a question or pacing her own answer. "Hmm, what did you ask me?" She laughs and without skipping a beat, prompts herself, "Oh, yes, how do I decide when to include myself? I don't really have a simple answer for that. The general and the particular fascinate me and I suppose I try to vary the pressure between them when I'm writing. So, probably, when I'm talking in some abstract way for a while and seem not at all to be involved, I like to change pace a little bit by including something very personal that seems to exemplify what I'm talking about."

It is in those personal moments of her work that a feeling of familiarity evolves and Diane Ackerman's fans feel that they know her. The impressions and detailed memories the author drops along her journey through the senses, for example, are perhaps more consequential in their abundance than in their intimacy.

Along with her pursuit of "improbable experiences" and unusual travels, her prose magnifies so much of life's domestic sensibility that sooner or later there comes a connection between what one encounters privately and what Ackerman poeticizes publicly. If you've ever taken a scented bath, smelled smoke, or heard Muzak, her prose profits from your experience. Yes, a reader might think, that very thing has happened to me, but I never knew it told such a rich story.

"Actually, I never think of an audience when I'm writing. I just try to write about what fascinates me and to contemplate what disturbs me or provokes me in some way, or amazes me. I suppose if I have a philosophy on this it's that if you set out to nourish your own curiosity and your own intellectual yearnings and use yourself as an object of investigation, then, without meaning to, you will probably be touching the lives of a lot of people."

For Ackerman, the writing process begins in her study—a lavender room complete with jungle-printed curtains framing the room's view of her backyard and woods. "What I usually do is walk down the hall, open the door to my study, invent my confidence, close the door and work from about nine in the morning to twelve." After a few errands or a long lunch with friends, she returns to her study for another two or three hours in the afternoon. More important than what she does at her desk seems to be the habitual act of sitting there. "I've found that if I don't do that, on the three or four days of the week when I'm actually inspired, I won't be in the right routine for it."

Although she travels a lot and spends a few days each month in New York City, she finds the rhythm of more metropolitan areas "jarring." At her home, she can resume her welcome habits as a naturalist. Ackerman enjoys living in a place where she knows almost everyone by name or face. A place where a herd of deer and a family of raccoons come into her back yard, along with a clan of squirrels, whom she knows one by one. A place where the constellations are in the sky, as she puts it, rather than on the ground.

"I really want both worlds," she admits. "I want the world of humans and the world of nature. Although, actually, I shouldn't have said it like that. I want the world of humans and the world of other animals, because I consider metropolises nature, too."

After traveling, she returns home and begins the large task of narrowing her wide experiential lens into language. Her topics—the animal world, the sensory world and her most recent topic, love—are virtually inexhaustible. I ask her how she begins to gather the broad array of experience and research into the writing of one cohesive book.

Each book begins with Ackerman becoming "willingly obsessed" with her subject. If, for example, she writes about a rare bird, she will need a lot of time to spend reading, looking at photographs, listening to recordings in a bio-acoustics lab. "I try to learn everything that can be learned, which takes a long time, but then I don't have to waste time with simple questions in the field. I can ask more subtle ones."

Ackerman has found the experts she has worked with eager to share their passion and knowledge. "I choose people who are going to be that way, not adversarial people. I have much contact with them by phone and letter before I go. I try to find a staff of people who are committed to learning more."

When working in the field, she writes down sensations that allow her to recreate a particular experience when she comes home. The narrative, she feels, can come later. The dialogue can be done through interviews. But the expression of an alligator, the color and light of an iceberg, the resonance of a singular sound—these are the details Ackerman records in small, yellow, spiral-bound notebooks. From these, she can review her surroundings in the Amazon, the Antarctic, or on a remote Japanese island as though her time there were preserved on film, stopped and replayed at will.

"And I've been doing it long enough that I know now how many of those little notebooks have to be filled to produce however many pages of prose." Still, the contents of one notebook have a habit of spilling into another.

"I once had three cats that all got pregnant at the same time and they all gave birth at the same time, within a day of each other," she says, seemingly out of nowhere. "And I thought it was very funny that they kept stealing each other's kittens. They would get confused about whose kitten was whose. My prose projects and my poetry projects steal each other's kittens all the time."

As glimpses of the private Ackerman are carefully revealed through the public narrator, so is the poet through her prose. One form becomes affected by the priorities of the other. During her reading a few months ago, she mused about the similarities between the genres that keep her working in both.

"A poem is so small a canvas on which to work, so compressed a form, that you're somehow reduced to taking contingency samples. You have to somehow capture the gesture or mood and that puts an enormous amount of pressure on every word, every space, every half-rhyme that you use. I love that. I would much rather do that than anything else in my life. Then, all of a sudden, I'll wake up one morning and I'll realize that there's something that I need to do that requires more elbow room and suddenly, I find myself working in prose. I don't think the goals are any different, and very often, the language isn't any different."

Although Ackerman doesn't get much of a chance to do what she calls "sport reading," there is a lot of reading to do before the writing begins.

"I always choose to write books that thrill me, about subjects that captivate me so deliciously, that the background reading I'm going to do is wonderful. It's fun, it's never a chore. So when you ask me: What do I read? Well, I have ten or twelve books going at the same time. Bookmarks are an important part of my life."

Before that last word has fully departed from her throat, the first side of the tape runs out and the recorder clicks off. She hands it back to me, and checks the time.

"I've got to go," she prompts kindly, yet clearly. "So, if you have one last question . . ."

I ask her about the novelist Paul West, who has been upstairs in the hotel while we've been talking. I wonder how living with another writer affects her own writing.

"Our engagement with the world is different. But he certainly taught me an enormous amount about prose. There's no doubt about that. Is it easy to live with a writer?" she asks. "No, it's difficult. It's difficult for any two people who are in the same field, regardless of what it is, because there are times in the life of one writer when things are going rough and they're going great for the other person, and vice versa. We have different editors, we have different agents, and we are working in different genres. That," she says, "helps a lot."

She asks me how my own work has been going and I see kindness in this gesture—now that we're done with the formality of an interview, she invites me into a brief conversation between writers.

And I answer, glad for the chance to tell her that I, too, went to Penn State and headed for an M.F.A. program in poetry straight from college. And like her, I used to consider prose "an unknown and frightening terrain." When I come to this last point in common, she asks me to turn the tape recorder back on.

Ackerman's ease with the artifice of an interview, with the broad questions hoping for definitive answers, convinces me. She has unfolded elaborate explanations at her own unhurried pace; explicated those that seemed, by her own standards, unclear, and concluded others when they met her needs. She is constantly and completely conscious of what she is doing. So, when she asks for the tape recorder, places it even closer to her mouth and begins talking about how hard it is for poets to live on poetry alone, I can feel her gently directing the ending of the interview. As an experienced writer and subject should, she knows that what will follow may be important for me.

Kathleen Veslany received her MFA *at the* University of Pittsburgh *and has had her work published in* Creative Nonfiction, Central Park, Sycamore Review, *and* Under the Sun. *She is finishing a collection of personal essays and lives in Tucson, Arizona.*

Courting the Approval of the Dead

TRACY KIDDER

I HAVE NEVER WRITTEN MUCH ABOUT MYSELF, BUT, LIKE MOST writers I know, I am interested in the subject. We live in an era surfeited with memoirs. This is my contribution to the excess.

My writing career began at Harvard College about thirty-two years ago, shortly after I enrolled as an undergraduate. I planned to fix the world by becoming a diplomat. I began by studying political science. Thinking I should have a hobby, I also took a course in creative writing. I didn't invest a lot of ego in the enterprise and maybe for that reason the first short stories that I wrote were rather sprightly. I think they contained some dialogue that human beings might have uttered. Anyway, the teacher liked them and, more important, so did some of the young women in the class. My first strong impulse to become a writer sprang from this realization: that writing could be a means of meeting and impressing girls.

The next year I got into a class taught by the poet and great translator Robert Fitzgerald. He admitted only about a dozen students from among dozens of applicants, and I seem to remember that I was the youngest of the anointed group. This mattered to me. In high school I had been addicted to competitive sports, and I conceived of writing in sporting terms. I figured I had won part of the competition already, by being the youngest student admitted to the class. The yearning for distinction is common among writers, and in that sense I had begun to become a writer.

I want to try to summon Mr. Fitzgerald back from the dead. I remember him as a small, elegant man, then in his sixties, I believe. Occasionally during office hours he smoked a cigarette, and did so with great deliberation, making every puff count—I think he'd been warned off tobacco, and had put himself on short rations. He would enter the classroom with a green book bag slung over his shoulder, and would greet us with a smile and a sigh as he heaved the bag onto the long seminar table. Mr. Fitzgerald's green bag contained our work, *my* work, with his comments upon it. I could not have been more interested in that object if Mr. Fitzgerald had been our adult provider, returning with food he'd found out in the world. But the way he sighed, as he heaved that sack onto the table, insinuated that what lay inside wasn't as valuable as food. Certainly it looked like a heavy load for one professor to carry.

I have always talked too much and listened too little. What is it about certain people that has made me pay attention to everything they say? Their confidence and wit, I guess, but most of all their interest in *me*. Mr. Fitzgerald paid his students the great compliment of taking us seriously. He flattered us, dauntingly. I remember the first day of that class. From his place at the head of the table Mr. Fitzgerald eyed us all. He had a pair of reading glasses, half-glasses, which he often used to great effect. He lowered them and looking at us over the top of them, said something like, "The only reason for writing is to produce something *classic*. And I expect that you will produce *classic* work during the term."

I recall thinking, "You do?"

Of course, none of us did, with the possible exception of one young woman who wrote a poem titled "The Splendor and the Terror of the Universe as Revealed to Me on Brattle Street." I don't recall the poem, but I still like the title.

Having told us of his expectations, Mr. Fitzgerald offered his first advice for meeting them. He jabbed an index finger at the wastebasket beside him and said, "The greatest repository I know of for writers. And I do hope that it will precede me."

After a few weeks of Mr. Fitzgerald, I gave up on political science. I quit right in the middle of a lecture by the then-not-very-famous professor Henry Kissinger. The lecture bored me. Professor Kissinger was only partly to blame. I now described myself as a writer, and I thought a writer shouldn't be interested in politics. I had not yet realized that a writer ought to know about something besides writing, so as to have something to write about. When I left that lecture I went right to the English department office and signed up. I'd already begun to do a lot of reading on my own, mostly fiction, which I was consuming at a rate I've never equaled since. At the same time, I had suddenly acquired an assigned-reading disability and a sleep disorder. I had trouble reading books that appeared on formal course lists, and I often worked all night on stories for Mr. Fitzgerald, then went to sleep around the time when my other classes began.

During the first part of Mr. Fitzgerald's class, he would talk about writing and read aloud to us, very occasionally stuff that a student had written, and more often works by wonderful, famous writers he had known, such as his old friend Flannery O'Connor. He read us one of her stories, and when he finished, he said, "That story unwinds like a Rolex watch." Listening to him read such estimable work made me want to try my hand. I think he aimed for that effect, because in the second half of every class he had us write. He warmed us up, and then made us exercise. It is a testament to those warmups of his that I can't recall ever being unable to write *something* in that room for him. In his presence, even poetry seemed possible. Mr. Fitzgerald insisted I try my hand at a poem now and then. I struggled but complied. Finally, I got one off that he seemed to like. It came back from him with this comment at the bottom: "This is very like a poem."

I prefer other memories, especially this one: I had written a short story, which an undergraduate, literary friend of mine had read and disliked. This was the first and at the time the only literary friend I'd acquired, and I thought him very wise and perspicacious, because he had encouraged me. I guessed that my friend must be right about my story. Once he'd pointed out its flaws, I saw them clearly, too. But I decided to show the thing to Mr. Fitzgerald, just so he'd know that I was working. He opened the next class by saying that he was going to read a student's story, a story that he particularly liked, and I remember sitting there wishing that he would some day single out a story of mine in that way and I recall vividly the moment when I realized that it was my story he was reading. The mellifluous voice that had read to us from the likes of James Agee and Wallace Stevens and Flannery O'Connor was reading something of mine! I felt frightened. Then I felt confused. I don't think it had ever occurred to me that intelligent people could disagree about the quality of a piece of writing. If my literary friend thought the story was lousy, Mr. Fitzgerald surely would, too. I see myself sitting at that table with my mouth hanging open, and closing it fast when I remembered the young women in the room. At first I wanted to ask Mr. Fitzgerald to stop, and then I hoped he never would.

I hoped, indeed expected, to have that experience again. I remember that I had given Mr. Fitzgerald a story I knew to be marvelous, a story I knew he'd want to single out in class. When I came into his office for the private visit all of us periodically received, I said to him, in a voice already exulting at his answer, "How'd you like that story, Mr. Fitzgerald?"

He performed the ritual of the reading glasses, pulling them an inch down his nose and looking at me over the top of them. "Not much," he said.

And then, of course, he told me what was wrong with the story, and I saw at once that he was right. I still have this problem. My judgment of my own work sometimes seems so malleable as not to rate as judgment at all. Any critic, no matter how stupid in praise or transparently spiteful in blame, convinces me, at least for awhile. Generally, harsh criticism tends to make me fear that the critic has an intelligence far superior to mine, and has found out things about my writing that I've been too blind to see myself. A person as easily confused by criticism as I am might well have quit writing after a few rejection slips came in for stories that my girlfriend and my mother thought were really good. Perhaps inadvertently, Mr. Fitzgerald taught me the value of trusting the judgment of just one person above all others—and of getting that judgment as the work is in progress, and a lot of help besides.

Which is the role I've inflicted on a single editor, Richard Todd, for more than two decades.

I took Mr. Fitzgerald's course again and again, right up until I graduated. After my first semester with him, I didn't perform very well. It wasn't for lack of trying or, God knows, desire. I had become self-conscious about writing. At one point I started a novel. I wrote twenty pages or so, but the most interesting parts were the comments and little drawings I made in the margins—and created with greater care than anything in the actual text—imagining, as I created these notes in the margin, my biographer's delight in finding them. During this period, almost all of the stories I wrote in my room late at night, and the pastiches I committed in class, came back with such brief comments as "O.K., but no flash" all written in an elegantly penned script, which I can still see in my mind's eye, my heart sinking all over again. Mr. Fitzgerald used to talk about something he called "the luck of the conception," an idea I still believe in, but no longer dream about. I used to have a dream in which I had come upon the perfect story. The dream did nor contain the story itself, just the fact that I possessed it. It was a dream suffused with joy, and I'd awake from it with a kind of sorrow that I haven't felt since adolescence. As a reader I felt then as I feel now, that any number of faults in a piece of writing are forgivable if there is life on the page. And there was no life in anything I wrote. Oddly, as the small natural talent I'd had for making up stories began to wane, my ambitions grew immense. Or maybe it was the other way around, and ambition stood in my way.

I can't blame Mr. Fitzgerald. He had only suggested that writing could be a high calling. I alone invented my desire to write for posterity. I am embarrassed to admit to this, but what I really had in mind was immortality. Once as a very young boy at a lecture at the Hayden Planetarium in New York, I learned that the earth would be destroyed in some two and a half billion years, and in spite of all my mother said, I was inconsolable for weeks. Maybe I was born especially susceptible to the fears that attend the fact of human mortality. Maybe I was influenced by certain of the English poets, those whose poems declare that their poems will make them immortal. Or it may be, as my wife suggests, that once a young man has solved the problem of how to meet and impress girls, it just naturally occurs to him that his next job is to figure out how to become immortal.

After college I went to Vietnam as a soldier—not the most likely way of gaining immortality, though I was never in much danger there. I came home with my body and my vaunting literary ambitions still intact and wrote a whole novel about experiences I didn't have in Vietnam. I designed that book for immortality. I borrowed heavily from Conrad, Melville, and Dostoevsky. About thirty-five editors refused to publish it, thank God. I went to the Iowa Writers Workshop, where it began to seem to me that the well from which I drew for fiction had gone completely dry. (I have written fiction since then, all of it published, but the sum total is three short stories.) I decided to try my hand at nonfiction. That term covers a lot of territory, of course, from weighty treatises on the great problems of the world to diet books—some diet books qualify as nonfiction, don't they? I dove into something then labeled The New Journalism. As many people have pointed out, only the term was new. I believe that the form already had a distinguished lineage, which included work by George Orwell and Joseph Mitchell and Mark Twain and Lillian Ross and Edmund Wilson and, my particular favorite, A. J. Liebling. This kind of nonfiction writing, whatever it's called, relies on narrative. Some people describe it by saying that it borrows techniques of fiction, but the fact is that it employs techniques of storytelling that never did belong exclusively to fiction. It is an honorable literary form, not always honorably used, but one can certainly say the same about fiction.

When I first started trying to write in this genre, there was an idea in the air, which for me had the force of a revelation: that all journalism is inevitably subjective. I was in my mid-twenties then, and although my behavior was somewhat worse than it has been recently, I was quite a moralist. I decided that writers of nonfiction had a moral obligation to write in the first person—really write in the first person, making themselves characters on the page. In this way, I would disclose my biases. I would not hide the truth from the reader. I would proclaim that what I wrote was just my own subjective version of events. In retrospect, it seems clear that this prescription for honesty often served instead as a license for self-absorption on the page. But I was still very young, too young and self-absorbed to realize what now seems obvious—that I was less likely to write honestly about myself than about anyone else on earth.

I wrote a book about a murder case, in a swashbuckling first person. It *was* published, I'm sorry to say. On the other hand, it disappeared without a trace; that is, it never got reviewed in the *New York Times*. And I began writing nonfiction articles for the *Atlantic Monthly*, under the tutelage of Richard Todd, then a young editor there. For about five years, during which I didn't dare attempt another book, I worked on creating what many writer friends of mine call *voice*. I didn't do this consciously. If I had, I probably wouldn't have gotten anywhere. But gradually, I think, I cultivated a writing voice, the voice of a person who was well-informed, fair-minded, and temperate—the voice, not of the person I was, but of a person I sometimes wanted to be. Then I went back to writing books, and discovered other points of view besides the first person.

Choosing a point of view is a matter of finding the best place to stand from which to tell a story. It shouldn't be determined by theory, but by immersion in the material itself. The choice of point of view, I've come to think, has nothing to do with morality. It's a choice among tools. I think it's true, however, that the wrong choice can lead to dishonesty. Point of view is primary; it affects everything else, including voice. Writing my last four books, I made my choices by instinct sometimes and sometimes by experiment. Most of my memories of time spent writing have merged together in a blur, but I remember vividly my first attempts to find a way to write *Among Schoolchildren*, a book about an inner-city schoolteacher. I had spent a year inside her classroom. I intended, vaguely, to fold into my account of events I'd witnessed in that little place a great deal about the lives of particular schoolchildren and about the problems of education in America. I tried out every point of view that I'd used in previous books, and every page I wrote felt lifeless. Finally, I hit on a restricted third-person narration.

The approach seemed to work. The world of that classroom seemed to come alive when the view of it was restricted mainly to observations of the teacher and to accounts of what the teacher saw and heard and smelled and felt. This choice narrowed my options. I ended up writing something less comprehensive than I'd planned. The book became essentially an account of a year in the emotional life of a schoolteacher. My choice of the restricted third person also obliged me to write parts of the book as if from within the teacher's mind. I felt entitled to describe her thoughts and feelings because she had described them to me, both during class and afterward, and because her descriptions rarely seemed self-serving. Believing in them myself, I thought that I could make them believable on the page.

Belief is an offering that a reader makes to an author, what Coleridge famously called "that willing suspension of disbelief for the moment, which constitutes poetic faith." It is up to the writer to entertain and inform without disappointing the reader into a loss of that faith. In fiction or poetry, of course, believability may have nothing to do with realism or even plausibility. It has everything to do with those things in nonfiction, in my opinion. I think that the nonfiction writer's fundamental job is to make what is true believable. I'm not sure that everyone agrees. Lately the job seems to have been defined differently. Here are some of the ways that some people now seem to define the nonfiction writer's job: to make believable what the writer thinks is true, if the writer wants to be scrupulous; to make believable what the writer wishes were true, if the writer isn't interested in scrupulosity; or to make believable what the writer thinks might be true, if the writer couldn't get the story and had to make it up.

I figure that if I call a piece of my own writing nonfiction it ought to be about real people, with their real names attached whenever possible, who say and do in print nothing that they didn't actually say and do. On the cover page of my last book I put a note that reads, "this is a work of nonfiction," and listed the several names that I was obliged to change in the text. I thought a longer note would be intrusive. I was afraid that it would stand between the reader and the spell that I wanted to create, inviting the reader into the world of a nursing home. But the definition of nonfiction has become so slippery that I wonder if I shouldn't have written more. So now I'll take the opportunity to explain that for my last book I spent a year doing research, that the name of the place I wrote about is its real name, that I didn't change the names of any of the major characters, and that I didn't invent dialogue or put any thoughts in characters' minds that the characters themselves didn't confess to.

I no longer care what rules other writers set for themselves. If I don't like what someone has written, I can stop reading, which is, after all, the worse punishment a writer can suffer. (It ought to be the worst punishment. Some critics seem to feel that the creation of a book that displeases them amounts to a felony.) But the expanded definitions of nonfiction have created problems for those writers who define the term narrowly. Many readers now view with suspicion every narrative that claims to be nonfiction, and yet scores of very good nonfiction writers do not make up their stories or the details in them—writers such as John McPhee, Jane Kramer, J. Anthony Lucas. There are also special cases that confound categories and all attempts to lay down rules for writers of narrative. I have in mind Norman Mailer and in particular his *Executioner's Song*, a hybrid of fact and fiction, carefully labeled as such, a book I admire.

Most writers lack Mailer's powers of invention. Some nonfiction writers do not lack his willingness to invent, but the candor to admit it. Some writers proceed by trying to discover the truth about a situation, and then invent or distort the facts as necessary. Even in these suspicious times, writers can get away with this. Often no one will know, and the subjects of the story may not care. They may not notice. But the writer always knows. I believe in immersion in the events of a story. I take it on faith that the truth lies in the events somewhere, and that immersion in those real events will yield glimpses of that truth. I try to hew to what has begun to seem like a narrow definition of nonfiction partly in that faith, and partly out of fear. I'm afraid that if I started making up things in a story that purported to be about real events and people, I'd stop believing it myself. And I imagine that such a loss of conviction would infect every sentence and make each one unbelievable.

I don't mean to imply that all a person has to do to write good narrative nonfiction is to take accurate notes and reproduce them. The kind of nonfiction I like to read is at bottom storytelling, as gracefully accomplished as good fiction. I don't think any technique should be ruled out to achieve it well. For myself, I rule out only invention. But I don't think that honesty and artifice are contradictory. They work together in good writing of every sort. Artfulness and an author's justified belief in a story often combine to produce the most believable nonfiction.

If you write a nonfiction story in third person and show your face in public afterward, someone is bound to ask, "How did your presence in the scenes you relate affect the people you were observing?" Some readers seem to feel that third-person narration, all by itself, makes a narrative incomplete. The other day I came upon a book about the writing of ethnography. It interested me initially because its bibliography cited a couple of my books and one of its footnotes mentioned me. The author spelled my first name wrong and gave one of my books a slightly different title from the one I chose. I swear I don't hold a grudge on account of that. My first name is a little weird, and the title in question is a long one. But those little mistakes did make me vigilant as I read the following passage:

> Writers of literary tales seldom remark on the significance of their presence on the scenes they represent, and this is in some instances a bothersome problem to field workers in addition to the common concerns for reactivity in any situation. It is, for example, very difficult to imagine that as famous and dandy a writer as Tom Wolfe was merely a fashionable but unobtrusive fly on the wall in the classic uptown parlor scene of *Radical Chic* (1970), or that Tracey [sic] Kidder did not in any way influence the raising of the Souweines' roofbeams in *House* (1985). Since writers of ethnographic tales have begun to break their silence on these matters, it is seemingly time for writers

of literary tales to do so too—especially when their accounts so clearly rest on intimacy.

I believe it's possible to learn something from anyone, including ethnographers who have begun to break their silence. But I can't work out the mechanics for calculating the *reactivity* that occurs during *field* work. As I imagine it, field work that is mindful to reactivity would have to proceed in this way: I'd open my notebook in front of a person I planned to write about, and I'd ask, "How did you feel when I opened my notebook just now?" Then I would probably ask, "How did you feel when I asked you that question about opening my notebook?"

I don't know for sure how my presence has influenced the behavior of any of the people I've written about. I don't believe that I can know, because I wasn't there when I wasn't there. To do the research for a book, I usually hang around with my subjects for a year or more. After a while, most seem to take my presence for granted. Not all do. It worked the other way with one of the carpenters I wrote about in *House*. I remember his saying at one point that he and the other builders ought to put a bell around my neck, so they'd know where I was at all times.

Obviously some readers expect to hear about the story behind the story. But all writing is selective. I think that a narrative should be judged mainly on its own terms, not according to a reader's preexisting expectations. As a reader, I know that I won't always sit still for the story behind the story. As a writer, I have often decided that it isn't worth telling.

I wrote my most recent book, *Old Friends*, which is about some of the residents of a nursing home, in the third person. I hope that I put my own voice in it, but I chose not to write about how I did my research and how I was affected by what I encountered inside the nursing home—never mind how my presence might, arguably, possibly have affected the inmates' behavior—mainly because what I did—asking questions, listening, taking notes—was much less interesting than what I observed. It is true, however, that my solution to the problem that the book presented did have something to do with my own experience of life inside that place. After writing for awhile, I realized that I wanted to reproduce, in a limited sense, the most important part of my experience there.

I entered the nursing home in the late fall of 1990. The place, which is situated in western Massachusetts, is called the Linda Manor Extended Care Facility. I went there with a notebook—I filled ninety notebooks eventually—and prowled around inside almost every day, and many nights, for about a year. And then for another year or so I spent about three days a week there. I chose a decent nursing home, not one of the very best but a clean, well-lighted place where residents weren't tied up and were allowed some of the trappings of their former lives.

I had visited a nursing home only once before in my life, and since then had averted both my eyes and thoughts as I passed by. That was part of the attraction; nursing homes seemed to me like secret places in the landscape. I went to Linda Manor tentatively, though. I was afraid that I might find it dull. I thought I might find myself in a kind of waiting room, a vestibule to eternity, where everything had been resolved or set aside and residents simply lay waiting to die. But waiting was the least of what went on in many of those clean, motel-like rooms. Nearly everyone, it seemed, was working on a project. Some were absurd: One resident kept hounding the office of a U.S. senator to complain about his breakfast eggs. Some were poignant: Many of the demented residents roamed the halls searching for exits, asking everyone for directions home. A lot of projects were quixotic. There was, for instance, one indomitable, wheelchair-bound woman who had set herself the task of raising about thirty thousand dollars to buy the nursing home its own chairlift van.

She intended to do so through raffles and teacup auctions and by getting other residents to remember the van in their wills. There was also an elderly actress who kept herself and the place somewhat invigorated by putting on plays. Staging those productions took great determination, because Linda Manor had no stage and most of the actors and actresses were confined to wheelchairs and walkers. In between plays, when things got dull, the old actress livened things up by starting fights. There were many residents working doggedly to come to terms with the remorse they felt for past mistakes and offenses. There was also a man in his nineties named Lou Freed who summoned up memories with what seemed like the force of necessity, reinhabiting his former life with something that resembled joy. And there were, of course, a number who knew their deaths were imminent and struggled to find ways to live in the face of that knowledge.

Even in a decent nursing home, the old often get treated like children. And yet many of the residents refused to become like children. The roommates Lou and Joe, for instance. Let me try to prove this point with a short passage from my book:

Joe and Lou could not control most of the substance of their life in here, but they had imposed a style on it. The way for instance that Joe and Lou had come, in the past months, to deal with matters of the bathroom. Joe had to go there what seemed to him like a ridiculous number of times each day and night. He and Lou referred to the bathroom as "the library." The mock-daintiness of the term amused Joe. The point was to make a joke out of anything you could around here. Up in the room after breakfast, Joe would say to Lou, "I gotta go to the library. I have to do my, uh, uh, prune evacuation."

This room was now their home, as in any household, people entering were expected to follow local rules. The nursing staff was overwhelmingly female. Lou and Joe referred to all of them as girls, and indeed, next to them, even the middle aged did look like girls. The staff had all, of course, been quite willing to talk frankly about matters of Lou and Joe's biology. Too frankly for Lou. Too frankly for Joe, once Lou had made the point. The aides, "the girls," used to come to the doorway, cradling opened in their arms the large, ledger-like Forest View "BM Book," and they'd call loudly in, "Did either of you gentleman have a bowel movement today?" It was Lou, some months ago now, who responded to this question by inviting in the girls who asked it, and then telling them gently, "All you have to say is, 'did you or didn't you.'" The way Lou did that job impressed Joe. Lou did it so diplomatically, so much more diplomatically than Joe would have. Lou, as he liked to say, had trained all the girls by now. Joe took care of reinforcement.

It was a morning in December. Joe had the television news on. He and Lou were listening to the dispatches from the Middle East. Joe wasn't waiting for the aide with the BM Book, but be had a question ready for her. When the aide came to the door, she asked, "For my book. Did you?"

"Yes." Joe tilted his head toward Lou. "And so did he."
Then, a little smile blossoming, Joe looked at the aide and
asked, "And what about you."

"None of your business!" The aide looked embarrassed.
She laughed. "Well, you ask me," Joe said.

"But I get paid for it."

"Goodbye," Joe said pleasantly, and went back to watching
the news.

Many residents insisted on preserving their dignity, in spite
of the indignities imposed by failing health and institutional
confinement. Many people in there were attempting in one
way or another to invent new lives for themselves. In the context of that place and of debilitating illnesses, their quests
seemed important.

So when I began to write *Old Friends*, I didn't lack for interesting characters or stories. I felt I had an overabundance. I
told myself before I started writing that I couldn't fit in everything, and then for about a year I tried to do just that. In the
end I had to jettison a lot of portraits and stories that I had
written many times and polished up. Among other things, I
wrote four or five times and finally discarded what in all modesty I believe to have been the most riveting account of a
session of Bingo ever composed. But the plain fact was that
about half of what I wrote and rewrote got in the way of the
main story that I wanted to tell.

Hundreds of articles and books deal with the big issues
that surround aging in late twentieth-century America. I read
some of them. But I didn't want to approach this subject in
a general way. It is useful, maybe even necessary, to imagine
that a definable group called *the elderly* exists. But all such
conceptions inevitably fail. It is accurate only to say that there
are many individuals who have lived longer than most of the
rest of the population, and that they differ widely among
themselves. For various reasons, some can no longer manage
what are called the activities of daily living at home, and, for
lack of a better solution, some of those people end up living
in nursing homes. I chose to write about a few of those people
partly because so much well-meaning commentary on old age
depicts white-haired folks in tennis clothes—a tendency, it

seems to me, that inadvertently denigrates the lives of the many people who haven't been as lucky.

About 5 percent of Americans over sixty-five—about one and one-half million people—live in nursing homes and, according to one estimate, nearly half of all the people who live past sixty-five will spend some time inside a nursing home. Obviously, they are important places, but nursing homes weren't really the subject I wanted to address. There were already plenty of published exposés of bad nursing homes. I decided to do my research inside a good nursing home on the theory that a good one would be bad enough, inevitably a house of grief and pain, and also because I didn't want to write about the kinds of policy and management issues that would have assumed primary importance in a story set in an evil place. I wanted to write from the inside about the experience of being old and sick and confined to an institution. I wanted to come at the subject of aging, not through statistics, but through elderly people themselves. I wanted to write an interesting, engaging book. The residents of even a decent nursing home are people in a difficult situation, and I think that stories about people in difficult situations are almost always interesting, and often dramatic.

In some ways, research in that place was easy work. In the course of every story I'd done before, I had run into people who hadn't wanted to talk to me. But people in a nursing home never have enough willing listeners. A nursing home like Linda Manor may be the only place on earth where a person with a notebook can hope to receive a universal welcome.

Various sights, smells, and sounds distressed me at first. But gradually I got used to the externals of the place and the people. Almost everyone who has spent some time inside a nursing home begins to look beyond the bodies of the residents. It just happens. But around the time when that happened to me, another problem arose. I remember leaving the room of a dying, despondent resident and stopping in my tracks in a Linda Manor corridor, and hearing myself say to myself, "This is amazing! *Everybody* dies." And, of course, my next thought was, "including me." I know that sounds silly.

One is supposed to have figured that out before pushing fifty. But I hadn't believed it, I think.

I arranged some other troubling moments for myself, during my research. At one point, I decided that I ought to check into Linda Manor for a couple of days and nights, as if I were myself a resident. I hate the kind of story in which a perfectly healthy person decides to ride around in a wheelchair for a day and then proclaims himself an expert in what being wheelchair-bound is like. But I believe in the possibility of imaginatively experiencing what others experience, and I thought I might learn something. With vast amusement, a nurse ushered me into a little room. My roommate, an ancient man who couldn't speak much, terrified me as soon as I climbed into bed. He kept clicking his light on and off. At one point I saw his hand through the filmy, so-called privacy curtain. His hand reached toward the curtain, grasping at it. He was trying to pull the curtain back, so that he could get a better look at me, and I had to stifle the impulse to yell at him to stop. Then, a little later, I heard a couple of the nurses in the hall outside, saying loudly, speaking of me, "Shall we give him an enema?" An old source of amusement among nurses, the enema.

I didn't learn much that I could use in my book, from my two-night stand at Linda Manor. Except for the fact that a few minutes can seem like eternity in a nursing-home bed and the fact that, from such a perspective, cheerful, attractive, average-sized nurses and nurse's aides can look huge and menacing. Those two nights I kept getting up and looking out the window, to make sure my car was still in the parking lot. I had planned to stay longer, but went home early the third morning in order to get some sleep.

At Linda Manor I got to know a nurse's aide who, when one of her residents had died, insisted on opening up the windows of the room. Asked why she did this, she said she felt she had to let the spirit out. All but a few of the staff were religious, at least in the sense that most believed in an afterlife. I think belief was a great comfort to them. At least I imagined it would be for me. But I possessed only a vague agnosticism. And I couldn't simply manufacture something stronger for the situation.

What troubled me most during my time at Linda Manor wasn't unpleasant sights or smells or even the reawakening of my fears about mortality. It was the problem of apparent meaninglessness. I watched people dying long before life had lost its savor for them or they their usefulness to others. I couldn't imagine any purpose behind the torments that many residents suffered in their last days. Sometimes I'd leave a resident's room feeling that everything, really everything in every life, was pointless. I remember thinking that we all just lie awhile and end up dying painfully, or, even worse, bored and inert. What meaning could life have, I'd find myself wondering, if the best of the last things people get to do on earth is to play Bingo? At such times, I'd usually find my way upstairs to the room of the two old men named Lou and Joe. Gradually, I began to notice that a number of the staff did the same thing, even giving up their coffee breaks to go and chat with Lou and Joe. I didn't usually plan to go to their room at these moments of vicarious despair. I'd just find myself wanting to go there. After about ten minutes in their room, I usually felt much better. Lou and Joe had been placed together in one of Linda Manor's little rooms, in what for both would likely be their last place on earth, and they had become great friends. Other residents had formed friendships inside Linda Manor, but none was durable or seemed to run very deep. Out in the wider, youthful world, this accomplishment of Lou and Joe's would have seemed unremarkable, but in that place it was profound.

The main thing I wanted to portray was that friendship, surrounded by the nursing home and all its varying forms of claustrophobia. I wanted to infuse the story of that friendship with sentiment, but not in a sentimental way. The difference, as I see it, is the difference between portraying emotion and merely asserting its existence, between capturing the reflection of something real on the page and merely providing handy cues designed to elicit an emotional response. It is, I realize, harder to depict manifestations of human goodness than manifestations of venality and evil. I don't know why that is. I do know that some people think that kindness, for example, is always superficial. That view is the logical equivalent of sentimentality. It's an easy way to feel and it gives some people a lot of pleasure. It has nothing to do with a tragic vision of life. It has about as much to do with an accurate vision of life as a Hallmark card. Anyway, that's how it seems to me. The world seems various to me, and depicting some of the virtue in it seems like a project worth attempting. I do not say that I pulled it off, but that's part of what I had in mind.

After my book was published, I continued to visit Linda Manor about once a week. I went partly because doing so made me feel like a good guy. But I had other reasons. Growing old with dignity calls for many acts of routine heroism, and some of the people I knew at Linda Manor were inspiring, admirable characters. All of them have died now, except for Lou, who has achieved the ripe old age of ninety-six. Joe died last winter. I visit only Lou now, but I used to go mainly in order to visit the two men. I *liked* visiting them. Their room was one place where I knew I was always welcome. They gave me good advice, on such subjects as child-rearing. They were funny, both intentionally and otherwise. Most important, their room was one place in the world where I could count on finding that amity prevailed. That was unusual, in my experience of the world. The crucial thing about Lou and Joe was that they remained very *good* friends, better friends every time I visited. They presented an antidote to despair, which is connectedness, and for me, I learned, it is only the connectedness of the human tribe that can hold despair at bay. Connectedness can, of course, take many different forms. One can find it in religion, or in family, or, as in the case of Lou and Joe, in friendship. Or perhaps in work, maybe even in the act of writing.

Harold Brodkey, who recently died of AIDS, wrote in an essay a couple of years ago, "I think anyone who spends his life working to become eligible for literary immortality is a fool." I agree. But I also think that only a fool would write merely for money or contemporary fame. I imagine that most writers—good, bad, and mediocre—write partly for the sake of the private act of writing and partly in order to throw themselves out into the world. Most, I imagine, *endeavor* for connectedness, to create the kind of work that touches other lives and, in that sense at least, leaves something behind. I don't dream of immortality or plant marginalia for my biographers anymore. But I do wonder what Mr. Fitzgerald would think of what I've written and especially, of what I'm going to write.

A few days after I got back from Vietnam, in June 1969, I traveled to Cambridge and called Mr. Fitzgerald from a pay phone. He invited me to lunch at his house the next afternoon. Of course, I didn't tell him this, but I wanted something from him, something ineffable, like hope. He had prepared sandwiches. I'm not sure that he made them himself, but I like to think that he did, and that he was responsible for cutting the crusts off the bread. I'm not sure why I remember that. It seemed a sweet gesture, a way of making me feel that I was important to him. It also made him seem old, older than I'd remembered him.

I saw Mr. Fitzgerald a few times over the next year or two, and then he moved away and I moved out west for a while. I fell under other influences. My dreams of writing something classic gave way to my little dreams of writing something publishable, of making a living as a writer, which seemed hard enough. But those early dreams were dormant, not dead. When, almost ten years later, a book of mine, *The Soul of a New Machine*, was awarded the Pulitzer Prize and the American Book Award, my megalomaniacal dreams of literary glory came out of storage. I could tell myself at moments that I'd achieved them. But I hesitated for awhile before sending my book to Mr. Fitzgerald. I was afraid. When I finally worked up the nerve, I wrote an inscription to the effect that I hoped this piece of writing began to approach his expectations. I soon received a letter from him, in which he thanked me, remarked upon the "modesty" of my inscription—no doubt he saw right through that—and apologized for his inability to read the book just now. I wrote right back, proposing that I visit him. He did not reply. I never heard from him again. I don't remember exactly when he died. I think it was a few years later.

His silence has bothered me for a long time, not immoderately but in the way of those embarrassing memories that suddenly appear when you're checking the oil in your car or putting a key in a door. Two summers ago I met one of Mr. Fitzgerald's sons and told him the story. He insisted that his father would never have failed to answer my last letter, if he'd been able to read and write by then. I believed him. And I believe that had Mr. Fitzgerald been able to read my book, he would have told me what he really thought. It's probably just as well that he never did. I've written other and, I think, better books since then. I'd rather know what he thought of *them*. I've been courting his approval ever since my first day in his class, and I continue to court his approval now, when he's certain to withhold it. That makes me sad sometimes, but not in my better moments. I'll never know if he'd approve of what I've written and am going to write. But I'll never know if he'd disapprove either. He's left me room to go on trying.

Tracy Kidder, contributing editor of The Atlantic Monthly, *was awarded both the Pulitzer Prize and the American Book Award for* The Soul of a New Machine. *He is also the author of* Among Schoolchildren, Old Friends, *and the best-selling* House.

A *Stylist's Delight*
A Conversation with Paul West

BARBARA ADAMS

WE'VE JUST SETTLED IN ON THE GREEN FLORAL COUCH IN THE garden room, and I'm explaining to writer Paul West—novelist, memoirist, essayist, reviewer, educator—that the article I'm interviewing him for profiles him as a writer rather less the work itself.

"But why?" he whispers incredulously, drawing out the vowel. "The work is the important thing. I'm irrelevant—I'm just a conduit." Suddenly we both laugh at this proclamation, and he pretends to end the interview: "That's it; it's over now—I'm just a conduit, that's all." I mime dutiful note-taking, and we enjoy the joke.

This afternoon at his home in Ithaca, New York, laughter punctuates Paul West's conversation, and later I find my notes repeatedly describing him softly chuckling, chortling, or crowing. A pleasant man, he chats playfully, his formal British courtesy tempered by half a lifetime in the U.S., so that what remains is easy-going and genial—as in genie? genius? ingenious, or perhaps disingenuous? One is tempted to echo the outrageous wordplay of his prose, but stops, shamed by the presence of a master juggler.

The master, the literary lion, has, at sixty-six, a high-flying mind but unassuming manner. Everything about him has converged toward comfort: his moderate height (5 feet 9 inches), his rounded middle (recalling his long-ago concern, as a nascent swimmer, for a perennially misplaced center of gravity), a gentle, broad face with light hazel eyes distinctly alert and kind. The wavy dark auburn hair adds a counter-touch of vanity, or spirit. Even his clothes today are soothing—a soft navy blue velour sweatsuit and elegant loafers on slender, sockless feet. One looks in vain for the sturdy boy fierce at cricket, finding instead a congenial, gracious man, compromised no more than most by the years and fueled, even renewed, this past decade, by a pacemaker. "I'm partly bionic, which is rather nice," he'd said a year ago, when we first met.

But if soul is manifest in the body, it's to be found not in Paul West's appearance but his deep, amiable voice—British still, yet broadened, soft yet commanding, courteous, interested, welcoming. "I think" politely prefaces many sentences, which string one to the next, compelling, murmuring, exploring. One hears, in his rhythmic speech, all the "elegant variation" West says he works to prune from his writing. Unless, of course, variation's the point—like the hyperbolic, self-deprecatory comparisons comically cascading in the opening chapter of *Out of My Depths: A Swimmer in the Universe*.

Of that 1983 book, on learning to swim late in adulthood, West recalls that writing it was great fun. So is revisiting his "sense of being an impostor, of all these people being able to swim—at the pool, in the ocean—while I was always pretending that I was swimming. It was a very humiliating feeling. I liked the sensation of the water—it was great . . . but how do you get from here to there?" Caught up in his mind's image, West describes the momentous day he accidentally first swam: "I ended up being carried off gently towards the center of the pool into the six-foot area, on my back, and not knowing how to get out of it. Very strange . . . I just floated and floated and floated, and thought, 'This is floating. Not bad, but what do you do NOW?' And so I made little cupping movements and gradually moved back to the shallow end." He motions this like a paddling puppy, laughing, recalling his elation. "Eureka!"

Perceiving his pleasure, I ask whether, while composing, he ever feels glee. "Oh glee! Enormous glee! I talk to fellow writers, and the one thing they seem to have in common is how miserable it makes them. Writers of all kinds—they mostly complain about the drudgery, the pain, the self-censorship and so on. I never feel that—ever!" He draws a light breath. "To me, there's absolute delight in doing it. I wouldn't swap it for anything. I think it's wonderful to be able to do it, and to require so few aids—I mean, a one hundred dollar type-writer and some paper. I don't need a word processor; I have one in my head."

He laments not being able to use a 2B pencil anymore, since he can't decipher his handwriting, even in his old manu-scripts. Then he's off again: "Somebody was telling me yester-day he writes eight hours a day. I thought 'My god, that's four times what I do, and it makes him so miserable.' So he's mis-erable a third of his day." His voice softens. "I never get that feeling. I get tremendous buoyancy from it."

Fluidity seems to be the essential word for West's writing—fluidity of style, content, genre, and even process. He de-scribes the act of writing as impetuous. "Whether it's fiction or nonfiction, it ain't that calculated, you know. . . . It's an overflow; it comes upon me. I still write at night, starting about midnight until, say, 2:30, and sometimes, if it's going well, I'll write an hour or two in the afternoon. I just go there, to my desk, and see what happens. Because if I don't sit down at the machine, nothing happens. There are lots of people who can be swimming or running or gardening"—here I won-der if he's thinking of his partner, essayist and naturalist Di-ane Ackerman—"and also be thinking about what they're go-ing to write. I can never do it—I have to go and sit down at the typewriter and it'll come. I can't do it anywhere else. I can't even prepare—my brain won't fix on it. There has to be that catalytic little clack-clack-clack thing—then I can go fine for several hours. And the instant I walk away, it stops—pecu-liar."

Equally peculiar, West says, is the internal voice he hears while writing: "It's as if some voice is singing the words to me. It's not my voice. It's a very strange effect, like an echo chamber—I can hear the words being said as they go down onto the page. And that's very useful, because I can tell if the thing sounds wrong—I stop." The voice saying his words aloud is remote, disembodied, he says, chuckling, "probably like the voice on answering machines. It's male, tinny—very strange." I ask if he couldn't provide himself with a more

pleasing voice, and he quips in return, "No, apparently not—
it just sort of squawks away." Because of this vocalization,
West rarely reads his work aloud as he writes, unless he's having trouble with a sentence, when, he says, it's "the infallible
test."

As he talks, West punctuates his thoughts, his left index
finger gesturing, almost conducting music, and then returning
to rest, pensively, at his lips. "I hear the words pronouncing
themselves as I pick them out and use them. It's rhythmical,
too—as I'm writing a page, I can hear the rhythms of the sentences that I haven't yet written lining up. All I have to do is
put the words into them." West recalls shocking some audience members at a lecture recently: "They said, 'Well you
know, you could be tempted by the rhythms into saying something you didn't mean,' and I said 'Absolutely—it's called fiction.' "

West looks puckish, reveling in the sovereignty of imagination, but concedes this interior rhythm happens to him while
writing both fiction and nonfiction. "I get this weird satisfaction of things falling into the right place. I tell you, I enjoy it;
it's full of activity." The effect is very musical, he says, and
finds it strange that he can't read music. (His formal music
education began and ended at age seven with his first piano
lesson from his mother.)

Writing is not a silent activity for West—not only because
of his inner voice, but because he surrounds himself with classical music. "I listen to music all the time—it drives Diane
crazy." While in Tucson in the late '80s composing *The Place
in Flowers Where Pollen Rests*, "the enormous Hopi novel," his
favorite, he listened to certain Busoni sonatinas one thousand two hundred times. Although he never experimented so
exhaustively with any other musical work, West finds music
a necessity: "I grew up listening to my mother's music pupils
playing all kinds of stuff—Beethoven, Brahms, Schubert—so
it's totally natural for me to be doing my homework to the
sound of music in the evenings. If I don't hear music while
I'm working, I don't get that feeling of stability or comfort."

Last summer, while writing *My Mother's Music*, his most recent nonfiction work, West listened to "lots of Delius—Delius
and Bach." His mother, the memoir's subject, who'd chan-

neled her gifts into her two children and her piano students ("her nest harmonic, and her passions proxy," he writes), had often told him he'd come to Bach one day. "She always thought Bach superb," West says, "and I could never get it, never. I said, 'The attitude's arid,' and she said, 'You're totally wrong.' And of course I was."

West finds music oddly catalytic: "I have my own rhythms as well, but here are these different rhythms, and I find listening to them propulsive and I don't know why. I have no idea." I ask if perhaps reading other people's work, hearing their voices, ever obstructs his own. "Yes, absolutely"—but what comes to mind for West is all the student work he's read in a lifetime of teaching. Some very good manuscripts, too, he says, "some of them of extraordinary ability—and that would get in the way. So I wouldn't ever write while I was teaching."

A little over a year ago, West retired from thirty-three years of teaching literature and fiction writing at Penn State in alternate semesters, with visiting stints at a wide range of other colleges—Brown, Cornell, Colgate, Hobart and William Smith, Arizona, Wisconsin, Wichita State. "I wouldn't write for five or six months," he says, "except book reviews and things like that. I certainly couldn't write fiction. And the instant I'd stop teaching in April, it was a great day—I would switch over and say 'That's it! I can put my mind back to writing.'"

But does reading published literature interfere with his own voice, I wonder. That's less trouble, says West. In fact, he rereads his favorite writers, mainly Proust, "to start the machine in some way. I keep Proust by me and if I feel a little stir-crazy or a little starved, I read some Proust. Also Faulkner, it's those two. I picked up a new *Absalom, Absalom* the other day—there's a book I keep around. But if I feel I've run dry, I just stop and look at them, and they sort of loosen up my rhythms again." He thinks, corrects himself: "There are four: Nabokov, Proust, Beckett, and Faulkner—I keep them by me as lifebelts, or something. They impress me tremendously— very refined."

Asked what nonfiction writers he values, West pauses at length, as if summoning up old spirits. Then he says firmly, "Thomas De Quincey, whom I admire enormously. I think De

Quincey is the real Coleridge." He goes on to mention the major British essayists of the last century—John Ruskin, Charles Lamb, William Hazlitt, Walter Pater. "These are all wonderful nonfiction models for anybody. I was a nineteenth-century specialist, and these people had an enormous effect on me. I think they wrote beautifully; they had tremendous symphonic reverberation—they wrote the last great visionary essays, I think, in English." He reflects a moment.

"That's the nineteenth century, anyway."

And the twentieth? We both laugh, guiltily. A voluminous reader and reviewer of fiction from different cultures, West admits, "I've got an awful suspicion I don't read a lot of [modern] nonfiction, for literary reasons anyway." He casts about, citing E. B. White, Colette, Virginia Woolf—"some of her nonfiction is very fine. I think she's one of the very best." And William Gass—"a real essayist. He has some of the best opening sentences: 'There is no o'clock in the cantina.'" West chuckles, repeating the line to himself. "He's very fine."

He recalls, "I used to like teaching literature because the text was always so good. I almost always taught fiction, and sometimes poetry. Once or twice I taught nonfiction, and we discovered that the essay was the most neglected form in the world, and there were so many people writing brochures."

Writing essays and nonfiction comes easily to West, for which he credits his rigorous undergraduate training at Oxford, where he studied literature and philosophy. "That's a tough discipline—every week an essay which you read aloud to two people, and then they tear it to bits. And this goes on and on and on and on, and eventually you become quite tough, accustomed to being criticized." Paul West's second severe schooling came not so much in acquiring his M.A. at Columbia but rather in writing for newspapers. His soft face starts to furrow at the memory of writing weekly book reviews, year after year. Many of these reviews, as well as West's essays, are republished in his 1987–94 volumes of *Sheer Fiction* I, II, and III. "They were all foreign books in translation, so I virtually had twenty years with the *Washington Post* of comparative lit."

West prefers the freedom of the essay to the constraints of writing reviews "with shoulders hunched." Spending a week or two perfecting a four-page review was "a terrible waste of time—in that time I could have written several chapters of a novel."

Fiction is West's first love, as his fifteen novels (and several in draft) may attest. Despite his two volumes of poetry, two critical studies, and twelve works of various nonfiction, he sees himself primarily as a "compulsive fictioneer." West pauses and then pronounces seriously, definitively: "I regard myself as a novelist writing occasional nonfiction, and not as a nonfiction writer writing the occasional novel."

For West, accessing memories seems much less laborious than the demands of invention. "If you can write good expository prose and some metaphorical, visionary prose, then nonfiction should be a real snap. I would never say that writing fiction is a snap; it's not. It's very difficult to balance all those things in the air. And you always have this shall I? shan't I? business of have I gone too far? How far and to what extent should I invent?—that's always the question. That's never the question for the nonfiction person: It's laid out, like music— and all you have to do is play it. But fiction is a much more complicated job—you have to create voices and lines of development that intersect."

West's quiet eyes sparkle as he describes the delight of writing novels. "I like writing nonfiction, but I really get off on writing fiction. It's more libidinous," he chuckles. But surely there are satisfactions unique to nonfiction, I venture. He has the impish answer ready: "You can irritate your family more. The fiction doesn't irritate anybody because they don't take it seriously, I guess. But nonfiction they go through with a fine-toothed comb, saying 'No, you got that wrong, and that! Why don't you give this up, because clearly you don't have any talent for it.'" He laughs, perversely gratified.

Writing memoirs, I say, is a double bind: Your subjects expect accuracy or literalism and at the same time may resent appropriation of any part of their lives. West nods, "Oh God, yes. They expect you to be them, to report events as if you were them, and then they completely ignore the fact that *a* you're a novelist and *b* you're a stylist, and this takes you very far from predictable lines of reportage. This doesn't bother me and never will. Because ultimately this is the big issue that I make of words, and that's more important than the basic facts. Writing is always a stylistic opportunity, and I'm sure that doesn't appeal to family members."

West finds the novel "always more open to manipulation," whereas nonfiction is more deliberate. "You are, I suppose, restricted to certain facts—you know, the way your father walked. You're not going to mess with that too much." But West admits to "messing with" his own thoughts and actions a great deal, and even inventing characters in nonfiction— "just to see what'll happen." In *My Mother's Music*, he introduces a fictional character, the allusively named Reyner Rilka, providing his mother, in her nineties, with an additional friend and neighbor. Always tinkering, the novelist argues for invention: "The grouping wasn't right; I needed a male wall to bounce things off."

Despite his restructuring of reality, West believes his mother would certainly have recognized herself in this memoir, in which he sought to make her "dominant on every page." Writing about his father, however, as West did in *I, Said the Sparrow* (1963), an autobiography up to age seventeen, was unappreciated. "He hated it—he said it exposed and revealed him. He hated to be depicted or even mentioned. And of course he shows up a lot in the recent novel *Love's Mansion*— with a sex life he never had, I'm sure. He would have been aggrieved, I think. So you can't really get away with it." He pauses, then hastens to a more positive thought: "My mother liked it; she liked being written about. She'd nod and say 'You've got a very accurate eye' or something. I say very little about my sister because she doesn't care to be written about either. If I'm writing about her, I know I'm getting it wrong, *ipso facto*, so I cut it to the minimum."

About his subjective elaborations, West turns almost apologetic: "There's a dreadful tendency to make your subjects perfect, you know, to make them even more imposing. You have to fight that like a demon." He's quiet for a moment. "I don't always win. Especially if it brings good phrases into being—I'm not going to give up good phrases for the sake of truth."

West sees the limits of fabrication as the essential distinction between writing fiction and nonfiction. "As a novelist I have much more freedom to take liberties, exaggerate and distort, and cook things up that weren't there." He finds this true "even if you're taking as your premise some historical personage, which I got into a habit of doing—Jack the Ripper, von Stauffenberg, et cetera. I take lots of liberties with my historical people." When people object to his fiddling with facts, he points out that he uses "these historical characters for their plastic, malleable quality. Claire Clairmont in *Lord Byron's Doctor* has a much richer life from me than she does from the fates. And that struck me as aesthetically appropriate. So it's no good saying to the novelist 'Well, you're inventing this; this isn't true,' because that's exactly right—the novelist is there to invent things that are not there."

At a reading last fall from *The Tent of Orange Mist*, a novel set during the Japanese invasion of Nanking in 1937, West described it as only nominally historical, rather more an opportunity to introduce his own particular "circus of ideas." This trait of welcoming a panoply of ideas and themes, as well as any stylistic and structural intrusion, surprise, juxtaposition, or excess, can be found in both West's fiction and nonfiction. His approach is like throwing an enormous party—opening the door and shooing everything into the mix in celebratory style. Swimming is only the infrastructure for *Out of My Depths*, which is as much philosophical speculation as memoir, and contains poems, charts (both Platonic and astrological), tables of passengers on the Titanic, and existential sketches. And in last year's A *Stroke of Genius: Illness and Self-Discovery*, in which he transcends his mid-1980s minor stroke and temporary paralysis through his own verbal surgery, he interweaves widely disparate lore on migraines, music, and cardiology.

"Paul West seems to have read everything and considered everything," Jean Stafford writes in the introduction to the much-acclaimed *Words for a Deaf Daughter* (1970). Even as a concerned father, writing this book "impulsively, in pencil, on the backs of old envelopes" as he watches his hearing- and mentally-impaired daughter, Mandy, West brings the world to bear on the experience—from Boadicea to Francis Bacon, amphibian physiology to Japanese hieroglyphs. His vast interests and knowledge complicate every subject he addresses, rendering it paradoxically more accessible, original, and deeply felt.

The eclectic interests and structures notwithstanding, what links all his works, West says, is their style. "Ultimately, they all belong together. The whole concatenation of books is a fabric made of words. And it varies enormously, but in some ways it's very consistent." West's habit of lush, erudite word-play is at times so baroque that one almost wants to call it febrile, were it not so sensuously grounded. Some sentences spin out for more than two hundred thirty words and a dozen ideas, and on such voyages you either trust the captain and enjoy his company, or you don't. The critics generally do: "No contemporary American prose writer can touch him for sustained rhapsodic invention," says a *Boston Phoenix* critic, while the *Chicago Tribune* identifies West as "possibly our finest living stylist in English."

"I always write in the same style," West says simply. "I don't know any other." He's defended it amply and inspirationally in his 1985 essay, "In Defense of Purple Prose." Neither his style nor subject matter has been influenced by his years in the United States, West believes, rather by reading Faulkner when he was fifteen and Proust when he was twenty. "I think I was fully formed and corrupted before I arrived. And I got much more sympathy here for the sort of thing I was doing than I would have gotten in England." Suddenly he's off on a mild rant about "minimalism, Puritanism, adapted social-ism." He deplores Britain's "very strange hatred of the color-ful, the flamboyant. I thought I should have perhaps gone to Latin America, where that sort of thing—stylish, exuberant, possibly flamboyant writing—is not just tolerated but is en-joyed and recommended.

"But there is a certain hospitality to it in America, other-wise Faulkner wouldn't be tolerated. Still, there's tremendous Puritanism in this country—'You mustn't enjoy things too much, you mustn't be seen to be enjoying them too much, you mustn't be luxuriating in the medium.' There are lots of people around who prefer the clipped, the lean, the terse— as if this were a question of morality." His voice softens. "It's got nothing to do with morality. It has to do with spellbinding, I think."

Occasionally an editor hasn't the patience for his prose, West says, describing one recently who crossed out twenty pages of a novel, line by line, in blue pencil. "Without a single explanation!" His tone is more astonished than indignant. "I simply reinstated all those pages. You've got to remain your own best judge—if you trust anybody else, then you've abdicated from a delicious responsibility." West is unquestionably his own most ruthless editor, having written entire books he's decided don't pass muster. He mentions deleting some sixty pages—"mostly about music"—from the memoir on his mother. His process seldom changes: "I get the first draft down, and if I don't like it, throw it out later. But when things start to come they come very fast. I type fairly fast. I revise slowly, which I think is probably a virtue. But composing is a swift process. So there's often a lot of revision to do." He routinely reduces a page to one line, and like Colonel Hayashi in The Tent of Orange Mist, types out corrected passages and then painstakingly glues them over the original manuscript.

While all West's novels are written impulsively, as was Out of My Depths and Words for a Deaf Daughter, most nonfiction works, such as My Mother's Music and A Stroke of Genius, are carefully mapped out. Urged by his agent to write a book about his mother, West doubted that he had enough to say; he "psyched out the ground" by diagraming the material. He points to the unusually elaborate table of contents and its subdivisions. "This is very carefully, almost musically planned, with motifs. It has a very finicky structure."

Once outlined, the book, written in three months, came to West easily and pleasurably, even though he was reaching back from ten to sixty years. "It was waiting to be done," he says. "I was amazed to find how much I remembered. But then I'm always amazed by how much more there is that you don't know about, and the problem is how to bring it into play. It's not a question of total recall, because there's no total. It's a sum with no addition at the end; you just keep adding and adding and adding and adding."

But memory is still quirky, elusive. "How can you make memory serve you?" he wonders. "You can't, as Proust pointed out. I think you always have to be receptive to memory, but never expect anything of it. Sometimes you can't get your hands on something—you're certain that there's more to the iceberg. Another day you'll probably get it, because you weren't trying so hard to find it. Memory is not a bag of sugar, you know, it's very mercurial. It pleases itself."

Has any city or location proved more conducive to writing, I wonder, and West says that he can work anywhere he goes, in any unfamiliar setting. Then a memory stirs: "The place I used to write a lot was in my mother's house in Derbyshire. In the living room, in an armchair, with a tray in front of me on my knees as a table. That's when I wrote by hand on a yellow tablet, and oh God, I must have written half a dozen books in that position—that's a lot of pages. She would be puttering around, doing her things, and cooking. That was a good place to write. It was soul food, or something."

West rejects the idea of writing another memoir, having written so much about himself and his family already. "I think I'm slowly cleaning out the granary; I don't think there's a lot left." Then he admits his agent is prodding him to write a nonfiction work about aviation, a lifelong obsession. And life is still traversing the boundaries of fiction: He's just completed a long autobiographical novel, about how he and Diane Ackerman met and became involved with Carl Sagan and the missions to Mars and Jupiter. Tentatively called *Life with Swan* (Swan is Diane, he explains), it "catches the euphoria of the '60s and '70s." He laughs. "The names are changed to protect the guilty. Everybody likes it, even Diane—as she says, it's a 'kissy' book. It was such fun to write, my god—it really has its own register, its own sound. It's first person and extremely straightforwardly written, for me."

Although West says he and Ackerman are "very much in sympathy with what the other is doing and respect it enormously," they usually don't read each other's work until it's published. "We're not talking the same language, certainly not if I'm writing fiction. Diane likes to get things right, and does, and half the time I don't care—I'm fudging it up anyway, concocting characters. She sees herself as a member of a group of responsible, concerned, natural historians who can't afford to play fast and loose. It's a different quest, and that's fine. But I think having a novelist on the premises always alarms her because she sees the sheer audacity of what they do." West describes astronomer Carl Sagan's delighted response to working on his own first novel. "For once he could please himself and do whatever he wanted. 'You have this freedom all the time?' He was absolutely astounded by it."

The early spring afternoon has waned, and our talk turns outward, to the squirrel hopping at the window—"she's almost a member of the family"—and the Siberian iris shoots in the garden. I ask to see where West writes, and he's pleased—but warns I'll be appalled. He whispers in awe, "Diane's study is very neat and tidy, and has pretty things in it. Mine is just a sewer. Come on . . ." Like a boy sharing his private hideout, he obligingly ushers me there, stopping in the kitchen to microwave me a cup of coffee and admire a sugarless cake Diane has baked him—"It's very sweet of her."

At the end of the long hall the matching study doors face each other, and Ackerman calls hello from behind the one on the left. Science and art have not stayed in their respective places, I notice—her door is graced with a Matisse poster of a purple-robed odalisque, while West's is covered by constellations—a dark blue chart of the night sky, courtesy of the London Daily Telegraph. Inside, I can't help commenting on the smallness of West's study. The room is windowless, the walls a half-hearted yellow; as expected, books and piles of paper are everywhere. By the door, a bright purple stepladder intended for reaching bookshelves serves as temporary lodging to some papers, books, and a pair of sweat socks.

"As you can see, this has to be reformed—it's a mess. Over-grown," West says, as much delighted as dismayed. Tripping on something just as he warns me to be careful, I assure him my own office is no less chaotic. On a high shelf I spot a white wooden model of the New York Public Library (both West and Ackerman have been recognized as Literary Lions), and he points out his father's medals from World War I. West's own medals and citations decorate the walls, and I'm drawn to the framed tribute from the American Academy and Institute of Arts and Letters, which begins "Paul West's speculative prose besieges the barriers of genre. . . ." Its words "resonant," "relish," and "joyous" remain with me, confirming my own experience of his work. We tour a series of old family photographs in silver frames, willingly sinking back into time.

In one, West's mother, Mildred, astonishes with her youthful beauty; in another, dwarfed in extreme old age, she stands wild-haired in her garden, her crooked, intense smile beckoning the photographer.

On a small desk sits an old blue Smith Corona electric, where, West says, "the little space there in front of the typewriter is always clear—except it isn't now—and there I work. It's very awkward." On the wall just above it hangs a faded advertisement featuring dozens of matchbook-sized photos of light aircraft. West points to one plane that looks like a white moth, a "supposedly uncrashable" Ercoupe that he and Ackerman had hoped to buy. He describes two trial flights fraught with mechanical failures. "I think that we're alive today because we didn't buy it."

We spend some time peering over a poor photocopy of *Esquire* magazine's literary pyramid, constructed of a series of movable Post-Its with an American writer's name scrawled on each. Saul Bellow is at the top. Sequestered off to the side, West's square appears, along with fellow immigrants Wilfred Sheed and Jamaica Kincaid, labeled "Brits?" "So I'm floating out here," he says, bemused at the vagaries of fashion and fame.

Moments later West is off to the kitchen—"Was I making tea or coffee?"—leaving me meditating on these objects, casual or cherished, and what they might explain. I think about having seen, in other places, fragments of writers' lives—Wordsworth's leather lunchbucket, Coleridge's opium pipe, Anne Bronte's first bible, on its flyleaf scrawled, "What where and how shall I be when I have got through?" And I wonder how the biographer or memoirist apprehends such things, knowing they sang such different songs to their owners.

What I'm seeking is, as Paul West promised, not here in his study, or even life, but in the works themselves, the memories transmuted. I recall what he said this afternoon—"I write nonfiction because I think ultimately some of the things that happened are of consuming interest . . . and are almost good enough for fiction." And then remember how last spring, in speaking of writing about his recovery from stroke and the outpouring of new work that followed, he defined his purpose even more ardently: "You write about the thing that sank its teeth into you and wouldn't let go. I find that a useful discipline."

For the past twenty-four years, Barbara Adams has been teaching writing at Ithaca College, where she helped found the Writing Program and now directs its technology initiative. She is also a freelance journalist and regional theatre critic.

How and Why

JANE BERNSTEIN

MOST IMPORTANT IS THAT I RUN. THIS IS NOT MERELY AN item culled from a list of my extracurricular activities, nor a boast meant as evidence that I am health conscious, but a beginning, a connection: if I did not run, I would not write essays. These two profoundly different activities are woven together for me: one physical, mindless enough so that dogs, rhinos, and rats do it, the other—How else can you say it?—cerebral, an activity reserved for the only animals capable of despair, delight, and reflection. I think therefore I am.

My body is an engine, a middle-aged engine, admittedly. The start-up is often rough; the beginning of the run, if I turned it into words, would be a litany of complaints. But inevitably, I get comfortable on the road, and shift into a kind of cruise control, in which my body moves forward of its own accord. A kind of forgetting washes over me then. It's not only that I forget the road, my beating heart, and tender knees, but what I think of as my daily self, the mother-teacher-datebook-keeper-member-of-the-community self. When this self is shed, my mind, another machine, begins to hum. The voice of my truest, most private self surfaces, and I drift into a kind of mulling state, a state in which I worry things. Not worry about them, the more sedentary, less productive activity done by my daily self. But "worry" as defined by Webster's Third: "to bite at or upon . . . to touch, poke, or disturb . . . To subject to persistent or nagging attention or effort . . . ."

"Why?" I ask, when I am out on the road. In this mulling state, I cannot will myself to address problems or think through things. I am dreamy and utterly unself-conscious, drifting through the easiest most trivial dilemmas—enough broccoli for stir fry? brown shoes or black?—until bigger things begin to rise.

Sometimes the *why* that surfaces is merely a question, not yet embodied. Or the *why* might be an image that continues to reappear, as if asking to be studied. Sometimes the why is embedded in a conversation that I replay or invent, a kind of auditory hallucination. Some of this mulling dissipates on these runs; the questions rise, float, and pop, ephemeral as soap bubbles. Other issues are played out later in conversation. But some of what surfaces on these runs keeps rising, demanding to be further mulled. These questions or voices become irritations, splinters beneath my skin.

WHY

I am running one day, wondering why running and mulling are so inseparable for me, when it occurs to me that even as a small child, I felt compelled to mull, to "subject to . . . nagging attention" questions that did not seem to plague others in my family. Long after the toddler years, I was still bugging my parents with why questions.

Three miles into my run, I remember the cemetery we drove past on our weekly visit to my ancient grandmother, how I looked out the car window each time and asked:

"Why do we die?"

I imagine my parents exchanging one of those oh-no-not-again looks in the front seat, my mother, bored, saying, "That's the way we're made."

"But why?"

"Because our bodies wear out."

"Why?"

My questions deemed a verbal tic, an attention-getting device. But, no, the need was real, the dismissive answers intolerable, even then.

Wearily: "Because that's the way it is."

"Why do they wear out?"

"Because I said so."

Several miles into my run, the questions I worry about are often just as unanswerable. I ponder the fact that the world has so little patience for mullers. There is no room for our questions on an ordinary day in the domestic world or the world of commerce. We are the object of fun if we voice our cosmic concerns too often. Cuckoos. Navel-gazers. Obsessed.

"Because," the world tells us.

"Is and always was," it says.

"Because I said so."

"Just because."

Back on the road, motor purring, I wonder why I wonder and think of my dog, a terrier, from the Latin *terre*, earth. He does not point or retrieve, could not pull a sled. But he needs to dig, this earth dog, at times so intent upon digging up a rock from beneath the soil that nothing can stop him once he starts. Passionate and fervent are the words that come to mind when I watch him dig. Is he looking for the rock of his dreams? Routing out the rock from hell? On the road I wonder if I am like my dog, born to dig. There is photographic evidence that this might be the case. Look! Here I am, in a photo at two years old, covered in mud, a literal digger. Perhaps there is a gene for mulling, the way some people feel there might be genes for patriotism and shyness. Maybe there's a strange trisomy that dooms the genetically challenged victim to ask and ask, incapable of accepting "because."

The teenage years: I did not outgrow it.

"Better not to dwell on such things," said my parents. "Leave well enough alone."

"Looking for trouble," my mother called my speculations. When my tenacity, my relentless digging, really irritated her, she would say, "Stop already. Stop analyzing everything!"

A second theory: Mulling in opposition to the style of the rest of my family, as a protest against the heavy door of "because," the wall of "stop analyzing."

HOW

And so: I am the kind of person who is predisposed to writing (and reading) essays and has found a way to shake free of the worldly stuff and hear the voice of my true self. What do I worry? What problems are persistent and irritating enough that I take them from the road to the desk? I'd like to say that my range of subjects is limitless, but in reality, much of my work fits into what essayist Nancy Mairs only half facetiously calls "the literature of personal disaster." To baldly list the disasters is an embarrassment to me—murder, senility, disability. But as Mairs points out, serious writers whose work fits into this genre don't write about adversity as a single monolithic event, the disaster as a disaster. While the adversity might become the background, the heart of the essay comes from one of what Mairs calls "the welter of little incidents" that make up the whole.

When I write about my daughter Rachel, who is blithely categorized by the world at large as a "special needs child," I don't write about her retardation itself. Nor do I replay secondhand sentiments that come in lockstep beside the word *retarded*. For instance, I neither write (nor think) of her as "one of God's Special Children." I don't write about how fortunate I am to be her mother, or how much she has taught me. I do not adhere to the party line by claiming that adversity has made me a better person. (It hasn't.) I write about my daughter competing in Special Olympics or about the times I regret her birth. My daughter is fundamentally unknowable, because she lacks the language to describe her own moods, desires, and dislikes. She lives in a world she cannot understand, and that often fails to accommodate what I believe to be her needs.

What I believe . . . "I am Rachel's interior voice," I tell people, as if there is something amusing in this. In fact, I take this quite seriously. If writing essays is a clear assertion of one's voice, I supposed I could say that I write about Rachel to make her voice heard, and in opposition to the sentiments that diminish her as an individual, make her an indistinguishable member of a fuzzy, barely human category.

But often, when I am mulling on the road, it occurs to me that there is something audacious and obnoxious in my presumption. Who am I to claim to be the keeper of Rachel's consciousness? And yet, if not me, then who?

This is the kind of tension that cannot be resolved on a run, that makes me want to take to my desk, to shape what is hazy and unformed into something comprehensible. Once

I begin to transfer my vague mulling into words on paper, everything changes radically. The private act of removing the splinter becomes an attempt to wrench meanings from my shapeless pondering. It is at my desk that I recall the the French root from which *essay* is derived. *Essaier*, to try. I will try not to solve the problem I wish to work out on paper, since the most vexing problems escape tidy solutions, but to work through it in a way that makes my tale of interest to people I have never met.

AN EXAMPLE

Some years ago, I found myself rather excessively mulling over the word *pleasure*, wondering as I ran what pleasure was for a child whose responses were muted, who never expressed what she wanted, never complained when deprived of what she had seemed to enjoy. First the word itself: pleasure. syn: delight, joy. Why was I stuck on this? I asked myself.

An image formed in my head one day, a picture of pure joy: my daughter, shrieking and flapping her arms in a swimming pool. Without question, the water was something she loved. All I had to do was provide the opportunity for her to swim, to put her in the water, and I could say, "Rachel knows pleasure." But a problem was locked inside this seemingly perfect picture, for her physician thought that swimming induced her seizures, and suggested that perhaps I keep her away from the water. If we no longer took her swimming, would she recall that she had lost something she loved? Would she experience deprivation? Or did experiences, even pleasurable ones, simply vanish without any traces? Was the evidence of her pleasure worth the possible risk that she might have the kind of dangerous, intractable seizures that once she'd had in a swimming pool?

How best to tell this modest tale? I did not aim to write a philosophical inquiry into the nature of human happiness. I wanted to tell a small story with larger questions embedded inside it, a story about one child, unable to speak up for herself, a well-meaning physician, and a mother caught between wanting her child to have pleasure and providing for her safety. I used the techniques of fiction for this piece when I opted to give the reader a glimpse of our life, to show Rachel in the pool, to set off the drama between the characters.

When the form of this piece made itself known, I began to draft away, flush with grandiosity, convinced that my tale would be meaningful to others. Then one day, in the midst of what seemed to be a final draft, I found myself clutched by modesty and terror. What a puny, deeply insignificant story it suddenly seemed.

"Who was I?"

"My trivial life!"

"Who could possibly care?"

"How could I presume?"

A struggle that I now realize is inevitable for me, permanent, sometimes crippling, and yet of value, too, for it creates a tension, twists my self-effacement ("Who am I?") into a fierce desire to get the story right ("I am no one, but I must be heard!").

Perhaps if I were bolder or quicker, if I could tug on someone's sleeve and say exactly what I meant, I would not need to punch through my modesty on paper. But I cannot do it in person, and therefore depend upon my written words to say to the reader, "This is what it's like," and "This is what I think. This is my daughter. This is me. This is how we traveled in our search for accommodation."

The rewards: no fame, not much in the way of recognition, but the immense satisfaction of a single reader who says, "You found the words for me." Or, "This is my life, too."

My satisfaction feels permanent when I hear this, my need to question feels forever quenched.

And it is, until I lace up my shoes and hit the road again.

Jane Bernstein started her writing life as a fiction writer but has become increasingly engaged by essays. Her essays have been published in such places as The New York Times Magazine, The Sun, Poets & Writers, Inc., Ms., *and* Creative Nonfiction. *She lives in Pittsburgh and is an Associate Professor of English and Creative Writing at Carnegie Mellon University.*

Seventh East

ELLEN FAGG

WHEN I FIRST MOVED TO SALT LAKE CITY, I WORKED NIGHTS, covering the night cops beat. At the newspaper—it was my first full-time reporting job—my desk was by the police scanner and I had to monitor it all the time. I carried a portable scanner whenever I went anywhere, whether it was out to cover a speech or over to the mall for dinner. At first, I was so nervous about missing some crime, something big, a fire or an aggravated assault or a murder, that I even carried the scanner with me to the bathroom.

I didn't know many people in town, and most of my friends worked during the day. Sometimes I would go for days without talking to anybody but police officers and dispatchers, strangers who were voices to me, the voices who ordered me around the city. I wasn't particularly good at police reporting, but I considered it a beginning, a place to start. When friends came to town I'd show off and give tours of the town based on stories I had reported. Fires and rapes and multiple-car accidents and bombings and murder.

"Cops have pulled dead bodies out of every house on this corner," I'd say, pointing to the street where I lived. Or:

"I covered a stabbing in that parking lot."

Some nights, I'd spend a whole shift chasing potential disasters, and still didn't report a story my editor considered important enough to deserve a byline. The photographers hated it when we arrived at a scene and there weren't any flames for them to shoot. And if a fire didn't cause at least fifty thousand dollars of damage, the story probably wouldn't make it into the paper anyway. So I learned to work the phones, calling dispatchers before I left the newsroom, asking for information that would help me prioritize the reports. "What's the condition on that auto-ped? How many trucks were called out on that fire? Is the structure fully involved? Anybody unaccounted for?"

Listening to the scanner, sometimes all that static drove me crazy. I'd listen to it for awhile and hear an endless run of dispatchers with eerily calm voices, potential emergencies on all the channels blurring into each other, like the cars in a chain-reaction pileup, skidding on the black ice of the highway on a dangerous night. Every report fades in importance until eventually I'd stop paying attention. I would. I'd forget to pay attention. And then there was an accident and I couldn't help but watch.

After a fiery motorcycle accident, Marty Hall, a star softball player, remained in a coma for three months, hovering between life and death.

Hall was twenty-seven in 1983 when doctors told his family there was little chance he would recover. More than 80 percent of Hall's upper body was covered with second- and third-degree burns, after the motorcycle he was riding spun out of control. He was trapped under the flaming vehicle in a pile of sewage. Hall's right arm was so badly burned it simply fell off, doctors said. His right leg was amputated at the knee—not due to burns, but from an infection that developed into gangrene.

Now thirty-eight, Hall has moved from Louisville, Kentucky, to Salt Lake City, where he lives with his wife, Shirley. He has undergone twenty-six operations to rebuild his face. Doctors built a nose from bone they took from his ribs. They grafted skin from his good leg onto his chest. In the most recent operation, surgeons sliced open his head and pulled his scalp forward in order to create a new hairline.

Hall, who speaks in a thick southern accent, says he misses his family and Kentucky. But he likes living in Utah, he said, "because people are too polite to stare."

The first time I saw Marty, he was watching me move in. While movers negotiated the traffic on Seventh East in order to park the van in front of my house, I noticed a guy watching me from the porch of the house next door. That's how it began. Him watching me, not the other way around. I didn't know yet that his name was Marty. I didn't know about his accident, a story that would spill out in bits and pieces during the months to come. From where I stood, I couldn't see the burns that covered most of his face and upper body. All I saw was a guy sitting in a white plastic lawn chair, his left arm resting on a metal cane, his face hidden behind mirrored aviator-style sunglasses. A guy sitting there on his porch, watching me.

I moved into a gray brick bungalow that faced the lake at Liberty Park, the largest park in Salt Lake City. Actually, the lake was a flood-control pond, and the best part of my view. First in my line of vision, though, was Seventh East, a collector street that was eight lanes of urgency, "an urban river," I would tell my friends. But that morning, I propped open the door so the movers could wedge my mauve sleeper-sofa up the front steps and inside the narrow front door. When I went outside later to label my mailbox, I glanced over at the neighbor's front porch and noticed my neighbor, the one I didn't know yet, was gone.

For a long time, I couldn't imagine not being a reporter. I used to say that growing up as the youngest of three sisters groomed me for the job. As a child, I played beauty school with my sisters, using Sabrina, my French doll with real human hair, as our model. My sisters learned to cut bangs on Sabrina's hair and when I learned that the doll's silky white curls wouldn't grow back, I started to cry. I couldn't help myself. When Mom asked what was wrong I told her. Being a tattletale prepared me to think that information equals power, and as I grew up, I learned to listen and ask questions, collect and add up the details of other people's lives. I watched, took notes, shaped the pieces into a story. I could have a conversation without thinking about making a story.

There was a detachment I felt when I was reporting, while I observed people I thought of as sources. Maybe specimens would be a more accurate word. Stick a pin through their guts, get some good quotes, add another story to the collection. I got bored sometimes, or annoyed, maybe, when a former source would call me after I had already moved on to the next breaking story. "Emotional hit-and-run drivers." That's how Anna Quindlen described journalists, before she won her Pulitzer and gave up reporting for *The New York Times* to write fiction, and that idea made me uneasy whenever I needed to ask a friend for an interview. Sometimes I felt as if I didn't really have any business messing around with the facts of people's lives. Of course, it was just a job, you might say. Which it was.

After I left the cops beat, years later, after I had covered suburbs and city hall and medicine, after I started writing and editing longer pieces, I still marked my life by my stories. The summer I met Marty for instance, was marked by Mango Bond. Bond was a female bodybuilder abducted from a local junior high school where she worked. While she was missing, her friends plastered posters all over town, and the picture was amazing, all kinky blond hair and bare shoulders and a cocky, crooked smile, as if Mango were a rock star's girlfriend. I became obsessed with the details of her life, her Wild Orchid lipstick, the way she exercised nude on her treadmill at home. A year after a nine-year-old kid found the body out in the desert, cops still didn't have a murder suspect. At the magazine where I worked, my bosses thought the story was dramatic enough to boost newsstand sales, and we wrote a cover blurb that went like this: *Mango Bond: Someone Is Getting Away With Murder*.

I worked long hours that summer, but no matter when I left for work, Marty was sitting on his porch. When I came home, ten or twelve hours later, he was still there, smoking or sometimes just watching the traffic pass by. I started greeting him in a wave when I pulled out of my driveway, and when I pulled in.

One night, I stopped by after I'd been jogging and Marty and I exchanged names. I peered into the mirrors of his glasses and noticed the puffy red blotches of new skin spreading out across his cheekbones and forehead. I told him I was a reporter, and I started asking questions, about his life, which he seemed eager to answer.

He had been a Kentucky hillbilly before the accident, he said, a beer-drinking, runaround lady's man. He had lived here for two years, since he married Shirley. I strained to catch the graphic details. Traffic roared behind us. Marty's words spilled out, garbled, thanks to the gasoline he had swallowed in the accident, and further complicated by his thick southern drawl.

While we talked, he stared across the street and pointed out the regulars at the park, and I realized how much Marty knew. "She always wears those red shorts," he said, pointing out one woman who was wearing a Jogbra top, and from this distance, it appeared as if she was being pulled forward by the leash connecting her to her big dog. "That dog's a mean one." It was the accident that caused Marty to sit out on his front porch. He used all his free time to become an observer, and it was unnerving to watch how good he was at it. I didn't even know what time the mail was delivered, and he knew the mailman's name and the names of all of our neighbors and the names of their dogs.

Because I was a woman who lived alone in Central City, I was constantly alert to the possibility of crime. So when Marty started asking me questions—What do you do all day? Why aren't you ever home? Why do you keep such odd hours?— I thought: Maybe he'd watch out for me. But he didn't. The white plastic chair on the front porch sat empty for a couple of months, and I didn't see Marty for a few months.

One night when I pulled into the driveway, he was sitting out there again, so I crossed the lawn. "Hey!" I called out. "Where've you been?"

"Me and Shirley got a divorce," Marty said, "so I moved back home to Kentucky. But a couple of Fridays ago, we went and got married again."

I listened to the roar of traffic that was the backdrop to all my conversations with Marty and fit my fingers inside the diamond links of the fence. "You're kidding, right?"

I kept asking Marty questions and they piled up in clumps, like grass clippings. "We can't live together and we can't live apart," Marty said. I was intrigued by the idea of remarriage, and wondered if it was an act of faith or familiarity. Everybody has a story, and I was curious about theirs. I wanted to know how they met, what they had in common. I kept thinking about fire and the transforming power of chemistry, how pressure and heat turn a lump of coal into a diamond, or oil.

But mostly I kept asking questions because I was glad my neighbor was back. I figured it would be a good time to ask for an interview, which I had wanted to ask him about for a long time. "I have to write one last story before I leave this town," I said.

"I'll be here," Marty said. "I don't go out much."

I laughed, awkwardly. But then he turned the tables on me. There was something he wanted to know first, he said. "Why do you always have men coming and going from your house?"

The question hung in the air like an accusation, and the way he shaped the word *men*, the way the word jumped out at me, I knew I didn't like what he was asking.

"There's that guy in the red Jeep."

"That's Ron," I said. "I've known him forever. We used to play on the same volleyball team. We still see each other sometimes."

"There's the guy who drives a little white car."

"Robert," I said. "My friend Robert is a radio reporter."

"And the other guy who drives the new car, the guy with blond hair."

"He's my best friend, another reporter. Mike."

"And the girl, the cute redhead," Marty asked, "the one who lives across the back alley?"

"That's Jill," I said, sucking in a deep breath.

"She was over here earlier, on your porch. I think she was reading your mail."

What else does Marty know? He had been watching me and watching my friends. And for a split second, I felt a tinge of something creepy. He was keeping track, and getting it wrong. I felt uneasy, then I felt guilty, protected, then invaded. This was my neighbor, after all. But what did I know about him?

That night I talked to Jill on the phone. Wing windows were open, and I was lying on my bed on top of my red-and-gold quilt, wearing a t-shirt and underwear, too hot to sleep.

I asked, "Did you enjoy reading my mail?"

The question startled her. "I stopped by to borrow your phone, and I read your *Esquire* while I waited for you to get home from work. You know, I could *feel* him watching me."

I didn't need to set an alarm clock when I lived on Seventh East. Mornings, I could tell time by listening to the stream of cars heading downtown building into a river of rush hour traffic. Nights, there was less traffic but cars passed at faster speeds. Whenever I couldn't sleep, I listened to the sound of gears shifting as cars accelerated from the corner of 13th South, and sometimes I could pick out the backfire of a motorcycle engine. I lay on top of my bed, listening to Jill, my shoulder scrunched to cradle the phone, and I imagined Marty sitting on his front porch right now, one quiet man alone in the dark.

"I always close my curtains when I see Marty sitting out back," Jill said.

"Isn't that a little paranoid?" I asked. "There's no way anyone could see into the back of your house. Your windows are too high."

"I don't care," she said. "You can't be too cautious. And besides. Just the thought of someone watching gives me the creeps."

"When I come home late, I look across the alley to see if your light is on," I said. "You watch for my light. We're watching each other."

"That's different," she said. "You know that's different."

There was something seductive about the newsroom, a big open space I could get lost in, the floor covered with squares of dirty blue-gray pile carpet, three police scanners turned up high, background noise, just like the phones that wouldn't stop ringing and the reporters, like me, who yelled that somebody else needed to answer the phone. My computer had a sticker that I inherited from the reporter who sat there before me—"No Wimps"—and I read those words hundreds of times everyday. *No wimps.*

For a while, before I quit reporting, I covered a string of murder stories. I worked with details, descriptions of the vulnerable, fleshy sites of entrance or exit holes, the pattern of bloody footprints stained in the carpet at the foot of a husband's bed or the long strands of sandy-colored hair blown into a horseshoe shape marking the head of a desert grave. Not that the details sickened me, because they didn't. I made use of them, using the adjectives, verbs, and clean declarative sentences that journalism taught me. In the newsroom, my desk and everybody else's was piled high with notebooks and newspapers and zoning plans and police reports and autopsy results, each of us building a fortress to shut the accidents out.

You sat in somebody's living room and heard about a tragedy, a son talking about the night his mother won the state bodybuilding title, back before she was murdered. And when you returned to the newsroom, you felt comforted to be among people who also knew the rules about organizing tragedy. A sixty-four-car pileup at the Point of the Mountain caused by an ice storm belonged on the front page. A motorcycle accident that inflicted burn injuries requiring twenty-five operations amounted, on a slow news day, to five paragraphs in the back of the local section. You filled a notebook with sprawling handwriting and read your notes later, looking for beginnings and endings, every other fact belonging somewhere in the middle. You learned the sympathy you felt sitting in the intimacy of a living room wasn't as important as how you would feel back in the newsroom, back in a place where you are part of a bigger cause, the public's right to know, where your loyalty was to the story, not the people who lived it. You were grateful for the urgent, flowing urban river of tragedy, grateful for the interesting work it provided, but observing all those stories set off the static in your head, like a pileup that kept growing, all the quotes and all the sources and all the shifting loyalties adding up, smashing into each other, slurring into background noise.

I did this, and tried to think it was only a job, but then, just by accident, something would remind me that being in control, being the person reporting the reaction, the observer in the middle of every tragedy, was one hell of a rush. What I didn't admit, even to myself, is how much I liked trying to control the view.

On another hot night, I opened the latch on my neighbor's metal gate. It was after nine P.M., too late to be starting this, but Marty sat on his porch, watching for me. Shirley came outside carrying tall glasses of ice water, the screen door banging closed behind her. The three of us sat under the light on the porch and swatted at gnats. We complained about the heat wave. We complained about living in old brick houses with no air conditioning. We stared at the view. Across Seventh East, the street lights reflected off the flood-control pond like fractured moons.

I asked how they met, starting the interview the way I always do with the small talk of background questions to put everybody at ease, the charm of my naked curiosity. Shirley, a tall woman with a red-painted smile and a shoulder-shock of frizzy, white-white hair, said her parents met Marty in Kentucky and asked her, back in Utah, to write to a guy in a wheelchair who sat alone in his apartment all day. "They never imagined," Shirley said, and shrugged. "I never imagined, either. We don't really have much in common."

"I'm a hillbilly," Marty said, "and she's a city girl. I'm crude. She's not. I'm a Baptist. She's a Mormon. I'm always in the mood, and she's . . ."

"Marty," Shirley interrupted. "She doesn't need to know everything."

"We wrote letters for a couple of months," Marty said, "and then we talked on the phone. She sent me a picture. One look, and I was gone." The door of their house was open, and I heard the whirring sound of the fans inside, all turned up to high.

"When did you know you were in love?" I asked Shirley.

It was quiet, except for the fans and bugs, and Shirley shrugged again. The way she looked away, didn't meet my eyes, embarrassed me. She thought my questions were too intimate, but her husband didn't seem to want to hide anything.

I hardly recognized Marty without his sunglasses. This was the first time I had seen his eyes, and I tried to be careful, but I was fascinated by the horror of his scars. I asked if he were sick of talking about his injuries. To answer, Marty lifted his t-shirt and proudly exposed the angry red patches of bubbled skin on his chest. I was surprised at how much he remembered, how much he was willing to offer. I got information that was even better, more revealing than I had hoped. "His mother says Marty's forehead was so charred that the skin was black," Shirley said. "His forehead looked like a piece of burned wood. The doctors said they didn't understand why he didn't die."

By now it was so dark I couldn't see anything but headlights streaking past. "Your friend dropped by the other night," Marty said. "The blonde." The night he was talking about was as sultry as this one. My friend used my computer while I went out to eat. She propped the front door open hoping to catch a breeze. "The blonde was scared, I think," Marty told me, "so I stayed outside, just to watch."

I couldn't quite make out what he was saying so I scooted my chair closer. "If I hadn't gotten hurt," he said and leaned over to aim his words right into my ear, "I'd be dead by now. Somebody's husband would have shot me."

"Marty!" Shirley said as she stepped back outside with three glasses of ice water on a tray. "I hate it when you talk like that."

One gnat buzzed around my head, and I felt sweat pooling on my neck underneath my ponytail. Sitting on my neighbor's porch, I was reminded of all the tragedies I had written about, the grieving mothers, the political scandals, the accident scenes. A transaction was going on every time, an exchange, but the part I tried to look away from was my own desire, how I was trying to control the view. I told myself that people chose to talk about their lives, to tell me their stories, chose to divulge their intimate secrets, and that they could choose *not* to if they wanted. I told myself that this was my job, that I had been trained to do this, that I asked first. But what I took away had nothing to do with what was offered. What was offered was intimacy, and the way I shaped a story, pulled out facts, seemed another kind of betrayal. Like everyone else, I was getting it wrong. Marty came of age in another body, and what wasn't burned in the accident, what he didn't lose, was desire. He seemed unsympathetic, a bit too proud of his sexual prowess, his bragging over the top, so I told him, "I have enough," and the interview was over. One morning, Marty called me over to his porch, and I could tell something was wrong. I didn't ask, but he told me anyway. Shirley wanted to get divorced again. "She said she realized the other night, when you were asking her all those questions, that she wasn't ever really in love with me." He said he would probably move back home to Kentucky.

The sunglasses were back, so I couldn't see much of Marty's face. I looked at the mirrors that covered his eyes and saw two reflections of me, centered right in the middle of his lenses. I couldn't tell how he felt: Was he upset? Was he mad? Mad at me? I wondered what he would do. I wondered if he would miss the traffic on Seventh East. I wondered if back home he would watch some other neighborhood like T.V.

All day at work, as I sat at my computer and edited stories, deleting words to eliminate widow lines, I thought about Marty and Shirley, how quickly things had fallen apart. I had gotten the promise of their remarriage wrong. I wondered about my part, how implicated I was in the divorce, if my questions were really to blame for starting the unraveling. I wondered: Should someone feel guilty for watching?

A couple of weeks later, I moved away. The morning I left, with the U-Haul parked out front blocking traffic in the far right lane, I ran up the sidewalk to Marty's house. For the previous week, as I stacked boxes on my front porch, I had avoided looking over, tried to avoid saying goodbye. But now I was ready. I stood on the front porch holding my camera, and I rang and rang and rang the doorbell, but nobody was home.

The column that I wrote about Marty, this is how it begins:

I live on Seventh East and Marty Hall lives next door.

This is how it ends:

Marty's life on the porch looks quiet, but his interior world seems urgent. I want to add up the details, to make a story out of his life.

As I pull out of town, drive south on Seventh East toward I–80, I see my neighbor Marty Hall reflected in my rear-view mirror. I already miss him and the view of Liberty Park we shared from our front porches.

After I moved, I posted pictures of friends above my desk. In one photo, my friend Mike and I are sitting on my stairs.

Mike has his arm draped around me. We're both laughing. You can't see how my mascara is smeared. In the picture, you can't see the street or the moving van or traffic passing by. You can't see that my house is empty. What you can see is a shadowy figure in the background of the photo. Standing on his porch, Marty looks frozen in position. He's staring at me, watching us, and I can't help myself. When I look at the picture, through a trick of photography, it always appears as if I'm staring back.

Ellen Fagg worked as a newspaper reporter, campaign manager, and magazine editor before attending the University of Iowa's Nonfiction Writing Program. Now she lives in Portland, Oregon, where she edits CitySearch, *an on-line community magazine.*